Review Journal of Political Philosophy
Volume 7, Issue Number 1

Review Journal of Political Philosophy
Volume 7, Issue Number 1

Edited by

J. Jeremy Wisnewski

Review Journal of Political Philosophy Volume 7, Issue Number 1, Edited by J. Jeremy Wisnewski

This book first published 2009

Cambridge Scholars Publishing

12 Back Chapman Street, Newcastle upon Tyne, NE6 2XX, UK

British Library Cataloguing in Publication Data
A catalogue record for this book is available from the British Library

ISBN (10): 1-4438-1109-2, ISBN (13): 978-1-4438-1109-5
ISSN 1752-2056

TABLE OF CONTENTS

ACKNOWLEDGMENTS

All journals benefit from the good graces of those academics who volunteer their time to make journals run smoothly and professionally. This Journal has had more of its share of good grace. The lion's share of thanks for the journal goes to members of the editorial board. In particular, I would like to thank the following individual persons for their continual help:

Thom Brooks, University of Sheffield
Janet Donohoe, West Georgia State University
R. D. Emerick, Palomar College
Gordon Hull, University of North Carolina, Charlotte
Glen Pettigrove, Massey University
Jose-Antonio Orosco, Oregon State University
Mark Sanders, University of North Carolina, Charlotte
P.A. Woodward, East Carolina University

I would also like to thank Meghan Lonergan and Dominique Thomas, my editorial assistants, for their assistance in preparing the manuscript, as well as the editorial staff at Cambridge Scholars Publishing, and in particular Amanda Millar, for continuing support of the journal.

Mathematics, Ontology, and Politics: The Work of Alain Badiou

Christopher Norris,
University of Wales-Cardiff

Abstract

With just a few exceptions Alain Badiou's work has been ignored or routinely dismissed by Anglophone philosophers and discussed at any length – or with an adequate knowledge of his large and demanding *oeuvre* – only by cultural and critical theorists. This is unfortunate in various ways, not least because Badiou is himself a philosopher by training and avocation, and also because his thinking is some of the most resourceful, inventive and potentially fecund (as well as most technically and conceptually demanding) to be found in present-day philosophy. Here I offer a summary account of that thinking with particular reference to Badiou's highly original work in the philosophy of mathematics and, more specifically, his exploration of those far-reaching ontological issues raised by developments in post-Cantorian set theory. His approach is more ambitious and adventurous than the kinds of discussion mostly carried on by analytically trained philosophers although – I should stress – none the less rigorous or mathematically accomplished for that. Indeed, when compared with most work in that 'other' (analytic) tradition, Badiou's shows a much higher degree of intellectual creativity as well as a far greater depth of engagement with the 'truth-procedures' (that is, the heuristics of problem-solving and paradox-resolution) that have typified the progress of set-theoretical methods and concepts.

My essay then goes on to explain – again with a view to allaying suspicions in the analytic camp – how Badiou can make the seemingly unwarranted leap from philosophy of mathematics, *via* a set-theoretically grounded ontology, to questions (some of them urgently topical) in the socio-political and ethical domains. Most significant here is the cardinal distinction – as in the title of his major book *Being and Event* – between the realm of ontology or that which pertains to some existing, preconstituted order of things and the realm of events or that which transpires in such a way as to radically disrupt, transform, or revolutionize the existing order. It is by way of this distinction that Badiou is able to argue his case for mathematics as the basis for a critical ontology not only of the formal and physical sciences but also of those social and political projects where progressive or emancipatory thinking is likewise bound up with material constraints

I

Alain Badiou is a French-domiciled Moroccan philosopher (born Rabat, 1937) who studied at the Ecole Normale Supérieure in the late 1950s, then taught at the University of Paris VIII (Vincennes) and returned to the ENS in 1999 to take up the Chair of Philosophy.[1] He has been – and remains – a committed left-wing activist and militant who, unlike many in the wake of *les évènements* of 1968, has not renounced his communist beliefs but sought to redefine them with greater precision while devoting his main political energies to extra-parliamentary campaigning on issues such as the treatment of asylum-seekers, ethnic minorities and other oppressed or marginalised groups.[2] Of his many and varied publications to date Badiou's book *Being and Event* (1988, English trans. 2005) stakes a strong claim as the single most original and challenging work to have appeared on the French philosophical scene during the past twenty years.[3]

I should say straight off that Badiou's thought is such as to resist and very nearly to defeat the best efforts of summary exposition. Indeed it has a depth, complexity, and range of reference – combined with a degree of conceptual rigour – that no commentator could hope to match. Still it is worth making some attempt since there are many aspects of Badiou's work that are apt to create problems of grasp for the first-time reader. They include his heterodox distinction between truth and knowledge, his likewise unfamiliar conception of truth in relation to issues of ethics and politics, and his idea of the event as a radically disruptive or world-transformative occurrence such as requires unswerving commitment on the part of faithful subjects or 'militants of truth'.[4] Among the latter are some – like Saint Paul – whose example in this respect Badiou finds very much to his purpose even though he is far from endorsing all or any of their doctrines or articles of faith.[5] However, what most needs explaining is the role of mathematics (more precisely: of post-Cantorian set-theory) as the basis of Badiou's philosophical ontology, that is to say, his approach to the fundamental question: what exists and what are its various structures, modes, or conditions of being? And again: how is it that truth can be discovered, manifested, or progressively revealed (as realists would claim) when subject to all the changing conditions of cultural or socio-historical time and place? Above all there is the question – central to Badiou's work – of the relationship between mathematics as the basis of ontological enquiry, philosophy as the discipline that draws out the implications of such enquiry, and those other kinds of theoretical and practical concern that make up philosophy's field of engagement beyond its more specialized – sometimes its overly self-occupied – interests and pursuits.

These questions go back to the ancient Greek origins of Western speculative thought and also, no doubt, to the sources of every cultural tradition that has taken the turn toward topics of a metaphysical or speculative character. Sufficient to say, for the moment, that Badiou comes at them from a standpoint at once profoundly attuned to those ancient sources and utterly distinctive in its own right. The attunement results from his engaging with problems – such as those of the one and the many, stasis and change, or (most crucially for Badiou's enterprise) the order of being and the order of events – which received their earliest incisive statement in the thinking of ancient Greek philosophers like Parmenides, Zeno, Heraclitus, Plato, and Aristotle. The distinctiveness has to do with his approaching them in a manner that draws upon various latter-day resources – principally those of set theory but also including Marxism, psychoanalysis, philosophy of science, and poetics – through a highly inventive synthesis that also displays an uncommon degree of conceptual and logical rigour. Indeed, it is Badiou's most emphatic claim that philosophy still has its work cut out despite all the nowadays fashionable talk of its 'end' or looming obsolescence. Nevertheless, he insists, that work is best done by maintaining a close and mutually productive contact with those other disciplines while refusing to be taken over by them or annexed to their own distinct aims and priorities.

Such has been the fate of philosophy at least since Hegel: to find itself invaded from various adjacent regions of thought with which it has a constant need to engage (since they define its very 'conditions' or means of involvement beyond its specialist domain) but from which it must always keep a certain distance so as preserve its autonomy and critical-emancipatory edge. As I have said those conditions are science, politics, art, and love, all of them conceived (reasonably enough) as basic components of human knowledge and experience whose special mark – what singles them out from the range of other possible candidates – is the fact that they involve a commitment to truth in its various modalities on the part of subjects for whom that truth is in some sense constitutive of their very being. 'Examples', Badiou writes: 'the appearance, with

Aeschylus, of theatrical tragedy; the irruption, with Galileo, of mathematical physics; an amorous encounter which changes a whole life; the French Revolution of 1792.' It is at junctures like these that the subject quite literally comes into existence as one who decides who decides to 'wager' on the truth of that event, or to take it as an axiom and follow out its consequences to the limit and (maybe) beyond. Thus philosophy has no choice but to address those four 'conditions' and define its project in response to their various, sometimes conflictual demands even if, by so doing, it is perpetually at risk of losing that critical distance. Amongst the temptations to which it has periodically been prone are scientific positivism, psychoanalysis in its more imperious (anti-philosophical) forms, poetic meditation when exalted (as by Heidegger) to a vatic or revelatory role, and political theory when likewise granted the kind of precedence that would keep philosophy very much in its subordinate place.

Badiou's way of countering this threat is to insist that philosophy take full account of developments in those other spheres while continuing to honour its ancient Greek inheritance as the discipline of thought whose proper task it is to draw out the various relationships between them. Beyond that, it has the task – one central to his own project – of explaining precisely how each bears witness to the polarity of being and event, or ontology and that which eludes or exceeds any specification in ready-to-hand ontological terms. All the same, as he is equally keen to stress, this sense of a distinctive vocation should not be taken as a licence for philosophers to fix their sights too high and hence to disengage from the business of reflecting on matters of real-world political and ethical concern.[6] For one of its more urgent responsibilities in the context of present-day socio-cultural-political developments is to hold out against what Badiou sees as the near-ubiquitous process of decline by which science degenerates into mere technique, politics into management, art into culture (or the 'cultured' discourse on or around art), and love into sexuality conceived as something like a synthesis of technique, management, and perpetual self-adjustment to perceived cultural norms. It is largely in order to resist this trivializing process – and also to resist philosophy's recruitment through sundry complicitous movements of thought, from hermeneutics, post-structuralism and postmodernism to the 'ordinary-language' and (some, not all) analytic schools – that Badiou presents his radical re-thinking of ontology *vis-á-vis* the unpredictable and world-transformative 'event' of truth.

Being and Event itself lays claim, immodestly but I think justifiably enough, to constitute just such a major event in the history of philosophic thought. Of course any claim of this order cannot be adequately gauged or assessed except through a sustained engagement with the text itself and a willingness, on the reader's part, to set aside the various kinds of prejudice – including those derived from very different conceptions of philosophy's proper role – that may well operate to block or to skew that engagement. What follows is of course no substitute for it but aims at least to prepare the way by dismantling a few of the prejudices.

II

What I have said so far should already make it clear that Badiou's project has little in common with other current modes of philosophical thinking, whether in the mainstream analytic (chiefly Anglo-American) or 'continental' (mainland-European) lines of descent. On the one hand it displays an ambitiousness and speculative range – especially in its treatment of mathematical themes – that will surely strike most analytic philosophers as well beyond the limits of intellectual propriety. On the other, as they would soon find out if persuaded to read him, Badiou's deployment of set-theoretical concepts, methods and proof-procedures has a rigour and degree of logical precision fully equal to anything achieved by thinkers in that other tradition.[7] Where his approach most notably contrasts with theirs is in its claim for mathematics as the basis of a general ontology with decisive implications for our thinking about issues across a great range of subject areas, from the natural sciences (unsurprisingly) to politics, ethics, aesthetics, and love. If this last term – here and on its previous appearance – caused my reader something of a jolt then this may perhaps serve as a useful measure of the extent to which Badiou's work challenges the norms of conventional academic discourse. After all, there is precedent going back at least to Plato for a link between philosophy of mathematics and philosophy of ethics, politics and art, even if the precise nature of that link – or its validity when subject to different, presumptively more rigorous standards of analysis – is nowadays considered far from self-evident. However, with respect to love, the fact of its having figured as a stage on the path to philosophic wisdom in Plato's *Symposium* and other texts will do little to offset the sense of its simply not belonging in a series that includes those other terms.

Yet it is just this notion of 'belonging' – and its precise relationship to that of 'inclusion' – that Badiou asks us to reconsider in the light of post-Cantorian set theory and the various problems it has had to confront in its development to date. Thus one of the most productive (though counter-intuitive) results of this development was the power-set axiom whereby it was established that the sub-sets of any given set would out-number the cardinality of that set by a ratio that increased exponentially and which also applied to the multiple orders of infinite (or transfinite) numbers.[8] That is to say, the members taken as *belonging* to a certain set will always be exceeded – sometimes massively so – by the constituent parts or the entities *included* in that set as a matter of everything that makes it up on whatever counting system. This discrepancy or disproportion between what is taken as truly or rightfully the case with regard to some existing situation and what it may harbour in the way of so-far unrecognised (i.e., included but non-belonging) sub-sets is a main theme of Badiou's writing and one that provides him with a bridge from mathematics to other (among them political) regions of enquiry. For instance, it gives him a strong point of purchase on the issue concerning the *sans-papiers* or immigrant workers whose vital contribution to the national economy (quite apart from their entitlement to due respect as human beings) counts for nothing in so far as they lack recognition by the state.[9] Badiou offers various terms by which to grasp the structure and workings of this discrepancy, among them the distinction between *members* and *parts* (where the parts always more numerous) and that between the *situation* and the *state of the situation*, where the latter contains everything excluded by the 'official' or currently legitimised count-as-one. What is counted-as-one is that which falls under any system – mathematical, political or other – whereby certain parts are treated as members in good standing while no such status is granted to those that fall outside it for this or that reason.

Hence Badiou's further distinction between 'inconsistent' and 'consistent' multiplicities, the former taken as ontologically prior since they include the full range of elements along with all possible relations between them rather than just the current (selective or exclusionary) order of membership. Thus Badiou takes his stand very much on the side of those pre-Socratic thinkers like Anaximander, Heraclitus and Empedocles for whom the one – that is, any principle of ultimate unity or reconciliation – must be seen as a fictive or illusory construct imposed upon an endlessly various, manifold, and shape-shifting reality. By the same token he comes out against those latter-day followers of Parmenides and Plato according to whom the one (in whatever derivative guise) is that which provides the grounding principle, the touchstone of reason or truth, and hence the basis for any reckoning with an otherwise unruly and unknowable multiplicity. So it is – on account of its raising this issue in an especially sharp and unavoidable way – that Badiou makes his claim for set theory as the discourse wherein one can best descry the various political structures of inclusion and exclusion. Or again, it enables the distinction to be drawn between that which is *presented* as part of a certain situation and that which may or may not be *represented* depending on whether it 'properly' belongs or qualifies for membership on terms laid down by the socially, politically or culturally dominant count-as-one. Badiou declares himself frankly impatient with mathematicians who would reject any such argument as merely an abusive extrapolation from their specialist subject-domain. On the other hand he is equally impatient with political philosophers and cultural theorists who take the supposedly 'abstract' character of mathematics and formal logic to justify their holding out against its claim on their attention. For it is just his point, and again one that most analytic philosophers would balk at, that the process should properly work both ways so that mathematicians have as much to gain by reflecting on these wider ontological implications of their work as philosophers have by acquainting themselves with developments in set theory.

Thus Badiou's philosophy of mathematics has a crucial bearing – albeit at a carefully specified remove – on his thinking about issues of politics, art, science, and love. These subject-areas must each be taken as exhibiting a distinctive relationship to truth, and hence as each requiring a different approach with regard to the radical dichotomy of being and event. Yet there is also a profound kinship between them in so far as each involves the irruption of a new and unprecedented kind of occurrence whose effect is to re-define the conditions – the terms of 'fidelity' or rigorous following-through – for subsequent thought or action. Just as truth surpasses the capacity of knowledge (since knowledge has to do with pre-established standards or criteria of judgement) so fidelity ensues upon certain events that transcend any previously adequate order of conceptual, ethical, techno-scientific, socio-political, or aesthetic representation. Where philosophy comes in is *not* as any kind of master-discourse that would somehow speak the truth of those other subject-areas from a higher adjudicative standpoint but rather as a discourse of critical reflection on and through their various specific sites or modes of practical engagement. Above all, its task is to point up the difference between *truth* as that which commands the allegiance of subjects beyond their current-best powers of ascertainment, proof or understanding and *knowledge* as that which by very definition falls within the bounds of achieved human cognisance. Thus the state of knowledge at any given time has this much in common with the state as a political entity: that it defines and constrains what legitimately counts as a proper object of cognitive enquiry or a legitimate subject whose status is a matter of meeting certain authorised or laid-down membership conditions. If the event – as Badiou defines it – is strictly unthinkable in ontological terms then this is because it initiates a radical change in what henceforth counts as a truth-conducive, scientifically warranted, politically enlightened, ethically just, or good-faith mode of proceeding.

This helps to explain his on the face of it improbable claim that set-theory is the only adequate means of re-thinking the relationship between being and event so as to leave sufficient room for an outlook of political activism and also for the prospect of genuinely innovative thinking in science, ethics, and the arts. Mathematics enjoys this privileged position not (to repeat) as some kind of master-discourse dispensing truths from a realm of absolute ideal objectivity outside and above the realm of contingent, might-have-been-otherwise events. Rather it serves to explain – by something more than suggestive analogy – how thought can transcend the limiting conditions of its own historically or culturally situated time and place. What set-theory is able to account for through its dealing with the various (often problematical) concepts of inclusion, belonging, and self-reference is the tension that exists between an 'inconsistent multiplicity' of subjects whose interests may or may not be acknowledged by the state and the 'count-as-one' by which the state identifies all and only those legitimate subjects whose interests it can more or less plausibly claim to represent. It is in this context that Badiou introduces his notion of the 'void' as that which occupies the zero-point of being, set-theoretically defined, and which also provides the conceptual bridge to a 'subtractive' ontology wherein the condition of absence or lack – that is to say, the representational deficit in any given political system – itself becomes a motivating force in the process by which unjust or oppressive socio-political orders provoke revolutionary change.

The point is nicely made by a passage from his essay 'Politics Unbound' where Badiou brings these various themes together in typically sweeping yet precise and by no means vaguely analogical way.

> Organised in anticipation of surprises, diagonal to representations, experimenting with lacunae, accounting for infinite singularities, politics is an active thought that is both subtle and dogged, one from which the material critique of all forms of presentative correlation proceeds, and which, operating on the edge of the void, calls on homogeneous multiplicities against the heterogeneous order of the State, which claims to prevent their appearance.[10]

Passages like this give a highly articulate but somewhat abstract and generalised account of what Badiou means, in the political context, by his use of mathematically-derived terms such as 'void', 'singularity', 'presentative correlation', 'homogeneous multiplicity', and so forth.

However, any suspicion that they serve merely to disguise a lack of detailed historico-political knowledge or engagement is amply dispelled when it comes to his treatment of those signal episodes – chief among them, in many ways, the Paris Commune of 1871 – that constitute genuine 'evental sites' in Badiou's precise sense of the phrase. Thus he fully endorses Marx's claim that '[t]he Commune was . . . the initiation of the Social Revolution of the 19th century', and that '[w]hatever therefore its fate at Paris, it will make *le tour du monde*' among the international working class as 'the magic word of delivery'.[11] It stands out above other, on the face of it more consequential or momentous events in so far as it marked the emergence of radically new possibilities which remained (and still remain) to be realised but the non-fulfilment of which up to now is no reason to consign them to historical oblivion or consider them of merely anecdotal interest when compared with great events such as the French or Russian Revolutions. According to Badiou, 'there exists no stronger a transcendental consequence than that of making something appear in a world which had not existed in it previously'.[12] On this reckoning the Paris Commune must be classed among the very greatest of world-political events despite the plain facts – as he grimly records them – of its having broken up in disarray and descended rapidly from the heights of popular power and massed resistance to the depths of bloody repression and brutal farce. For these facts of the matter, though no doubt 'decisive' from the standpoint of conventional historiography or hard-headed worldly wisdom, are beside the point when one raises questions concerning the long-term deeper implications or ethico-political significance of the Commune. In this alternative perspective '"March 18" gets instituted . . . as the exigency of a new political appearing, as forcing an unheard-of transcendental evaluation of the political scene'.[13]

Here we might recall W.H. Auden's line from his great, although as some (including Auden himself later on) have felt, morally flawed or ambivalent poem 'Spain 1937': 'History to the defeated/May say Alas but cannot help or pardon'. What Badiou proposes in place of this drastically foreshortened outlook – this idea of present success or failure as the be-all or end-all of hope for better things – is a conception of politics that locates the significance of past events not so much in their demonstrable impact on the course of history to date but rather in their standing as singular examples and reminders of that which has yet to be achieved. 'We can identify a strong singularity', he writes, 'by the fact that, for a given situation, it has the consequence of making an inexistent term exist in it.'[14] How this relates to Badiou's understanding of the relevant set-theoretical concepts – principally those of the void and inconsistent *vs.* consistent multiplicity – is a topic that I have broached already but will later discuss in more detail. The most important point to make in this context is that the Commune figures as one of those strictly nonpareil events or evental sites which could neither be predicted before their occurrence/emergence nor explained with the help of received concepts and categories. That is to say, '[t]he value of the site's existence cannot be prescribed from anything in its ontology', since here – as in the case of mathematics – the advent of a radically innovative way of thinking or acting is such as intrinsically to draw upon resources that elude the grasp of any presently existing conceptual, descriptive, or explanatory scheme. Just as set theory has typically advanced through a process of transforming paradox into concept or some newly encountered obstacle into the spur for renewed efforts of creative thought so likewise politics has typically achieved its most significant moments of advance through the kinds of apparent setback or seemingly decisive (even terminal) setback that have been such a prominent feature of its history to date. And just as this process is constantly at risk of betrayal or derailment through the inertial force of received ideas so likewise the post-history of any event – in Badiou's strongly evaluative sense of that term – will always most likely be subject to evasions, distortions, or betrayals that none the less allow its true import to appear through a reading (like that which he devotes to the Paris Commune) sufficiently attuned to its 'singularity' as just such a signal event.

March 18th 1871 is therefore an evental site 'because it imposes itself on all the elements that help to bring about its existence as that which, on the basis of the indistinct content of worker-being, "forcibly" calls for a whole new transcendental evaluation of the latter's intensity'.[15] The word 'forcibly' bears something like its everyday meaning but also a more specific (and specialised) set-theoretical sense which, again, I shall return to later. Meanwhile it is worth noting that the major theme of Badiou's highly detailed and also highly partisan (that is to say politically, ethically, and philosophically involved) writing on the Paris Commune is the way that this event stands strikingly opposed to the subsequent history of compromise or sell-out whereby working-class movements have been hijacked by the parliamentary 'socialist' or even 'communist' left. This in turn goes along with his vehement rejection of present-day accommodationist strategies on the part of nominally left-wing parties and his decision to make common cause with those on the extra-parliamentary communist left who represent or embody that 'worker-being' that he invokes when discussing the Paris Commune. 'Today's task, being undertaken notably by the Organisation Politique, is to support the creation of such a discipline subtracted from the grip of the state, the creation of a thoroughly political discipline'.[16] And it is precisely this 'subtractive' component – whatever doesn't count or has to be discounted according to some dominant conception – that, according to Badiou, can be seen to constitute the driving force of every major advance in every major field of human creative (whether artistic, ethical, political, natural-scientific, or mathematical) endeavour. Like all such landmark events, he writes, 'the Commune had not *realized* a possible, it had created one. This possible is simply that of an independent proletarian politics.'[17]

Thus the failure of the Commune – its having been put down in blood and fire, not to mention those near-farcical aspects of its ending that have struck even the most sympathetic and politically well-disposed commentators – is a matter of all-too-plain historical fact but not one that in any sense revokes or invalidates its creation of a new possibility. Indeed Badiou goes so far as to posit the existence of something like an inverse relation between what history routinely treats as major or truly consequential episodes and those which merit just a footnote or passing mention. Hence his cryptic proposal that a *fact* should be defined for such purposes as 'a site whose intensity of existence is not maximal', while the term *singularity* designates a site that does bear witness to such maximal 'intensity'. Among the many illustrative contrasts offered by Badiou is that between the Commune (or March 18th 1871) as a striking and utterly 'singular' example of the latter and the date of September 4th 1870 which marked the collapse of Second Empire and inauguration of the Third Republic. This is not, as Badiou points out, a matter of the politics or class-allegiance of those most directly involved since on that occasion also it was the working people of Paris who marched under a red flag, 'illegally' occupied strategic buildings, and showed every sign of gearing up for a full-scale violent confrontation. What sets it apart from a genuinely epochal event such as the Commune is the fact that 'September 4 was to be confiscated by bourgeois politicians primarily concerned to re-establish the order of property, while the Commune, Lenin's ideal referent, will inspire a century of revolutionary thought'.[18] In this respect it stands as a veritable emblem of the seemingly inexorable process by which any major innovation or radical departure from the norms of a dominant political order will at length be drawn back into established modes of party-based 'representative' pseudo-democracy.

III

So, to recall Auden once again, if history indeed says 'Alas' to the defeated of the Commune – as likewise to those of the Spanish Civil War – then it is not so much a question as to whether they can now be 'helped or pardoned' with the dubious (scarcely encouraging) benefit of hindsight but rather a question as to what remains, after and despite such knowledge, of the prospects for social and political transformation held out by the event. Where orthodox history comes back with the confident answer 'Nothing whatsoever!', Badiou invokes a different historiography whose difference consists not only in its cleaving to a sharply opposed political valuation of events but also in its radically divergent sense of just what constitutes the true (as distinct from the retrospectively censored) order of relationship between an event and its aftermath. Moreover, he devotes some passages of detailed and intricate, at times mathematically-based argument to the task of setting that relationship out in terms of the varying degrees of 'intensity' that establish a more-or-less tight or rigorous – subjectively speaking, a more-or-less binding or obligatory – linkage of the kind here at stake.[19]

Thus in the context of politics as in those of mathematics and the physical sciences it is always – according to Badiou – a matter of truths that are fully objective in so far as they transcend any merely *de facto* state of knowledge or belief but whose discovery, maintenance, and later development involve an irreducibly subjective component of fidelity, that is, of *truth to* the epochal event in question. As Badiou puts it in one of his most resounding statements:

> [t]he proclamations of the Commune, the first worker power in universal history, comprise a historic existent whose absoluteness manifests the coming to pass in the world of a wholly new ordering of its appearing, a mutation of its logic. The existence of an inexistent aspect is that by which, in the domain of appearing, the subversion of worldly being by subjacent being is played out. It is the logical marking of a paradox of being, an ontological paradox.[20]

So likewise with regard to the history of science in its various specialist fields or disciplinary domains where any major paradigm-shift will occur as the upshot of a heterodox truth-procedure that exists to begin with only through fidelity to a barely discernible (since unpredictable) event. This event must be thought of as eluding any means of prior ontological or conceptual specification since it breaks altogether with existing standards of accredited knowledge or representation. Moreover – Badiou claims – there is a close and not merely fanciful analogy between the kind of fidelity that keeps enquirers on the path of scientific truth or political justice and the kind that leaves its mark on certain significant (especially erotic) human encounters. What these instances all have in common is the occurrence of a truth-event that, when it first appears, finds no place within the range of admissible facts, theorems, hypotheses, ethical precepts, or inter-subjective commitments.

Let me stress once again – for those of a sceptical mind – that Badiou's treatment of set theory in its technical, i.e., logico-mathematical as well as its wider philosophic aspects is highly impressive for its depth, lucidity, and strength of intellectual grasp. Thus anyone who comes to *Being and Event* with a vague recollection of the subject from school days and otherwise little in the way of background knowledge will leave it – if their reading is sufficiently attentive – with a much improved understanding of the maths along with a keenly developed sense of how it relates to those other truth-conditions under which its logic can be seen to unfold. Indeed one could claim with ample warrant from his writings that rigour of thought is a prime ethical value for Badiou as well as a matter of philosophic, intellectual, and academic-professional responsibility. The most striking example is his brief but intensely admiring commentary on the life and work of Jean Cavaillès, a young mathematician who showed exceptional courage as a member of the French Resistance and, in consequence, was captured, tortured and shot by the occupying Nazi forces. What most impresses Badiou about Cavaillès' actions is the fact that, on all the evidence, they were performed not so much out of moral conscience, love of country, or personal heroism but rather as the upshot of clear-headed logical thinking with regard to the wartime situation and his own best, most effective way of affecting the course of events.

Any attempt to relate Cavaillès' philosophical outlook with his Resistance activities has to face the 'apparent enigma', as Badiou terms it, that 'Cavaillès was working quite some way from political theory or committed existentialism, in the field of pure mathematics'.[21] Moreover he himself had a good deal to say, in his more philosophical writings, about the need to renounce any remnant of the old intuition-based or consciousness-oriented way of construing mathematical thought and in stead adopt a more austere conception whereby it is identified with purely logical, formal, or conceptual procedures. Yet this is just the point, according to Badiou: that 'Cavaillès was resistant *by logic*' (a phrase that he borrows from Georges Canguilhem),and hence that in such a case any question of distinguishing motives from reasons, or personal from political considerations, or indeed the circumstantial causes of actions from the principles and values embodied in those same actions becomes merely otiose or misconceived.

> This 'by logic' contains the connection between philosophical rigour and the political prescription. It is not moral concern or, as we say nowadays, ethical discourse that have, it seems, produced the greatest figures of philosophy as resistance. The concept appears to have been a better guide on this matter than consciousness or spirituality.[22]

And again: 'a Resistance figure "by logic" obeys an axiom, or an injunction, which he formulates in his own name, and whose major consequences he lays out, without waiting to win over other people, in the objective group to which he belongs'.[23] In this connection Badiou, like Cavaillès before him, singles out Spinoza as the greatest exemplar of a thinking that acknowledged the extent of the intellect's subjection to various kinds of necessity, among them those of its physical embodiment, its historical or socio-cultural situation, and (not least) the manifold sources of formative, even determinative influence that have shaped its development.[24] To acknowledge so much – in marked opposition to the emphasis on freedom, autonomy, and conscience that has typified post-Kantian moral debate – is (again like Spinoza) to adopt a very different view of the relationship between on the one hand mathematics, logic and the formal as well as the physical sciences and, on the other, philosophy in its ethical and socio-political dimensions.

Badiou takes issue with Spinoza on various grounds, notably concerning the Spinozist conception of a thoroughly monistic ontology wherein 'mind' and 'nature' are merely two attributes of a self-same substance that includes and determines every occurrence in both of these parallel or strictly indissociable domains. Thus any 'event' – in Badiou's distinctive sense of that term – would be put down to the illusion of freedom or independent agency created by our relative lack of knowledge with regard to the operative causal forces or motivating factors involved. Badiou devotes some probing pages of *Being and Event* to a careful teasing-out of the problems and tensions that result from Spinoza's attempt to make good this radically determinist conception while none the less allowing – or seeming to allow – sufficient room for the cultivation of active (or 'joyful') as distinct from passive (or 'sad') emotions. Still he is very much in sympathy with Spinoza as regards the idea that what are usually taken as moral virtues manifested in action through the exercise of autonomous will can more plausibly (or less self-deludingly) be treated as issuing from a no doubt unfathomably complex concatenation of causal, circumstantial and rational-deliberative factors. Hence Badiou's tribute to

Cavaillès as an avatar of the same Spinozist tradition, that is, the somewhat exclusive tradition of those whose fidelity took the form of a clear-headed and resolute acceptance of necessity linked with the courage of their own moral and political beliefs.

It is the same combination of jointly intellectual, moral and personal qualities that Badiou admires in those various thinkers across a great range of disciplines – mathematics, physics, philosophy of science, logic, ethics, political theory, psychoanalysis, philosophy of art, and poetics – whose sole common attribute is just this commitment to a truth that cannot (so to speak) be cashed out in the present or known as a matter of demonstrative warrant on the best evidence to hand. What he seeks to bring out, most of all through the sequence of set-theoretical meditations n *Being and Event*, is the way that thinking is inexorably drawn beyond the limits of intuitive, received, or orthodox, knowledge by the effect of those at present barely discernible conflicts or anomalies whose long-term consequences cannot yet be grasped even though they exert a constantly unsettling or destabilising pressure. This is, for Badiou, undoubtedly a matter of truth – of truth in a sense irreducible to any linguistic or constructivist account – yet also a matter of subjective fidelity in so far as the subject is here defined precisely in terms of such intensive commitment to bearing out the truth (or perhaps the falsehood) of the theorem, proposition, or hypothesis in question. Thus:

> I call *fidelity* the set of procedures which discern, within a situation, those multiples whose existence depends upon the introduction into circulation (under the supernumerary name conferred by an intervention) of an evental multiple. In sum, a fidelity is the apparatus which separates out, within the set of presented multiples, those which depend upon an event.[25]

To which he adds – lest this be taken as implying any kind of subjectivist or psychologistic approach – that 'a fidelity is always particular, in so far as it depends on an event', that 'there is no general faithful disposition', that it 'must not be understood . . . as a capacity, a subjective quality, or a virtue', and should be thought of rather as consisting in 'a functional relation to the event'.[26] All of which suggests that Badiou aligns himself firmly with that realist or objectivist conception of mathematical truth that Frege defended against what he saw as the creeping malaise of a subjectivist outlook represented by the project of Husserlian phenomenology.[27] However, as we have seen, this would be to ignore the presence of that countervailing emphasis in Badiou's work on what has to be called (for want of a better, less misleading term) the *subjective* component that is always bound up with any faithful and rigorous commitment to establishing the truth of certain theorems, conjectures, or hypotheses. For it is just his point – brought out with particular force in his writing about Cavaillès but also implicit in his own more 'technical' mathematico-philosophical work – that the appeal to subjectivity in this context-specific and carefully delineated sense has nothing in common with those psychologistic tendencies that Frege claimed to expose and discredit in the project of Husserlian phenomenology.

I have argued at length elsewhere that Frege got Husserl seriously wrong in this regard and that his misapprehension has badly distorted the subsequent history of relations between 'analytic' and 'continental' thought.[28] Suffice it to say that that a chief motivation of Badiou's work in philosophy of mathematics and other fields has been to challenge the very idea that there can or should exist such a drastic distinction between rigour, objectivity, and truth on the one hand and commitment, fidelity, and truthfulness on the other.[29] Along with this goes his likewise principled refusal to accept any version of the widely-held idea – mostly put about by analytic philosophers – that the virtues of conceptual rigour and logical precision simply don't mix with the kind of thinking (more typical of work in the 'continental', i.e., post-Kantian mainland-European line of descent) that stresses the virtues of speculative range or inventiveness. On the contrary: the most remarkable feature of *Being and Event* is the way that it manages to bring together a sustained and highly original meditation on the history of Western philosophy from Plato to the present with a first-rate critical-expository account of developments in post-Cantorian set-theory and also an adventurous, imaginative, at times well-nigh visionary sense of intellectual and political vocation. Certainly the contrast will strike any reader who approaches *Being and Event* with expectations primed by acquaintance with the kind of debate that typifies philosophy of mathematics in the mainstream analytic tradition. In that context the agenda is far more tightly defined – for the most part concerned with issues such as rule-following and the realism *versus* anti-realism dispute – and often restricted to a far more basic or elementary range of working examples or 'problem'-cases Thus it typically turns on questions like 'what does or should count as "following a rule" given the need for some higher-order rule that determines the first-order standard of rule-following correctness', and so on, or 'what can be the status of mathematical "objects" such as numbers, sets or classes given that, if objectively conceived, they must *ipso facto* be thought of as transcending the utmost limits of human knowability?'.[30]

To be sure, Badiou has a good deal to say on these and related topics, some of it quite capable of showing them up in a new and highly revealing philosophical light. My point is simply to remark that his take on them involves a degree of speculative freedom (rather than licence) that goes well beyond the limits laid down by received analytical ideas of what counts as serious, constructive, or genuinely problem-solving philosophy of mathematics. Yet Badiou is very clear in *Being and Event* that if there is one lesson to be learned from developments in post-Cantorian set-theory it is the fact that they can only be grasped – or yield anything like their full measure of mathematical as well as philosophic insight – on condition that thinking be prepared to explore regions of speculative ontology beyond those preconceived limits. Such, he maintains, is the chief advance brought about by this way of thinking as compared with previous, vaguely formulated ideas concerning the relationship between mathematics and some ultimate order of reality or truth. It is because that relationship is here conceived as always and by its very nature involving a passage beyond what is presently knowable toward those truths that are offered to thought through a process of often highly speculative yet not, for that reason, any less disciplined or rigorous enquiry.

Indeed the distinction between knowledge and truth – between what *counts* as 'knowledge' at some given stage in the history of knowledge-acquisition and what *will or counterfactually would* so count once all the evidence is in – is absolutely central to Badiou's claim for mathematics as the basis of ontology and therefore (in a time-honoured sense going back to the ancient Greeks) as 'first philosophy'. Moreover, it is a precept that he shares with those in the analytic community who espouse a realist conception of mathematical truth, that is, a conception according to which our best present state of knowledge (or best available proof-procedures) may always fall short of ascertaining or establishing the truth of any given proposition.[31] For Badiou this applies across all subject-areas, no matter how diverse in other respects, where there is a need to respect the elementary distinction – 'elementary' at least from a realist perspective – between the way things stand as a matter of objective reality and the way they are considered to stand as a matter of existing opinion, rational consensus, or expert (even optimal or best attainable) human judgement. On this point at least he is in agreement with some (if not most) analytic philosophers of mathematics, logic and the formal sciences: that the truth or falsehood of statements in the relevant class is decided, quite apart from our state of knowledge, as a matter of objective or (in the jargon) verification-transcendent warrant. And if it is then asked – as very often it is by anti-realists – how we could possibly gain epistemic access to truths that by very definition might always surpass the utmost limits of human knowledge then Badiou's response is again very much in accord with the standard realist rejoinder. That is to say, the chief lesson that emerges from the history of advances in mathematics to date – not least through the various extensions and refinements of set-theoretical method – is that any state of knowledge at any given time might always fall short of objective truth and yet point the way to some further, as yet scarcely conceivable stage of progress. Such advances can be seen to occur solely by virtue of the fact that mathematical thought is subject to constraints – along with a sense of inventive or exploratory-creative possibilities – that enable just such a passage beyond the limits of present (even best-attainable) knowledge.

Nevertheless it needs saying that Badiou is not a 'realist' or 'objectivist' about mathematics in the sense of those terms commonly adopted by analytic philosophers. On their account, typically, one is faced with the choice between a theory of truth that places it inherently beyond the furthest power of human conceptual grasp and an alternative (anti-realist, constructivist, or intuitionist) theory that brings it safely back within epistemic reach but only the cost of renouncing any claim to objective, i.e., recognition-transcendent truth. Indeed he sees this as a downright false dilemma and one that has all too often been foisted onto Plato in the name of a typecast mathematical 'Platonism' presumed to entail just such a drastic (and drastically disabling) dichotomy of truth and knowledge. Hence his objection to the statement by two analytic philosophers that '[i]n general, the Platonists will be those who consider mathematics as the discovery of truths about structures which exist independently of the activity or thought of mathematicians'.[32] After all, as Badiou does well to remind us, when Plato raises this issue most directly – as in the famous scene of instruction with the slave-boy in the *Meno* – he makes it very plain that mathematical knowledge can be acquired only through a grasp of objective (and in sense mind-independent) truths that is none the less a grasp in and by the active power of human intelligence. 'What the metaphor of anamnesis designates is precisely that thought is never confronted by objectivities from which it is supposedly separated. The idea is always already there and would remain unthinkable were one not able to "activate" it in thought.'[33]

Thus philosophers quite simply get it wrong and turn a puzzle into a full-scale paradox or epistemic crisis by approaching these topics in an abstract, disengaged way and consequently failing to achieve and communicate any such demonstrative power. Why else – one might ask – could they become so engrossed or preoccupied by problems (like that of following-a-rule or providing a justification for the axioms of elementary arithmetic) which may have a certain philosophical interest as formal variations on an age-old sceptical theme but would scarcely command the attention of thinkers at the cutting edge of mathematical research. It is in this respect chiefly that Badiou offers an instructive contrast by actually explaining and working through a representative range of those set-theoretical problems, challenges, and stages of conceptual advance that have played such a central role in the development of his own thinking. What they mostly have in common is the character of turning obstacles and setbacks to advantage by using them as a springboard – a standing provocation or source of renewed creative and intellectual impetus – whereby to devise more powerful means of set-theoretical treatment. Such, for instance, were the various solutions put forward in response to Bertrand Russell's discovery of the paradox that followed from constructing self-referential expressions like 'the set of all sets that are not members of themselves', or (in homelier terms) 'the barber who shaves every man in town except those who shave themselves' (in which case who shaves the barber?). For Badiou, these cases should not be seen as mere distractions – however puzzling or intriguing – from the straight high road of mathematical progress but rather as a chief and indispensable means of bringing such progress about. Besides, as he remarks, they are just the sorts of problem that have often cropped up in the path of metaphysical thought or ontological enquiry ever since the issue of the one and the many was first raised by speculative thinkers like Parmenides, Zeno, Heraclitus, and Empedocles.

It is this pattern of advancement through repeated encounter with threats to its own conceptual, logical, or structural consistency that has typified set-theoretical research throughout its history to date. It thus provides Badiou with his favoured example of how thinking can achieve its most impressive discoveries in this or other fields of investigation as a result of coming up against just such blocks to its smooth development or steady progress toward an ever greater power of conceptualisation. Moreover it provides him with a paradigm instance of the *active* and *heterodox* power of thought, that is, of the way that thinking can break with received, established, or conventional habits of belief. Thus '[t]hose who practice the mathematical sciences are "forced" to proceed according to the intelligible, rather than according to the sensible or to *doxa*'.[34]

IV

Among the most recent of these discoveries – and one that is of central importance to Badiou's whole project – is precisely the concept or procedure of 'forcing' which received its canonical formulation by the mathematician Paul Cohen.[35] In brief, this involves the capacity of thought to exceed to the limits of present-best knowledge or attainable proof through a grasp of those procedures and truth-conditions that *will* or necessarily *would have* been satisfied if this or that statement, theorem, or conjecture is eventually to count as verified. Thus:

> [y]ou certainly cannot straightforwardly name the elements of a generic subset, since the latter is at once incomplete in its infinite composition and subtracted from every predicate which would directly identify it in the language. But you can maintain that *if* such and such an element *will have been* in the supposedly complete generic subset, *then* such and such a statement, rationally connectable to the element in question, is, or rather will have been, correct.[36]

That is to say, any rendition of Cohen's thesis must be couched in the future-anterior tense and also in the conditional or subjunctive mode since it has to do with what cannot yet be formally proved or verified while none the less following by the strictest necessity from certain other propositions which, if true, will be recognised as lending decisive support to the given hypothesis or theorem. And again: any gaps, inconsistencies, or contradictions in some given state of knowledge may force the invention (in a somewhat archaic but aptly ambiguous sense of that word: the creative devising but also the discovery) of a new working hypothesis. This latter is then subject to further testing, refinement, and elaboration until the stage when its validity – if and when confirmed – will retroactively endorse whatever led up to it in the way of conjectural (though none the less rigorous and faithful) truth-procedures. Cohen's thesis therefore offers Badiou a means of sharpening his own distinction between being and event, or explaining how events which exceed the utmost limits of conceptual specification can none the less bring about a decisive change in the state of mathematical knowledge. Thus: '[f]oreclosed from ontology, the event returns in the mode according to which the undecidable can only be decided therein by forcing veracity from the standpoint of the indiscernible'.[37]

It is here precisely that the subject makes its entry since, on Badiou's account, the subject can best be defined as 'that which decides an undecidable from the standpoint of an indiscernible . . . or that which forces a veracity, according to the suspense of a truth'.[38] That is, the subject is here conceived as the locus of certain commitments, attachments, priorities, hypotheses, research agendas or projects, and so forth, any one of which may properly be said – in some particular, well-defined context – to constitute their very identity or mode of existence. What this involves – in the language of *Being and Event* – is a capacity to grasp those as-yet strictly 'indiscernible' elements that reveal the constant (and at times critical) excess of inconsistent over consistent multiplicity, subsets over sets, parts over members, inclusion over belonging, or the 'state of the situation' over the situation as currently rendered according to the dominant count-as-one. As Badiou writes:

> [a] subject alone possesses the capacity of indiscernment. This is also why it forces the undecidable to exhibit itself as such, on the substructure of being of an indiscernible part. It is thus assured that the impasse of being is the point at which a Subject convokes itself to a decision, because at least one multiple, subtracted from the language, proposes to fidelity and to the names induced by a supernumerary nomination the possibility of a decision without concept.[39]

It is important to recognise that Badiou is not here adopting any kind of ultra-nominalist, constructivist, cultural-relativist, or linguistic-descriptivist stance with regard to the process by which thinking decides between the various events – or the various possible modes of fidelity to them – that confront the subject in some given context of enquiry or commitment. Nothing could be wider of the mark, as will be obvious to anyone who has read his often caustic remarks about the stultifying effect of the 'linguistic turn' in its manifold forms and guises. Above all he rejects the version of it to be found in Wittgenstein where the idea of language as an ultimate horizon of intelligibility goes along with the idea of mathematics as just another cultural practice or 'form of life' that necessarily adheres to the conventions laid down for its own 'correct' (i.e., communally warranted) conduct. On this view, quite simply, mathematics 'doesn't think' in so far as its standards of validity and truth must be taken to consist either, as the early Wittgenstein believed, in a series of empty since merely tautologous propositions and linkages between them or, as he later came around to believing, in conformity with the 'rules' that generally hold sway within this or that, more-or-less expert community.

'Here', Badiou comments, 'with customary radicality, Wittgenstein merely restates a thesis that is common to every variety of empiricism, as well as to all sophistry. It is one which we will never have done refuting.'[40] So we should not for one moment read the above-cited passage, or others like it, as betraying some residual lapse into a language-first, 'continentally' inflected (that is, hermeneutically inclined or post-structuralist) way of approach these issues. Rather we should take it as a vigorous assertion of Badiou's claim that mathematics does indeed 'think', and also that the kind of thinking most aptly exemplified by certain major advances in mathematics is a kind that goes far beyond anything accountable on those or such-like terms. This is also why he rejects

Heidegger's view of 'Western metaphysics' since Plato as mortgaged to a technocratic drive for mastery over nature and humanity alike, and of the various sciences – whether 'applied' or 'pure', thus including mathematics and logic – as likewise the product of a strictly unthinking since somehow pre-destined movement of thought in that same direction. On the contrary, Badiou argues: such a failure to perceive the frequent creativity, depth, and ethical resonance of scientific thought is one that could result only from Heidegger's having been in the grip of a distorted philosophic, historical, and socio-political perspective. Moreover it had much to do with Heidegger's intense (but intensely one-sided) identification of philosophy – or authentic 'thinking' – with poetry alone among those salient 'conditions' that Badiou regards as setting the terms for its effective engagement with issues outside a narrowly self-occupied sphere.[41]

This recurrent inclination of philosophers to throw in their lot exclusively with one or another of those conditions – whether poetry (with Heidegger), science (with the positivists), or politics (as with Stalinist or other such attempts to dictate philosophy's ideological content) is, according to Badiou, one major cause of their having so often gone ethically, politically, and intellectually off the rails. Indeed it is just the kind of aberration that he pinpoints in his book *Ethics: an essay on the understanding of evil* as the source of much moral corruption and one that is liable – as in Heidegger's case – to infiltrate thinking even (or especially) at points of maximum concentration or intensity.[42] Such is that particular 'romantic' temptation of thought whereby 'art is presented as the sole free form of descent from the infinite Idea to the sensible and, with Heidegger and certain fascisms, requires itself to prostrate philosophy before art'.[43] This is one reason why Badiou insists on the equiprimordiality – that is, the jointly and equally vital contributions – of those four conditioning factors that between them constitute philosophy's proper and enabling sphere of concern. Above all he rejects the commonplace idea (given its most philosophically articulate expression by Heidegger) that mathematics and science are somehow inimical to the kind of inventive or creative-exploratory thinking that typifies poetic thinking.

Thus '[t]he tautest, most unremitting, and truest art6 of the twentieth century made an attempt to test out the notion . . . that "Newton's binomial is as beautiful as the Venus de Milo", which is to say: this art tried to seize the real with the same impersonal rigour as that of mathematics'.[44] On the one hand this conviction comes across to very striking effect in Badiou's commentary on Mallarmé in *Being and Event*.[45] On the other it is conveyed with equivalent force by his sustained and intensive meditation on set theory and related mathematical, logical, and scientific developments. Again what Badiou is most anxious to communicate is the close kinship that exists between these developments and the kinds of creativity that are more often taken to characterise significant achievements in poetry and the other arts. So it was – by venturing beyond the range of propositions that found any room within existing norms of intelligibility – that mathematicians from Galileo to Cantor and Cohen have challenged the limits of intuitive (received or 'common-sense') judgement and hence succeeded in 'turning a paradox into a concept', or using obstacles as springboards for inventive and transformative thought. So it was likewise that Cantor 'had the brilliant idea of treating positively the remarks of Galileo and Pascal . . . in which these authors had concluded in the impossibility of infinite number'.[46] This he achieved simply by remarking that since there was a term-by-term correspondence between the whole numbers (integers) and squares – that for every whole number there existed a square – therefore one might as well state that there are *just as many* square numbers as integers, despite the strong (and still-persisting) commonsense-intuitive conviction to the contrary, i.e., that the whole must always be greater than its parts.

Hence the decisive set-theoretical advance whereby it became possible to think of the one not as the foundation or precondition of all mathematical reasoning but rather as a product of the count-as-one, and moreover, to think of inconsistent (rather than consistent) multiplicity as that which underlies and may always turn out to exceed or disrupt any unifying order thus imposed. Thus:

> because the set theory doctrine of the multiple does not define the multiple it does not have to run the gauntlet of the intuition of the whole and its parts . . . . We will allow, without blinking an eye, that given that it is a matter of infinite multiples, it is possible for what is *included* (like square numbers in whole numbers) to be as 'numerous' as that in which it is included . . . There is a subversion herein of the old intuition of quantity, that subsumed by the couple whole/parts: this subversion completes the innovation of thought, and the ruin of that intuition.[47]

So Badiou is very firm – as against many adversaries, present and past – in maintaining the absolute and principled independence of mathematical thought from any conditions having to do with the scope and limits of linguistic-symbolic expression or the deliverances of intuitive judgement. Where the former brings him out squarely at odds with Wittgenstein and likeminded present-day thinkers the latter flags up not only his distance from Kant and any notion of synthetic *a priori* mathematical truths but also his rejection of certain intuitionist (which, in this context, most often also means anti-realist) approaches to issues in philosophy of mathematics. For instance, Badiou takes a strong line against the intuitionists' refusal to endorse the logical axioms of bivalence or excluded middle, that is, their claim that for certain mathematical statements – those belonging to Michael Dummett's 'disputed class' of formally unproven theorems, hypotheses, or conjectures – these classical axioms simply don't apply.[48] This follows directly from the intuitionist (and anti-realist) precept that truth cannot possibly be thought to exceed the scope of warranted assertibility, in which case any statement of this type that we venture to assert cannot be rendered true or false by the way things stand in mathematical reality quite aside from the issue as to whether we are now – or shall ever be – suitably placed to decide either way. In other words truth is 'epistemically constrained' by our various perceptual, cognitive, or conceptual capacities and cannot be thought of (in objectivist or realist terms) as always potentially transcending or eluding our present-best state of knowledge.[49]

Along with this goes their rejection of another basic classical axiom, namely that of double negation elimination, or – simply put – the principle that two negatives always make a positive. Here again their revisionist stance results from the belief that unproven conjectures are neither true nor false to the best of our attainable knowledge and hence neither true nor false *sans phrase*. So, consistently with this, they have to deny the validity of any argument – for instance, any use of *reductio ad absurdum* – which purports to derive its demonstrative force from precisely that axiom, i.e., to establish the truth of some given hypothesis by establishing the falsehood (or absurdity) of its negation. For Badiou, conversely, such principles of deductive reasoning are a *sine qua non* of mathematical thought and cannot be abandoned without, in the process, renouncing all claim to be concerned with discovering *truths* of mathematics rather than convenient working fictions or handy techniques for fixing any problem in line with the current-best state of knowledge or opinion. Badiou is quite clear that the axiom of double negation elimination – and along with it the force of *reductio*-type or apagogic arguments – can readily be made to seem artificial and unconvincing by the standards of everyday-commonsense thought. Thus:

> [t]he strict equivalence of *A* and ~~*A* – which I hold to be directly linked to what is at stake in mathematics, being-qua-being (and not sensible time) – is so far removed from our dialectical experience, from everything proclaimed by history and life, that ontology is simultaneously vulnerable in this point to the empiricist and the speculative critique.[50]

That is, it might seem wide open to the kinds of objection mounted not only by empiricists like Hume but also by a speculative thinker like Hegel who sought to overcome the charges of tautology, vacuity, vicious regress, circularity, and so forth, through a different, i.e., dialectical logic with substantive rather than abstract or merely formal content. However Badiou comes back most emphatically against that whole range of arguments – as likewise against the intuitionist refusal to countenance those classical axioms – by claiming that mathematics simply cannot do without such resources unless at the cost of triviality or (*contra* Hegel) giving up any claim to engage with matters of real-world ontological concern. Indeed, 'it is on the basis of the ontological vocation of mathematics that one can infer the legitimacy of the equivalence between affirmation and double negation . . . and, by consequence, the conclusiveness of reasoning via the absurd'. In which case 'the use of apagogic reasoning signals the belonging of mathematical deductive fidelity to ontological concerns'.[51]

Badiou introduces a number of related set-theoretical concepts, along with that of 'forcing', some of which derive from Cohen's work and others from the broader development of post-Cantorian mathematical thought but all of which bear directly on this issue of how advances come about in the formal (as well as the physical) sciences. More specifically, they hold out the prospect of explaining how truth can be conceived as running ahead of some current state of knowledge while not losing touch so completely with the powers and capacities of human reason as to conjure up the threat of epistemological scepticism or – as a supposed escape-route from it – the fallback appeal to various kinds of anti-realist, intuitionist, or constructivist doctrine. Among them are the concepts of the void, the generic, the indiscernible, the ultra-one, the evental site, and the supernumerary, which between them can be seen as laying out the groundwork of Badiou's ontology and his account of what exceeds or transcends any power of ontological reckoning. Thus the *void* – like the null set in mathematics – is that which is included in every situation or every set-theoretical ensemble but the presence (or determinate absence) of which can be felt to exert a destabilising pressure only at moments of challenge to the dominant count-as-one. That is to say, it achieves its maximum impact or its power to transform the *status quo ante* – whether in the formal, the natural, the social, or the human sciences – at just those times when the reign of 'consistent multiplicity' gives way to the irruption of an 'inconsistent' (i.e., anomalous and crisis-inducing) multiplicity. The *generic* (again from Cohen) is a term for that which derives from some anomalous even though, to begin with, *indiscernible* element in this or that given situation – one that doesn't figure or qualify for membership according to the count-as-one – yet which turns out to possess just that kind of long-range transformative or paradigm-shifting power. What enables those elements to acquire such power is their existing as *supernumerary* parts of a situation whose total state – including its various constituent sub-sets – must always be reckoned as greatly in excess of whatever is recognised or counted as belonging to it by current membership criteria. The *evental site*, as Badiou defines it, is a multiple or sub-set that exists within some given larger or more numerous situation yet none of whose members are taken as belonging to it.

It is here – with the emergence of anomalies, excrescences, or 'supernumerary' elements – that the situation comes under strain or confronts an as yet scarcely visible challenge from that which it contains yet cannot properly accommodate. It is here also, in the wider context of Badiou's work, that the discourse of mathematics – that is to say, of fundamental ontology as he conceives it – provides the point of juncture for all those concerns and involvements that have occupied his thinking over the past three decades. Thus the entire conceptual *ensemble* of count-as-one, event, void, evental site, the generic, forcing, consistent *versus* inconsistent multiplicity, situation *versus* state-of-the-situation, and so forth enables him to make the crucial link between issues in the realm of mathematics or the formal sciences and issues of political power, agency, and representation. That is to say, 'what the State strives to foreclose through its power of counting is the void of the situation, while the event always reveals it'.[52] Moreover, as we have seen, this allows for the extension of those same heuristic concepts to a range of other fields – including certain aspects of arts and the natural sciences – where he shows them to apply with equal pertinence and force. Here again it is a question of doing justice on the one hand to truth-conditions or validity-claims that transcend any merely *de facto* state of knowledge, understanding, or best judgement and on the other to those various procedures whereby the dedicated subject affirms his or her commitment to the truth in question. For Badiou is absolutely insistent on the point that we are *not* then faced with any version of the false dilemma so eagerly touted by some occupants of the 'nothing works' camp in philosophy of mathematics. Rather there is just too much evidence – for anyone who works through *Being and Event* with sufficient attentiveness to detail – that in this field especially sceptical doubt of the kind professed by some philosophers can only be the product of a failure to engage with the activity of real mathematical thought as distinct from reflecting on the nature of that activity from a disengaged standpoint.

Nor is this approach by any means confined to his treatment of issues and developments in the set-theoretical domain. Indeed one of the most striking features of Badiou's work is the sheer wealth of illustrative cases – mathematical, scientific, political, artistic, and (not least) 'amorous' or psychoanalytically oriented – that he offers by way of substantive support for what might otherwise seem some highly abstract and often quite exorbitant claims.

V

What makes his project altogether unique in contemporary terms is its cleaving to truth as an indispensable standard across these diverse regions of enquiry and yet – consistently with that – its stress on the irruptive or unpredictable nature of those epochal events that impose new demands of fidelity on subjects who have known or experienced their impact. Thus Badiou proposes nothing less than a radical reconfiguration of issues and concerns that are central to every major branch of philosophic thought and have rarely been exposed to so remarkably acute and original a mode of questioning. It is through the privileged role assigned to mathematics that his work stands apart from all the chief currents of post-war (though not, as he is quick to point out, of pre-1940) French philosophy.

This is also where it comes most directly into contact with a chief preoccupation of philosophy in the mainstream analytic or Anglo-American line of descent, albeit from a very different angle of approach. Still one should bear in mind Badiou's firm insistence on the strict separation of realms between mathematics as the basis of any first-order ontological project of thought and those other projects whose task it is to articulate the truths of our contingent or situated being-in-the-world. For there is, he reminds us,

> the vast question of that which subtracts itself from ontological determination, the question of that which is *not* being qua being. The law of subtraction is implacable: if real ontology is set out as mathematics by eluding the law of the One, it is also necessary, lest one allow this norm to re-establish itself at a global level, that there be a point at which the ontological (i.e., mathematical) field is detotalized or caught in an impasse. I have called this point *the event*. Accordingly we could also say that, beyond the identification of real ontology . . . philosophy is also, first and foremost, the general theory of the event. That is, the theory of that which subtracts itself from ontological subtraction. Or the theory of the impossible proper to mathematics.[53]

Thus philosophy should take its lead from mathematics with respect to ontological issues but should also draw attention to those epochal events – among them events in the history of mathematics itself – which by their very nature elude or exceed any such purely onto-mathematical account. After all, as Badiou remarks, 'the mathematical elaboration of thought is not of the order of a mere linear unfolding or straightforward logical consequence', but on the contrary displays an evental character in so far as it 'comprises decisive but previously unknown gestures'.[54] Moreover, philosophy must always maintain its critical distance from the various regions of scientific, political, ethical, or aesthetic enquiry that none the less provide its most significant subject-matter. These have to be approached with a due regard for their relative autonomy lest philosophers make the not uncommon mistake of exceeding their own particular fields of competence or special expertise.

Thus one main reason for Badiou's intensive engagement with field-specific questions of natural science, political theory, aesthetics, and psychoanalysis is to disabuse philosophy of any such overly ambitious or grandiose claims. On the other hand his project stands out in the context of recent 'continental' (not to mention a good deal of recent analytic or 'post-analytic') thought for its uncompromising stance with regard to the need for philosophy to re-assert its own distinctive character as the precondition for its relevance to work in those other disciplinary fields. This places him squarely at odds with various present-day assaults on the notion that truth might transcend or surpass the limits of some given language-game, discourse, cultural life-form, or whatever. That is to say, it goes against some prominent strains of post-1960 French philosophy but also against some conspicuous anti-realist, constructivist, or framework-relativist trends in recent analytic debate. Hence Badiou's outright opposition to those various present-day movements of thought that would claim to have emerged on the far side of all that endless and pointless squabbling over misbegotten topics like the 'problem of truth'. Hence also his rejection of the widespread 'linguistic turn' (whether in its mainstream-analytic, Wittgensteinian, or continental-hermeneutic variants) as merely a sophistical means of distraction from those core issues – such as the relationship between being and event – which properly occupy the focus of philosophical attention. Badiou's project can thus be seen as an eloquent call for philosophy to regain a due sense of its legitimate purpose and priorities in response to various internal as well as external threats or pressures. Yet just as important in the context of present-day debate is his stress on philosophy's absolute need for close and reciprocal involvement with those other equiprimordial dimensions of human experience where truth is always in question, even if arrived at (as he is careful to show) through very different paths of thought. Indeed the most striking aspect of Badiou's work is this ability to think across and between disciplines – mathematics, politics, philosophy of science, psychoanalysis, ethics, theory and history of art – while none the less maintaining a strong sense of their distinctive character and truth-content.

Notes

---

[1] See Jason Barker *Alain Badiou: a critical introduction* (London: Pluto, 2002); Peter Hallward, *Badiou: a subject to truth* (Minneapolis: University of Minnesota Press, 2003) and Hallward (ed.), *Think Again: Alain Badiou and the future of philosophy* (London: Continuum, 2004).

[2] Alain Badiou, *Metapolitics*, trans. Jason Barker (London: Verso, 2005); *Polemics*, trans. Steve Corcoran (London: Verso, 2006); *Century*, trans. Alberto Toscano (Cambridge: Polity Press, 2007).

[3] Badiou, *Being and Event*, trans. Oliver Feltham (London: Continuum, 2005).

[4] Badiou, *Manifesto for Philosophy*, trans. Norman Madarasz (Albany, NY: State University of New York Press, 1999); *Infinite Thought: truth and the return to philosophy*, trans. Oliver Feltham and Justin Clemens (London: Continuum, 2003); *Theoretical Writings*, ed. and trans. Ray Brassier and Alberto Toscano (London: Continuum, 2004).

[5] Badiou, *Saint Paul: the foundation of universalism*, trans. Ray Brassier (Stanford, CA: Stanford University Press, 2003).

[6] See entries under Notes 2 and 4, above.

[7] See especially Badiou, *Being and Event* and *Theoretical writings* (Notes 3 and 4, above).

[8] For a lucid account see Michael Potter, *Set Theory and its Philosophy: a critical introduction* (Oxford: Oxford University Press, 2004).

[9] See Note 2, above.

[10] Badiou, 'Politics Unbound', in *Metapolitics*, pp. 68-77; p. 77.

[11] Cited by Badiou, 'The Paris Commune', in *Polemics* (Note 2, above), pp. 258-90; p. 284.

[12] Ibid, p. 285.

[13] Ibid, p. 278.

[14] Ibid, p. 286.

[15] Ibid, p. 278.

[16] Ibid, p. 290.

[17] Ibid, p. 288.

[18] Ibid, p. 284.

[19] See especially ibid, pp. 278-89.

[20] Ibid, p. 287.

[21] Badiou, *Metapolitics*, p. 3.

[22] Ibid, p. 4.

---

[23] Ibid, p. 5.
[24] Spinoza, *Ethics*, trans. Edwin Curley (London: Penguin, 1996; Badiou, *Being and Event*, pp. 112-20; also – for relevant discussion from various philosophic and political perspectives – Etienne Balibar, *Spinoza and Politics* (London: Verso, 1998); Jonathan Israel, *Radical Enlightenment: philosophy and the making of modernity, 1650-1750* (Oxford: Oxford University Press, 2002); Christopher Norris, *Spinoza and the Origins of Modern Critical Theory* (Oxford: Blackwell, 1991).
[25] Badiou, *Being and Event*, p. 232.
[26] Ibid, p. 233.
[27] See Gottlob Frege, 'Review of Edmund Husserl's *Philosophie der Arithmetik*', trans. E.-H. W. Kluge. *Mind*, Vol. 81 (1972), pp. 321-37; also – for a subsequent episode in this history of misunderstandings – Gilbert Ryle, 'Phenomenology' and 'Phenomenology versus *The Concept of Mind*', in Ryle, *Collected Papers*, Vol. 1 (London: Hutchinson, 1971), pp. 167-78 and 179-96. A range of more balanced and better-informed views may be found in Leila Haaparanta (ed.), *Mind, Meaning, and Mathematics: essays on the philosophical views of Husserl and Frege* (Dordrecht and Boston: Kluwer, 1994).
[28] Christopher Norris, *Minding the Gap: epistemology and philosophy of science in the two traditions* (Amherst,. MA: University of Massachusetts Press, 2000).
[29] For a very different but not entirely incompatible approach, see Bernard Williams, *Truth and Truthfulness: an essay in genealogy* (Princeton, NJ: Princeton University Press, 2002).
[30] See for instance Paul Benacerraf, 'What Numbers Could Not Be', in Benacerraf and Hilary Putnam (eds.*), The Philosophy of Mathematics: selected essays*, 2nd edn. (Cambridge: Cambridge University Press, 1983), pp. 272-94; also W.D. Hart (ed.*), The Philosophy of Mathematics* (Oxford: Oxford University Press, 1996) and Hilary Putnam, *Mathematics, Matter and Method* (Cambridge University Press, 1975). On the rule following issue, see Ludwig Wittgenstein, *Philosophical Investigations*, trans. G.E.M. Anscombe (Oxford: Blackwell, 1951), Sections 201-292 *passim*; Saul Kripke, *Wittgenstein on Rules and Private Language: an elementary exposition* (Oxford: Blackwell, 1982); Alexander Miller and Crispin Wright (eds.), *Rule-Following and Meaning* (Chesham: Acumen, 2002).
[31] See especially Kurt Gődel, 'What Is Cantor's Continuum Problem?', in Benacerraf and Putnam (eds.), *Philosophy of Mathematics* (op. cit.), pp. 470-85; also Jerrold J. Katz, *Realistic Rationalism* (Cambridge, MA: M.I.T. Press, 1998).
[32] Benacerraf and Putnam (eds.), *Philosophy of Mathematics* (op. cit.), p. 15.
[33] Badiou, *Theoretical Writings*, p. 49.
[34] Ibid, p. 30.
[35] Paul J. Cohen, *Set Theory and the Continuum Hypothesis* (New York: W.A. Benjamin, 1966).
[36] Badiou, *Theoretical Writings*, p. 127.
[37] Badiou, *Being and Event*, p. 429..
[38] Ibid, p. 407.
[39] Ibid, p. 429.

[40] Badiou, *Theoretical Writings*, p. 53.
[41] See especially Martin Heidegger, *Early Greek Thinking*, trans. David F. Krell and Frank Capuzzi (New York: Harper & Row, 1975); *'The Question Concerning Technology' and Other Essays*, trans. William Lovitt (Harper & Row, 1977); *What Is a Thing?*, trans. W.B. Barton and Vera Deutsch (Chicago: Regnery, 1969); *The Principle of Reason*, trans. Reginald Lilly (Bloomington, IN.: Indiana University Press, 1991).
[42] Badiou, *Ethics: an essay on the understanding of evil*, trans. Peter Hallward (London: Verso, 2001).
[43] Badiou, *Polemics* (Note 2, above), p. 135.
[44] Ibid, p. 140.
[45] Badiou, *Being and Event*, pp. 191-8.
[46] Badiou, *Being and Event*, p. 267.
[47] Ibid, p. 267.
[48] Michael Dummett, *Elements of Intuitionism* (Oxford: Oxford University Press, 1977); also *Truth and Other Enigmas* (London: Duckworth, 1978) and *The Logical Basis of Metaphysics* (Duckworth, 1991). For a critical account of these and related developments, see Christopher Norris, *Truth Matters: realism, anti-realism, and response-dependence* (Edinburgh: Edinburgh University Press, 2002) and *Philosophy of Language and the Challenge to Scientific Realism* (London: Routledge, 2003).
[49] For further discussion, see Crispin Wright, *Realism, Meaning and Truth* (Oxford: Blackwell, 1987) and *Truth and Objectivity* (Cambridge, MA: Harvard University Press, 1992).
[50] Ibid, p. 248.
[51] Ibid, p. 250.
[52] Badiou, *Metapolitics*, p. 119.
[53] Badiou, *Theoretical Writings*, p. 98.
[54] Ibid, p. 19.

THE PRACTICAL-AMBIGUOUS SUBJECT (COPING IN AND WITH THE WORLD)

MARK SANDERS, UNIVERSITY OF NORTH CAROLINA AT CHARLOTTE

The Death of the Subject?

Michel Foucault and Jacques Derrida have both famously heralded the death of the subject. In *The Order of Things*, Foucault claims that "man is in the process of disappearing" (Foucault, p. 385). In "The Ends of Man," Derrida states, "The thinking of the end of man, therefore, is always already prescribed in metaphysics, in the thinking of the truth of man" (Derrida, p. 121). But what does it mean to say that man (or woman) is in the process of disappearing or coming to an end? What are the ramifications of the end or death of the subject for philosophy?[1]

"Man" conceived of as a subject seems crucial to the discourse of philosophy. While the concept of the subject may require alterations, such a process is nothing new for philosophy, which by its nature is constantly adapting to new ideas and transforming itself. Luc Ferry and Alain Renaut propose that the concept of the subject must be reconsidered, but this should not entail its wholesale destruction. According to Ferry and Renaut, "After Marx, Nietzsche, Freud, and Heidegger, it is philosophically impossible to return to the idea that man is the owner and controller of the whole of his actions and ideas . . . the real task today . . . is to rethink the question of the subject" (Ferry and Renaut, p.17).

I agree that the subject should be re-thought in a manner that criticizes certain aspects of the Cartesian cogito, but the subject should not be overwhelmed by the deconstruction of Heidegger, Derrida, Foucault, and others. Specifically, the subject must be disentangled from the theoretical abstract mental space of Descartes and connected to the practical space of the everyday world. The subject must sever ties to the Cartesian notion of certainty and embrace a sense of ambiguity.

Descartes' subject is a cognitive concept concerned with the mental act of acquiring certainty of itself. It is separate from the body and the world, existing only in a theoretical mental space. Descartes' mind/body dualism removes the subject from the world, which is clouded by imperfection and uncertainty. This act of disengagement entails that we objectify the world as something clearly separate from us. This subject/object dichotomy will cause problems for all conceptions of subjectivity that remain stuck in the Cartesian framework. The result of Descartes' mind/body dualism and subject/object dichotomy is a concept of an abstract mental subject which expunges the concrete practical subject.

In what follows I hope to show the importance of both the practical and the ambiguous, and their connection, in formulating what I have named the *practical-ambiguous subject.* In doing so, I will draw upon a wide range of sources stressing the value of the practical and the ambiguous in understanding the subject. These will contribute to the formulation of the practical-ambiguous subject, which should be understood as a living human being involved in, and coping with, the practical-ambiguous world.

The Practical World is Ambiguous

The notion of *practice* is an essential component for any conception of subjectivity because it opens up possibilities for human solidarity and community, which are vital to the very explanation of the concept of subjectivity.[2] The subject is something that must be understood in and through practice, i.e. in and through one's interactions with others in the world.

It is my contention that the real reason for maintaining a notion of the subject is because one must, and in fact does, act in the practical world. This is crucial because those philosophers who call for the death or elimination of the subject seem to overlook the fact that the subject acts and is ethically judged in the practical world of everyday experience. As Fred Dallmayr explains, "the abolition of man, as counseled or intimated by end-of-man arguments, may carry a price which outweighs its benefits," pointing out that one of the casualties would likely be "moral responsibility" (Dallmayr, p. 30). To erase or replace the subject is to erase or replace the center of practice and moral responsibility, which is not something to be taken lightly, at least not by those of us who want to defend a conception of the subject. What is at stake here is articulated by Vincent Descombes in a discussion about the theoretical and practical aspects of the subject:

> As for the defenders of the subject, they seem to assert the 'primacy of practical interest' in philosophy. For them, the 'philosophy of the subject' cannot be totally invalid in its theoretical aspect since it is valid in its practical aspect. If we no longer had the possibility or the right to consider ourselves, even if only partially, as subjects, we could no longer pose ethical questions. (Descombes, pp. 121-122)

The subject must be understood as an actual person who makes choices and acts on them in the practical world. Furthermore, when one realizes that the practical world of everyday experience is governed not by certainty but by ambiguity, then one realizes the connection between the practical and the ambiguous and the subject must be understood accordingly. The subject that grapples with the ambiguity of the practical world is a subject that grows in fullness and richness in ways that a subject that is analyzed from a purely abstract mental standpoint can not. The practical-ambiguous subject is an involved participant in the world that accepts the uncertainty of their ever-changing circumstances and continues to make choices. This acceptance and ability to cope defines the growth of the practical-ambiguous subject.

Ernst Tugendhat differentiates between "epistemic self-consciousness and the practical relation of oneself to oneself" (Tugendhat, p. 23). The practical relation of oneself to oneself is connected not just to one's mental states, but to one's ability to act as well. The notion of the practical relation of oneself to oneself is preferable because it links the subject to the practical world, and because in doing so it allows the conception of subjectivity to be understood as a *process*. In epistemic self-consciousness, represented by the Cartesian cogito, the subject gains immediate knowledge of itself upon self-reflection. The problem here is that knowledge should not be thought of as something immediate or instantaneous, but as something that is acquired through a process. As Tugendhat states, "The talk of immediate identification is meaningless if it is supposed to represent an achievement of knowledge" (Tugendhat p. 49). The notion of the practical relation of oneself to oneself, allows the subject to be understood as an evolving entity whose growth is accomplished through the process of being involved in the practical world.

This idea is illustrated by Fichte's contention that the subject should not be regarded as a fact *(Tatsache)* but as a fact-act *(Tathandlung)*. By conceptualizing the subject in this way, Fichte is expressing the idea that, "The I is not to be understood as a thing but as an activity" (Neuhouser, pp.106-107). This idea is further elaborated by

Alfred North Whitehead, who recognizes nature as an evolving process in which things are understood in and through their changes. Understanding the subject in the world as a continually unfolding process helps give a more complete picture than one could get from taking a snapshot that captures a static thing at a particular time and place. This viewpoint sees the subject as an entity involved in the process of living.

Whitehead understands process as progress without teleology. That is, he conceives of the process of the subject in the world as one that moves along in a manner that can be described as progress, but has no end point. It is not the case that human beings are propelled along by a random set of events and actions. Rather, there is a rational structure that guides people's actions and helps them progress, but without certainty and without finality. According to Whitehead, "Mankind never quite knows what it is after. When we survey the history of thought, and likewise the history of practice, we find that one idea after another is tried out, its limitations defined, and its core of truth elicited." He then concludes that, "The proper test is not that of finality, but of progress" (Whitehead, p. 14). This lack of certainty and finality means that the subject is an ever-changing and ambiguous entity in an ever-changing and ambiguous world.

The relationship between the subject and the world, then, is at its core practical and ambiguous, and the nature of this relationship is the focus of phenomenology, but is perhaps best described by existentialism. Most existentialists argue against the philosophers of the absolute, and embrace the plurality of the concrete, particular human beings enmeshed in their own unique situations and engaged in their own projects. "In order for this world to have any importance, in order for our undertaking to have a meaning and to be worthy of sacrifices," writes Simone de Beauvoir, "we must affirm the concreteness and particularity thickness of this world and the individual reality of our projects and ourselves" (de Beauvoir, p. 106). Many existentialists describe this "concreteness and particularity thickness" in terms of *ambiguity*, including de Beauvior, who proposes that we embrace it: "Let us try to assume our fundamental ambiguity. It is in the knowledge of the genuine conditions of our life that we must draw our strength to live and our reason for acting" (de Beauvoir, p. 9).

The concept of ambiguity is also extremely important to Maurice Merleau-Ponty, who draws upon Heidegger's notion of "throwness," in which individuals are thrown into the world and find themselves always already in the world with others. This inter-subjective relationship, according to Merleau-Ponty, is necessarily ambiguous in that it is indeterminate and inexact, but not irrational. Reason must be understood as something that is *not* based on necessity and *not* accomplished by a subject in isolation. Instead, reason must be understood as something accomplished by a subject in the world with others. For Merleau-Ponty, reason is not a subjective process but an inter-subjective one born out of the struggle that goes on between two or more beings:

> To seek harmony with ourselves and others, in a word, truth, not only in a priori reflection and solitary thought but through the experience of concrete situations and in living dialogue with others apart from which internal evidence cannot validate its universal right, is the exact contrary of irrationalism, since it accepts incoherence and conflict with others as constants but assumes we are able to minimize them. (Merleau-Ponty, 1969, p. 187)

Reason is founded on the uncertain communication between people because despite this uncertainty—and in a sense even because of it—they succeed in making mutual agreements. Reason is dependent upon the risk of communicating with others, which is never certain, and so it is in this sense that for Merleau-Ponty, reason is ambiguous. However, this does not render reason meaningless or useless—far from it. This more practical conception of ambiguous reason helps us to make choices and act in the world.

Merleau-Ponty's conception of an embodied subject is also relevant here. For him, the subject must be understood as the result of the connections and confluences of several diverse elements—namely, the body, consciousness, the world, and others. It is crucial to understand that the body does not exhaust the possibilities of the subject; the body is inextricably linked to consciousness in that neither can exist without the other, but neither is reducible to the other. The body and consciousness interconnect or intermingle with each other and with the bodies and consciousnesses of others. These interconnections form a social milieu that is constantly evolving. No one side of the relationship is ever in complete control and it is this condition of their relationship that defines the existence of the subject. As Merleau-Ponty says,

> To the extent that I have 'sense organs', a 'body', and 'psychic functions' comparable with other men's, each of the moments of my experience ceases to be an integrated and strictly unique totality, in which details exist only in virtue of the whole; I become the meeting point of a host of 'causalities'. In so far as I inhabit a 'physical world' in which consistent 'stimuli' and typical situations recur – and not merely the historical world in which situations are never exactly comparable – my life is made up of rhythms which have not their *reason* in what I have chosen to be, but their *condition* in the humdrum setting which is mine. (Merleau-Ponty, 1962, pp. 83-84)

The subject is a meeting point that is made up of many different but connected parts, and the connections help define the parts and form an inter-subjective pattern that defines subjectivity. Consciousness is linked to the body because consciousness is the understanding of one's place or situation in the world. This situation is defined through the spatial and mental connections with others in the world, which are essentially ambiguous. Upon realizing this, the practical-ambiguous subject resists the attempt to escape from the ambiguity of everyday life and instead chooses to embrace it.

The subject understood as an evolving entity helps define the nature of its moral responsibility and character. People are defined by their actions in the world, and making choices and acting on them is an ongoing process fraught with ambiguity and uncertainty, and is therefore fallible and revisable. This notion of ambiguity can cause a certain amount of anxiety, and so this ongoing process should be understood as a process of coping with that anxiety. The ability of someone to cope with the ambiguity of the world is what propels that person through life in the practical world.

The Formulation of the Practical-Ambiguous Subject (Coping with Ambiguity)

The practical-ambiguous subject comes into existence in two distinct but related steps: the first is to realize that the subject cannot be established on a foundation of absolute certainty and the second is to be able to *cope* with the anxiety that results from the above realization. There is a deep yearning for certainty and absolute foundations, and the practical-ambiguous subject recognizes their appeal. However, the practical-ambiguous subject rejects the idea that absolute certainty is in fact available or possible in the real world of everyday experience.

The quest for certainty in philosophy stems from the idea that absolute certainty would supply a final answer and put one's mind at ease. The absence of an absolute foundation or lack of certainty would understandably result in a certain amount of anxiety. The practical-ambiguous subject anticipates this anxiety and attempts to cope with it. The attempt to cope with this anxiety requires a fundamental shift in philosophical perspective. Such a shift is explicated by Richard Rorty in *Philosophy and the Mirror of Nature*, where he calls for the transformation of traditional philosophy—ahistorical, absolute, foundational solutions—into revolutionary philosophy which recognizes that philosophical problems have historical, contingent solutions. The goal of this new philosophy is not foundational, but therapeutic. For Rorty, an individual must be committed to pragmatic principles and attempt to establish a community consensus without recourse to a foundation of absolute certainty. This is accomplished by replacing the *either-or* thinking of traditional philosophy with *both-and* tensionalist thinking, which can also be thought of as a *more-or-less* thinking. Such a tensionalist thinking is therapeutic in that it can adapt to ambiguity.

The practical-ambiguous subject is a result of taking Rorty's therapeutic point seriously, embracing fallibility and understanding it not merely as an epistemological theory but as a pragmatic virtue. The practical-ambiguous subject entails a certain moral character or disposition that requires not simply a high tolerance for plurality and ambiguity but an active engagement with plurality and ambiguity. This engagement is vital to coping with the anxiety of ambiguity. We must find our way through the fog of the ambiguity of everyday life and realize that it is just as crucial to make ethical choices without the benefit of having them rest on absolute foundations.

The notion that ethical judgments must be based on absolute foundations of certainty is rejected and replaced with the idea that in order for one's choices to have moral significance they must be made with free will, which requires a pluralistic world where the future is open-ended. This follows the thinking of William James who needed to believe in free will in order to believe that his choices carried any meaning at all. He made the choice to believe in free will, and came to understand philosophy not in terms of certainty but rather in terms of coping with a world (or more correctly for James, a universe) that is pluralistic.

James chose to believe in free will after going through a period of severe depression. He emerged from his depression after reading Renouvier's *Essais*, concluding that he saw no reason not to believe in free will. "My first act of free will shall be to believe in free will," he wrote in a letter (James, 1920, p. 147). Reading Renouvier not only rescued James from his mental darkness, but it taught him some valuable lessons that would guide his pragmatic philosophy. According to Louis Menand, "Renouvier had taught James two things: first that philosophy is not a path to certainty, only a method of coping, and second, that what makes beliefs true is not logic but results" (Menand, pp. 219-220).

Choosing free will was important to James and his pragmatic philosophy because "determinism denies the ambiguity of future volitions" (James, 1956, p. 158). By affirming free will, James affirmed the importance of the ambiguity of one's decision-making process. Free will, the exercise of chance, and the acceptance of ambiguity are clearly vital to

James' philosophy and indeed to life in general. The presence of chance is the "vital air which lets the world live, the salt which keeps it sweet" (James, 1956, p.179). Indeed, for James the belief in free will, the belief that our choices matter, is the crucial belief that makes life worth living for everyone.

Any analysis of the choices one makes in everyday life should examine Aristotle's notion of *phronesis*, which he defines as knowledge wisely applied to conduct. Phronesis connects thought and reason to the moral choices of everyday life. It is not based on certainty or objective, absolute foundations but is knowledge that is subject to change because it deals with the world of practice, where situations are ever-changing. For Aristotle, phronesis is not the highest form of knowledge, but he stresses its importance in helping one make everyday choices in order to bring about the ultimate goal: happiness.

In *Truth and Method*, Hans-Georg Gadamer provides an insightful analysis of Aristotle's theory of knowledge, and of phronesis in particular. Gadamer distinguishes phronesis from *techne* and *episteme*, defining it by the essential characteristics of particularity and application. "The task of making a moral decision," Gadamer writes, "is that of doing the right thing in a particular situation—i.e., seeing what is right within the situation and grasping it" (Gadamer, p. 317). The particularity of the situation makes phronesis the type of knowledge that, unlike techne, can not be learned once and then applied, and unlike episteme is not knowledge of an absolute, unchanging truth. There are no objective laws to be followed, but rather guidelines to be applied differently depending on the given concrete situation. "The law is always deficient," Gadamer writes, "not because it is imperfect in itself but because human reality is necessarily imperfect in comparison to the ordered world of law, and hence allows of no simple application of the law" (Gadamer, p. 318).

Phronesis does not command the moral individual to act in a certain way, but it does provide a certain amount of guidance in making ethical choices and helping one attain happiness. In other words, it is a process that helps us cope with an ambiguous world. The practical-ambiguous subject attempts to cope by seeing the connection between knowledge and practice based on the concept of phronesis, which does not give one certainty in terms of what actions to choose but gives one guidelines for actions in the practical world.

The Ongoing Movement of the Subject (Why the Subject Can Not End)

The practical-ambiguous subject corrects the problems with traditional philosophical conceptions of subjectivity by actively participating in the practical world as opposed to being a detached, mentally reflexive spectator. Reversing what Charles Taylor has referred to as the "turn inward" the practical-ambiguous subject demonstrates that the subject is something that is understood in and through practice—i.e., through its interactions with others in the world—and that these interactions or relations are governed by a certain ambiguity that never allows for a complete and final conception of the subject.[3]

In opposition to the statements by Focault and Derrida quoted at the beginning of this essay, the subject, properly understood can not come to an end. What has been overlooked by those who wish to bring the concept of the subject to an end, is that there has never been an accepted static conception of the subject. Those that herald the end of the subject are guilty of the same mistake made by those who call for the end of philosophy. Rodolphe Gasche claims, "Philosophy comes to a close, paradoxically, because its heterological presuppositions constitute it as, necessarily, always incomplete" (Gasche, p. 251). The problem with Gasche's statement is that it presupposes that philosophy always considered itself an autonomous discipline. Gasche makes it seem as though it is only with Derrida and other postmodern thinkers who announced the end of philosophy that the autonomy of philosophy is called into question. On the contrary, the questioning of the autonomy of both philosophy and the subject has been going on in philosophy since its inception. Peter Dews also points out that Derrida's deconstructive critique of transcendental philosophy is "not entirely unprecedented" in the history of philosophy:

> The assumption—central to the whole pattern of post-structuralist thinking—that the concept of the subject implies an immobile, self-identical and constitutive center of experience seriously underplays the complexity and subtlety of the ways in which subjectivity has been explored within the Western philosophical tradition. (Dews, p. xv)

The formulation of the practical-ambiguous subject pays heed to the exploration of the complexity of the subject that has taken place throughout the history of philosophy. Descartes' formulation of the cogito is a central signpost in the history of the subjectivity, but it did not arise out of the blue, nor did it go unchallenged until the emergence of postmodern critiques of it. The subject must be seen as a concept that has changed and will continue to do so.

While one can not establish an absolute foundation for the subject or the world, by seeing the subject as connected to the world one can understand the subject resting on a foundation that allows for movement. The absence of a fixed ground does not mean one necessarily loses their balance and falls down. Rather, the shifting ground shows the necessity of movement, and in practical terms reflects the movement of life—never certain, but always moving along.

The subject understood as a living person immersed in the practical world evades a final and complete definition because the practical world is defined by imperfections and ambiguities, which do not allow for certainty or finality. This view is shared by George Herbert Mead, who claims, "The 'I' is something that is never entirely calculable" (Mead, p. 178). Likewise, Charles Taylor points out, "The issue of our condition can never be exhausted for us by what we *are*, because we are always also changing and *becoming*" (Taylor, pp.46-47). The subject must be understood as an open-ended question. "There can be no end to the traversing of the question of the subject," writes Caroline Williams, "not because there is no end to the subject, but because the subject is sustained by, endures, and persists in, all the questions posed of its existence" (Williams, 197).

The practical-ambiguous subject should be understood as a movement akin to the way that Merleau-Ponty conceived the subject as a chiasm or intertwining, as an ambiguous dialectical movement. The subject is defined by one's relationship to the world, and that relationship is a movement held together by an inextricable connection that never completely coincides. This meeting point of non-coincidence may seem paradoxical, but that paradox is the essence of the subject. Instead of trying to force the subject into a clear and precise meaning, Merleau-Ponty tries to capture the essence of the subject, which he believes is an ambiguous movement.

The subject is constantly changing because one's situation in the world is always changing. The subject, as a human being interacting with others in the world, moves along from one situation to the next, from one relation to the next, making ethical decisions and coping along the way. This practical process and ambiguous movement is what we all are, namely practical-ambiguous subjects.

Works Cited

Bernstein, Richard. *Philosophical Profiles.* Philadelphia: University of Pennsylvania Press, 1986.

Dallmayr, Fred R. *Twilight of Subjectivity.* Amherst: The University of Massachusetts Press, 1981.

de Beauvoir, Simone. *The Ethics of Ambiguity.* Trans. by Bernard Frechtman. New York: The Philosophical Library, Inc., 1948.

Derrida, Jacques. "The Ends of Man." in *Margins of Philosophy.* Trans. Alan Bass. Chicago: The University of Chicago Press, 1982.

Descombes, Vincent. "Apropos of the 'Critique of the Subject' and of the Critique of this Critique." in *Who Comes After the Subject.* Ed. Eduardo Cadava, Peter Connor, Jean-Luc Nancy N. Y. : Routledge, 1991.

Dews, Peter. *Logics of Disintegration.* New York: Verso, 1987.

Ferry, Luc, and Alain Renaut. *Heidegger and Modernity.* Chicago: The University of Chicago Press, 1990.

Foucault, Michel. *The Order of Things: An Archaeology of the Human Sciences.* New York: Random House Inc., 1970. (Vintage Books Edition 1994).

Gadamer, Hans-Georg. *Truth and Method.* Second, Revised edition. Translation revised by Joel Weinsheimer and Donald G. Marshall. New York: The Continuum Publishing Company, 2003.

Gasche, Rodolphe. *The Tain of the Mirror.* Harvard University Press, 1986.

James, William. *The Will to Believe and Other Essays in Popular Philosophy.* New York: Dover Publications, Inc. 1956.

—. *The Letters of William James.* Vol. I Ed. Henry James. Boston: The Atlantic Monthly Press, 1920.

Mead, George Herbert. *Mind, Self, and Society.* ed. Charles W. Morris. Chicago: The University of Chicago Press, 1934, renewed by Charles Morris 1962.

Menand, Louis. *The Metaphysical Club.* New York: Farrar, Straus and Giroux, 2001.

Merleau-Ponty, Maurice. *Humanism and Terror.* Trans. John O'Neill. Westport, Connecticut: Greenwood Press, 1969.

—. *Phenomenology of Perception.* Trans. Colin Smith. Routledge: New York, 1962.

Neuhouser, Frederick. *Fichte's Theory of Subjectivity.* Cambridge University Press, 1990.

Taylor, Charles. *Sources of the Self.* Cambridge: Harvard University Press, 1989.

Tugendhat, Ernst. *Self-Consciousness and Self-Determination.* Cambridge, Massachusetts: MIT Press, 1986.

Rorty, Richard. *Philosophy and the Mirror of Nature.* Princeton University Press, 1979.

Whitehead, Alfred North. *Process and Reality.* Corrected Edition ed. David Ray Griffin and Donald W. Sherburne. New York: The Free Press (Macmillan Publishing Company), 1978.

Williams, Caroline. *Contemporary French Philosophy: Modernity and the Persistence of the Subject.* New York: The Anthlone Press, 2001.

Notes

[1] In other writings, Foucault and Derrida curb their radical critique of the subject. However I maintain that they represent a standpoint that seems more interested in critiquing or de-constructing, as opposed to re-constituting the subject. One of my aims with the practical-ambiguous subject is to make the turn from de-construction to re-construction.

[2] This idea is derived from Richard Bernstein who warned against the danger of Heidegger's attempt to reduce philosophical activity to the activity of thinking, because it "virtually closes off the space for attending to the type of thinking and acting that can foster human solidarity and community." (Bernstein,, p. 208).

[3] See Charles Taylor's *Sources of the Self*, especially Part II for an explanation of the "turn inward" in modern philosophy.

THE PAST, PRESENT AND FUTURE OF GLOBALIZATION: COLONIALISM, TERRORISM, AND THE NEED FOR DEMOCRATIC SUPRANATIONAL GOVERNANCE[1]

DAVID IGNATIUS GANDOLFO
FURMAN UNIVERSITY

> Forgive me my foul murder,
> That cannot be, since I am still possess'd
> Of those effects for which I did the murder. . . .
> May one be pardoned, and retain th' offense?
> (King Claudius in *Hamlet*, Act iii, Scene iii)

Abstract

I argue that the governing structures (economic, political) of today's world were put in place during and through the ascendancy of the West; that the process governing that ascendancy was colonial in nature; that the logic and force of that process is still at work in the structures it created; that moving definitively beyond the colonial structures means moving beyond the logic of colonialism; that doing so entails putting in place democratic supranational structures; that the powerful states, for reasons of both justice and self-interest, should participate in this emergence; and finally, expanding on the last point, that unless and until we move beyond the structures fashioned by colonialism the fight against terrorism will be hamstrung by an appearance of hypocrisy as that fight is perceived by many of the people living under the enduring colonial structures.

Introduction

Globalizing *economic* regimes, such as the GATT, the World Bank and the IMF, have been emerging in a formal manner since the end of World War II. Over the past decade, as these economic regimes have moved to a new level of development, breadth and penetration (c.f., the WTO), theorists have begun to discuss the desirability of globalized *political* regimes. Broadly speaking, the argument can be made in two ways: one should promote democratic supranational governance for reasons of efficacy, or one should promote it for reasons of justice. In the first category are those theories that argue that the world is now facing problems – e.g., global warming, depletion of ocean fish stock, nuclear proliferation, disease pandemics – that are global in scope and which will not be resolved without globalized political coordination. In the second category are the theories arguing that the injustices of the current world, are an affront to human dignity and thus e.g., the continued, grinding poverty of the Global South, demand coordinated world-wide action. There is not strict separation between these two views, and both may be present in a single theory. There is a tendency for theories in both categories to be forward looking, i.e., they avoid looking at international governance as away of addressing past injustice. They do this for good reason: a focus on past injustice tends to impact the powerful states more than the weaker ones (for the simple reason that the weak states did not have the power to inflict much injustice), thus alienating from the discussion precisely those states which need to be on board in order for movement towards *democratic* supranational governance to proceed.[2]

However, I wish to add to the arguments in favor of the emergence of some form of democratic supranational governance one that *is* premised on the need to redress past injustices. Since the historical structures that constitute today's world were created, to some significant degree, by unjust practices and, I will argue, thus "contain" and thereby continue the injustice, a just world can only be built by directly addressing the injustices of the past. I shall argue that the definitive overcoming of the past injustices of colonialism requires the establishment of a regime of democratic supranational governance and that, short of such a move, the world remains fundamentally unjust. I will argue, further, that it is important to consider past injustices in order to de-fuse a widespread, though not thereby legitimate, justification for terrorism.[3] The primary reason we should be motivated for moving in the direction of a democratic supranational political regime is to establish a world that is more just for having finally and definitively overcome the injustice of colonialism. A secondary motivation for making the move, however, is that the particular kind of injustice such a move would overcome provides the *appearance* of legitimacy for terrorist strikes against the powers maintaining the current world system. Past injustices, left un-redressed, provide an *effective*, though again not thereby legitimate, justification for terrorism. And since the kind of terrorism involved tends to target the powerful states, it will be in their interest to heed this argument.

Formal colonialism is not *in practice* today, but its *effects* endure – to the extent that we are still living in a colonial world. The premise that colonialism has not yet been overcome, and that it, thus, exists in some way, presumably strikes many as a surprise. In the second half of the Twentieth century, the world traversed a momentous period of struggles for decolonization that would appear to have succeeded, for it issued in a community of nations more than double its previous size. And yet, colonialism remains with us in the following, crucial way: the distribution of power in the world today – i.e., the parts of the world where power resides, and the parts of the world that are exploited – was decided during *and through* colonialism. This has not been overcome.

As long as the colonial distribution of power exists, our world is still a colonial world and, thus, an unjust world because colonialism was, and its enduring effects are, fundamentally unjust. We should, therefore, be interested in overcoming it. There is only one way to definitively overcome colonialism: the overcoming of the enduring structures created by colonialism.[4] The creation of democratic supranational political regime moves us definitively beyond colonialism because this amounts to a sharing that which colonialism sought, successfully, to hoard for the colonists: power.

My paper is thus, principally concerned with an argument for why it is just to move towards democratic supranational governance. Secondarily, I also argue that failure to move in this direction leaves the powerful more vulnerable to terrorist attack because the continued hoarding of power unjustly gained presents proto-terrorists with what can be construed as a 'prima facie justification'[5] for terrorist acts which we will explore, below. I hasten to add that such construal does not confer legitimacy to such terrorist acts. But the struggle against terrorism cannot be won by pointing to the illegitimacy of terrorism: such a move amounts to preaching to the choir and reaches neither the perpetrators of terrorism nor, more importantly, their sympathizers. It seems to me, here, that the situation faced by a powerful country in its efforts against terrorism is similar to that faced by a judge: both should seek to avoid even the hint of impropriety. Otherwise, their actions and decisions are viewed as suspect and, to that extent, are perceived as lacking legitimacy. Actions *perceived* as illegitimate aid in the recruitment of terrorists.

My paper proceeds in three parts: First, I will present the metaphysical foundations of the claim that colonialism is still with us in the socio-politico-economic structures it built. The second part explores the logic of colonialism in order to show how the move towards democratic supra-national governance is a way to definitively move beyond colonialism. And the third section argues that the failure to make this move leaves the powerful vulnerable to terrorism and that, therefore, this element of a traditional social contract argument, greater security, is applicable at the international level. A number of conclusions regarding the movement towards democratic supranational governance are then drawn.

I. Foundations of the Argument

As might be expected from an argument about the distribution of wealth and power in the world, we are starting from the materialist assumption that matter matters.[6] Reality is material – if not exclusively then at least in a fundamentally important way. Prior to the advent of human beings, reality developed in a manner that can be described as automatic: according, first, to the forces of physics and, later, adding the force of evolution. However, this automatic development of reality changes with the introduction into reality of an additional force, the human force: praxis, free conscious action to change reality. Since the essence of praxis is freedom, once human beings arrive on the scene the further development of reality is no longer strictly automatic.

Human beings came into existence through the logic and causation of evolution as the animal with a nascent ability to respond not merely automatically (instinctually) with a pre-programmed spectrum of scripted responses but, rather, to respond after reflecting on the possible outcomes of various possible actions, and after choosing which of the real possibilities present will be actualized and brought into reality. Praxis is circumspective: it eyes up the situation, taking in the part of reality that it can influence, and decides how to manipulate reality and towards what end.

The development in reality, from the physical to the biological to the human, represents a progression of higher, more developed forces in that the subsequent forces build upon and go further than the prior ones, opening up new possibilities in reality. Praxis, the most developed force in reality, is the primary determinant of the further development of reality because its effects far outstrip those of the other two forces. Its action cannot contradict physical and evolutionary forces, for these prior forces have not gone out of existence. But within the limits imposed by these prior forces, praxis is responsible for the further development of reality. Thus, praxical beings, i.e., human beings, have to reflect on and decide the direction in which to take reality. We are the part of reality responsible for its further development, i.e., we are the responsible part of reality.

Praxis is informed by its experience of what is possible. In its creative acting to realize possibilities present in the situation, praxis has an effect on reality: its actions to realize certain of reality's possibilities create a new reality with new possibilities. The succession of these actions by praxical beings is human history: praxis accretes as history.[7]

The fundamental task of human intelligence is to size up reality in order to identify the possibilities therein so that it can decide which of the possibilities to realize. In so far as human history is the furthest reach of reality, an understanding of reality demands an understanding of history, i.e., an understanding of the succession of human actions in reality, actions that have bequeathed to us the possibilities that constitute the world we live in. Failure to ground our comprehension of reality in history means that the intellect has not fulfilled its task: the task of identifying the possibilities present so that we can decide which to realize. Without the grounding in history, human understanding is stuck in an a-historical ideology. Thus, we can see a need for ideology-critique as a way to recognize this ground of truth in history. The Ellacurian approach ensures that intellect is tethered to history and not simply spinning an ideology that does not have to answer to history.

Thus, human actions, upon their accomplishment, do not simply vanish into nothing. Rather, they leave effects, structures built by those actions. Further, because of our human finitude, our reality must be structured, and these structures result from the more or less consciously coordinated actions of many human beings across time; hence, the structures are both social and historical. Our current reality is the accreted accumulation of the actions of past humans. The structures of human reality shape individuals and are, in turn, shaped by social/historical individuals.[8]

The conception of history as the accretion of human praxis allows us to understand the continuing presence of colonialism in the world: past human actions during the colonial era built structures and these structures are still the controlling structures of reality. The current distribution of power has a history, and that history must be acknowledged if we are to have an adequate grasp of reality. Given that our reality is social and historical, if we are to understand reality fully, i.e., if our understanding is to make effective sense of reality and orient us appropriately within it, then we must know the history and the social formations that brought about this reality. *Acting in the present to transform the unjust structures inherited from the past is how socio-historical human beings build a more just future.*

It is difficult to solve a problem for which the origin is not understood. We need to understand our history in order to be able to make sense about what should happen in the present. This seems like common sense, but it is not practiced. Why not? When power is obtained unjustly, clarity about the past conflicts with the needs of the powerful in the present which are centered around the maintenance and, therefore, legitimation of the unjustly obtained power. Most people in the powerful countries are ignorant of the history of colonialism, so it is difficult to appreciate the claim that the ruling structures of the present were put in place during and by colonialism. The vacuum created by ignorance of history allows ideology to win the day: the gap is filled with such narratives as Manifest Destiny and American Exceptionalism. But regardless of the ideological spin one wants to place on the facts, the reality is that the power of the present is built, to a significant degree, on injustice: millions of people were enslaved, billions of hours of labor went unrecompensed, millions of acres of land were stolen, millions of people were killed in wars of aggression. It will be very difficult for the powerful to consider the past honestly. But since the present is structured by the past, we will not understand the present, its opportunities and challenges, unless we consider the past honestly.[9]

Before passing to the next part of the argument, a few points of clarification are needed about a claim that I am making, viz., that the distribution of power in the world today is due, *to a significant extent*, to colonial practices. First, note that I include under "colonial practices" the settler colonialism that triumphed in the United States. A typical version of American history sees the American Revolution as a triumph over colonialism. But that view is facile and inaccurate. By 1776, colonists had been in what became the United States for 150 years, and they never left. The US war of independence did not defeat colonialism. Rather, it moved the seat of colonial power from London to Philadelphia, New York, and Washington. Second, note that my claim uses the deliberately vague phrase, "to a significant extent." I am not trying to quantify the exact contribution of colonial practices to the current power of the West, though that would be a useful, if difficult, exercise;[10] I am only suggesting that the contribution is significant and that it, therefore, should not be ignored.

II. The Logic of Colonialism, and How to Move Beyond It

Colonialism aims to use a colonized people, along with their land and their resources, for the good of the dominating country without regard for the effect on the colonized. Colonial practices include such things as land theft, theft of other natural resources, slavery, and genocide, the last two being perhaps the most heinous acts that human beings can commit. Colonialism does not always go so far as slavery and genocide, but the general logic is that of using the Other without concern for the Other, and such degradation can slip into the extremes of slavery and genocide. This was certainly the case in the North American experience vis-à-vis Native Americans and Africans, and in the European colonization of Central and South America, Africa, the Middle East, South Asia, South East Asia and Oceania.[11]

Colonialism *seems* to be now definitively in the past, a problem that the world has solved and moved beyond. However, the areas of the world that are powerful, i.e., the areas that control and benefit from the world=s resources, were determined during and *by* colonialism.[12] Colonialism did not just leave some countries worse off; it positively benefited other countries and left them in a position of privilege. To put this point baldly: The power of Europe and its progeny, the United States, would not have been possible without the labor, gold, diamonds, timber, rubber, etc., taken unjustly from Africa, Latin America and Asia, and the land and other resources taken in North America. The power of the West was forged through, and rests on, these injustices. To the extent that the structures of today were formed by particular practices in the past, the effects of those practices endure. So long as their effects endure, the practices have not been definitively overcome. Thus, although First Worlders tend to think of colonialism as dead and gone, it lives on in the enduring colonial structures that form the basis of the contemporary international distribution of wealth and power. In *effect*, therefore, the world is still colonial.

One obvious objection to this position is the claim that the powerful countries and people have *earned* their power. One cannot deny that hard work and talent went into the success of the powerful nations. But so too did slavery, land-theft and genocide. To say that one has *earned* something entails the idea that what one has earned was obtained fairly, not solely because one was powerful enough to accomplish the end gained. Were this not the case, one could argue that Saddam Hussein had earned the right to rule Iraq in the 1970s-90s, that the US has now earned the right to rule Iraq, and that Osama bin Laden earned the right to dance on the destruction at Ground Zero. Arguments that Hussein and bin Laden had earned such a right would be grounded solely in the logic of power; an argument that the West has earned its position of power and privilege may be similarly grounded, since these were got, to a significant extent, through the most heinous of actions.

Another objection to the position being presented might be called the "realist objection:" there is nothing wrong, after all, with the powerful imposing their will on the powerless, or, in other words, there is nothing wrong with colonialism. This objection begins from the assumption that the world is run by power, and that that is not going to change. The response to this objection is two-fold. First, a world based on might-makes-right leaves everyone, ultimately, insecure since the legitimating logic of such a world states that if you are powerful enough to do X then X is right. By that logic, anything that one succeeds in doing is right, including the terrorist actions of September 11, and such heinous acts as slavery and genocide. Secondly, that the world is run by power is true by definition. What is at stake, however, is the legitimate versus illegitimate use of power. If might-makes-right is the criteria by which the use of power is to be judged, then we are back with the first response.

The logic of colonialism is the self-aggrandizement of the agent at the expense of the Other. Moving beyond this means acting with regard for the consequences to *all* others – not just with regard for "me and mine" – i.e., acting with the whole in mind.[13] Since colonial practices contributed in a significant way to the current distribution of power in the world, the legitimating logic of the current distribution of power is an imperial, colonial logic by which the powerful care only about their power and not about its effects on others.[14] And moving beyond it will require acting to create structures that empower the whole, i.e., democratic structures.

Colonialism was the rule of self-interested power, the goal of which was to hoard for the colonial powers as much power as possible. The *only* way to definitively move beyond this hoarding of power is to *share* that power. Democracy is the most legitimate alternative to the rule of self-interested power: self-interested power, by definition, promotes the good of the agent; what is needed in its stead is a rationality that promotes the good of the all. The latter is the only alternative to the former: either one acts with a concern only for "me and mine" (where the "me" gets to decide the extent of the "mine"), or one acts with a concern for the whole. And a concern for everyone reaches its fulfillment in the demand for democracy, the demand that everyone have an equal say in the structuring of the regimes that rule our lives.

At the level of the individual, self-interested rationality moves us beyond a capricious licentiousness, and we move beyond this by some sort of social contract, the creation of a regime of laws that constrain the capricious exercise of power by individuals. Within a *democratic* regime of laws, all individuals are not only equal before the law but are also equal in the structuring of the laws that bind them: that is the superiority of democracy.

At the level of states, however, capricious licentiousness still reigns: powerful states work to prevent the emergence of supranational regimes that would constrain the will of the sovereign, and they ignore, or follow selectively, those supranational regimes that do emerge.

What is at stake in the contest between a self-interested rationality and a rationality that takes into account the common good is the illegitimate versus legitimate use of power. What we are arguing for here is the idea that the exercise of power by all in the interest of all is more legitimate than the exercise of power by the few for the few, or even by the few for all. The argument rests on the premise that the source of power in the socio-historical structures that govern our lives is human beings. And the decision that the democratic exercise of this power is the most legitimate rests on the idea that all people are essentially equal. The claim by the powerful few that they are somehow more deserving to rule than are the all is a rule of might; it does violence to the idea of essential equality.[15] It should not be surprising, then, under the rule of the few, if those who have been thereby deemed inferior choose to fight back, even by any means necessary.

The argument here is perhaps circular: the defense of democracy as the most legitimate structure for the regimes that govern us rests on the democratic premise that people, as such, have the right to rule themselves. But although circular, it is instructive to present because it makes clear that the claims of the powerful few that they somehow have a right to rule translates into the claim that people do not have the right to rule themselves. The final defense of democracy is a faith in the proposition that human beings have the right to rule themselves within social structures that respect a similar right of all others.

The competition between a rationality that looks out for "me and mine" and a rationality that looks out for the good of all is a zero-sum game. The democratic exercise of power needs to become more powerful if the rule of dictatorial power is not to carry the day. Thus, failure to strengthen supranational regimes of law that hold the powerful states accountable to the same rules that less powerful states must follow automatically promotes the rule of the few.

The empowerment of reason depends on placing power in the service of reason. Those who currently control power have a choice: either they recognize that their long-term interest is tied up with the interests of everybody else and thus work for the emergence of the rule of all rather than a rule of the powerful few, OR they encourage, if only unintentionally and indirectly, the all to revolt against the current regime of rule by the few. If those with power do not use it to move towards structures that empower the whole in the interest of the whole, they will be encouraging increasingly desperate attempts by the unpowerful to take the situation into their own hands.

Empowerment comes from the stores of power. Proximally, that store is with those who currently hold power, but ultimately that store is the people. So those who now hold power have the choice of using it to empower democratic regimes (in effect, using their power to end their monopoly on power), or they legitimate efforts, if only indirectly and unintentionally, by increasingly desperate people to find ways of by-passing the powerful. Those with power have to decide that building democratic institutions is preferable to ruling by force of arms. The strategy of ruling by force of arms can win battles, but not the war; it will ensure the proliferation of increasingly nasty battles.

The foregoing argument suggests that the United States' response to the tragedy of 9/11 has been precisely the opposite of what is needed. On the morning of September 12, 2001, the United States enjoyed the sympathy and cooperation of nearly the entire world. On that morning it faced the choice of responding through the rule of force or the rule of reason, the rule of unconstrained power or the rule of power constrained by reason. In defining the events of 9/11 as an act of war, the United States chose the path of unconstrained power. Had it chosen to define the problem as a crime, rather than an act of war, it could have turned the case over to the International Court of Justice and asked countries everywhere to cooperate in the apprehension and punishment of those responsible for the crime. This would have had the effect of strengthening an international regime against terrorism. The danger with fashioning such a regime of law is that it would render all nations equal before said regime. The powerful do not want to be equal to all others, they want to enjoy the privilege their power grants them. Strengthening a regime of international law might mean that some of the actions of the United States could possibly be found to be terrorist. Note, I am not stating that any particular American actions have been terrorist actions; I am only arguing that the possibility that a powerful country could be held to standards by an international body is one that powerful countries do not want to face. By defining the attacks as an act of war, the US reserved to itself the right to use violence to achieve its ends, which is, of course, the same right the terrorists claim. In doing so, the US missed an opportunity to galvanize the world around standards that could have more forcefully and clearly delineated the boundaries of acceptable international behavior. The path the United States chose to pursue, rather than clearly placing the taking of innocent lives for political purpose beyond the pale has brought into the pale "collateral damage" and "enhanced interrogation techniques." The rule of law is based on reason; the will of the sovereign is based on power. If one=s policy is not strengthening the international framework of institutions, it is strengthening the rule of power; there is no middle ground.

In order for those with power to be able to empower the rule of reason, they have to see reality from the perspective of the colonized; seeing what the world looks like to those without power is the necessary first step towards seeing beyond the interests of the powerful to the interests of the whole.

Consider, for a moment, what September 11, 2001, looks like from the perspective of one who takes into account *all* the world's people and holds each of their lives to be equally precious. On that day, at least 38,000 innocent people died.[16] Some 3,000 of these deaths occurred in the tragedy that has been preserved in memory as 9/11. These 3,000 deaths are very close to us. We know the victims, who they were, their stories. We have heard what they were like as fathers and mothers, daughters and sons, lovers and spouses. This is entirely appropriate. They were human beings, each one unique and irreplaceable.

The other 35,000 innocent people who died that day were children under the age of five. They died in the Global South from diarrhea, hunger and malnutrition. They were human beings, each one unique and irreplaceable, but we do not know their stories. We do not know the infinite hole their deaths left in the lives of those who loved them. The powerful want to focus almost exclusively on the 9/11 deaths, which has the effect of elevating those deaths, an elevation that implies that these deaths are somehow more important, more meaningful, than the others. This can become infuriating when one recalls that 35,000 innocent children under the age of five *also* died on September 10, 2001, from diarrhea, hunger and malnutrition, and on September 12, 2001, and on every day since. The total from this on-going carnage now reaches the staggering, unfathomable, almost unbelievable amount of *ninety million* innocent victims since the tragic deaths in New York, Washington, and Pennsylvania. Let me stress that I am in no way suggesting that we should not commemorate, and be outraged by, the deaths of the innocent people who perished in New York, Washington and Pennsylvania on September 11, 2001. But we should remember that the innocent lives lost that day in the Global South are equally as precious as those lost in the United States.

The unspeakably horrible toll in deaths of innocent children is even more outrageous in the world of plenty in which we live. Such a situation can drive those who are conscious of it, or suffering from it, to desperation. The US, as the chief organizer and enforcer of the politico-economic regime in which one finds starvation amidst plenty, is particularly vulnerable to this kind of frustration.[17]

To move definitively beyond the world bequeathed to us by colonialism we have to once-and-for-all recognize the illegitimacy of the rule of the few and embrace the rule of all, i.e., we have to reject the legitimacy of decisions made for the good of the sovereign in favor of decisions made for the good of all. This would entail acknowledging that the unfair and unreasonable distribution of power and wealth in the world was brought about unjustly, and that, therefore, efforts expended on behalf of maintaining that distribution are unjust and unreasonable. It would entail fostering the growth of democratic supranational institutions that place the powerful on the same level as the powerless.

III. Considerations for the War on Terror

The current distribution of power in the world was put in place during the colonial era. This is not merely coincidental. The current socio-econo-political structures were built, to some significant degree, through colonial practices, i.e., through land-theft, slavery, and genocide. Thus, the current regime of power was built, to some significant degree, through the most heinous acts imaginable. We in the West have developed the habit of telling ourselves, in the presence of evidence of our past atrocities, "yes but . . . in the end . . . it was worth it."[18] The atrocities, we tell ourselves, were a deplorable, regrettable, but necessary price to pay for progress. And so we must face the following genre of questions:

> If it's OK to obtain power through land-theft, slavery and genocide, then why not through hijacking airplanes and flying them into buildings? If land-theft, slavery and genocide are not too high a price to pay in the quest for power, what would be?

These questions throw into stark relief the hypocrisy implicit in the struggle against terrorism as it is currently structured. Obviously, neither the path of genocide nor the path of hijacking is a legitimate path to power. The problem is that it is not good enough to say, now, that *henceforth* no advantages gained through genocide or hijackings will be allowed to stand.

Because of this hypocrisy implicit in the current regime of power in the world, terrorism has available to itself a ready-made "legitimacy claim" for why it commits its acts: *The current regime of power in the world was brought about unjustly, and this regime refuses to acknowledge that fact and open negotiations on a just redistribution of power within a new regime; this refusal effectively forecloses the possibility that change can be achieved through peaceful procedures that take into account the interests of all the world's people.* The availability of this legitimacy claim does *not* mean that all terrorists are so motivated, nor does it mean that those terrorists who are so motivated are justified. But its existence does establish a climate in which terrorism can grow because it opens the possibility that terrorism be *perceived* as legitimate by the critical mass of people needed for its propagation.

Bat-Ami Bar On has noted that the "leadership" of the United States in the war on terror is "not merely military but also ethicopolitical." She observes that while she wants to be able to criticize the evil done by terrorists like those responsible for 9/11, it is hard to do so without playing into the hands of the powerful in their continuing domination of the world. "And yet," she continues, "why should I let the Bush administration seize and control an extremely powerful ethical term, . . . the notion of 'evil.'"[19] There needs to be a space in which one can recognize as evil the indiscriminate killing of 9/11 while not accepting the response that has been enacted; at the same time, there has to be a space for recognizing the legitimacy of the complaints of the oppressed without accepting all of the solutions they have engaged in. But my point is slightly different. What can be classified as legitimate and illegitimate from the calm of an academic office or the safety of the White House briefing room is not what counts in the effort to contain and ultimately eradicate terrorism. What counts is the perception on the street. And because of the enormous expansion of access to information, the hypocrisy of an "ethicopolitical" leader atop a mountain of gold gained via the most heinous acts of which human beings are capable is obvious. There is, in Bar On's phrase, "an official discourse of 'evil'" that is being "deployed manipulatively."[20] It is being deployed, I would suggest, so as to focus only on the use of power against the powerful, not the use of power by the powerful to gain and maintain their privilege.

I hasten to add a clarification to forestall misinterpretations of the argument. Note that the claim about the "*perception* of terrorism as legitimate" is not a claim about the moral status of terrorism; it only means that enough people find terrorism to be an acceptable alternative to the status quo that it succeeds. Further, note that finding terrorism to be an acceptable alternative does not entail being willing to strap a bomb onto one=s own body; it only entails turning a blind eye to those who do strap on the bombs, or the willingness to aid them in finding housing, in opening a bank account, in caring for their loved ones, etc. The pool of people who are willing to assist (if only by their willful ignorance) those who engage in terrorism is surely influenced by the hypocrisy of the West's refusal to admit the unjust aspects of its rise to power; that pool is probably growing, and this should be of primary importance to those who seek to curb the spread of terrorism.

Consider the following example. At the local bar, one of the regular patrons, the bully, regularly hauls off and slugs some of the smaller patrons, day in and day out, for one reason or another (to have quicker access to the pool table, the dart board or the tap). One evening, in a completely unprovoked attack, one of the smaller regulars sneaks up behind the bully and knocks him unconscious with a bat. The general consensus around the bar, about what happened to the bully, is going to be, "yeah, well, he kinda had it coming." It is that general consensus, not the legal fine-points about whether the bat-swinger was justified in that particular instance in attacking the bully, that must concern those who are interested in putting an end to terror.

I am not attempting to identify the conditions under which terrorism could be justified. Other theorists have tried to do that.[21] My argument is concerned with why terrorism can have an appeal wide enough as to render it feasible. In order for the struggle against terrorism not to be hamstrung by the legitimacy claim that is readily available to terrorists, it must act to take the claim away from the terrorists by taking steps towards redressing the grievances therein. This is difficult to do for many reasons, not least because it seems to grant the effectiveness of terrorism and because, more importantly, it involves the surrender of some power, albeit ill-gotten power. Nevertheless, without taking such steps, the powerful countries make themselves vulnerable to a terrorism that, in the eyes of far too many, has a *prima facie* case for legitimacy.

Joseph Stiglitz, in his influential work, *Globalization and Its Discontents*, argues that the history of the United States going through the period of industrialization and economic integration is relevant to what the world now faces.

> The experience of the United States during the nineteenth century makes a good parallel for today's globalization.... Today ...we have a process of "globalization" analogous to the earlier processes in which national economies were formed. Unfortunately, we have no world government, *accountable to the people of every country*, to oversee the globalization process in a fashion comparable to the way national governments guided the nationalization process. Instead, we have a system that might be called global governance without global government, one in which a few institutions – the World Bank, the IMF, the WTO – and a few players – the finance, commerce, and trade ministries, closely linked to certain financial and commercial interests – dominate the scene, but in which many of those affected by their decisions are left almost voiceless.[22]

Although Stiglitz's main point is that there are lessons to be learned by studying the role of government during the period in which national economies were forged in order to be able to apply those lessons to the international scene, we can mine a deeper lesson from this passage. *National* economies emerged during the period in question precisely because *national* governments asserted their authority. Otherwise what would have emerged would have been larger and larger private fiefdoms. Even if one of the fiefdoms became co-extensive with the territory of the nation, it would still not have been a national economy, but a very large private fiefdom. The difference is the presence of an overarching authority, in the national economy, that can regulate the economy, through fiscal and monetary policies, towards ends decided upon by the nation, not just and only ends delivered by the free market. At the global level, the absence of an overarching authority means that we are left with ever larger private fiefdoms, many of which overwhelm the size of most small nations. The large private fiefdoms act to maximize return to themselves, and there is no supra-fiefdom authority looking out for the interest of *all* the world's people in the way that national governments were able to act against the market in the interest of all the nation's people.

Similar to Stiglitz, Lewis Coser considers the experience of England during its industrial revolution, paying special attention to the social function of violence:

> Violence and riots were not merely protests: they were claims to be considered.... It is not to be doubted that legislative remedies, from factory legislation to the successive widening of the franchise and the attendant granting of other citizenship rights to members of the lower classes, came, at least in part, in response to the widespread disorders and violent outbreaks that marked the British social scene for over half a century.... The often violent forms of rebellion of the laboring poor, the destructiveness of the city mobs, and other forms of popular disturbances which mark English social history from the 1760's to the middle of the nineteenth century, helped to educate the governing elite of England, Whig and Tory alike, to the recognition that they could ignore the plight of the poor only at their own peril. These social movements constituted among other things an effective signaling device which sensitized the upper classes to the need for social reconstruction in defense of a social edifice over which they wished to continue to have over-all command.[23]

Coser concludes that violence by the oppressed, in that it announces something wrong in society, has frequently lead to improvements in that society. Nevertheless, Virginia Held points out, after reviewing Coser's work, that "[v]iolence on other grounds than self-defense and law enforcement is not in fact found justifiable or legitimate by most advanced legal systems because an acceptable set of legal rules should rule it out."[24]

Perhaps it is assumed by most Americans, and most Westerners, that political violence is illegitimate because it is unnecessary: there exist other means of making political changes. But is that a reasonable assumption for the kind of change in question? There exist a large group of poor, oppressed, disempowered people, constituting more than half of humanity, many of whom think that they have good reason for seeing their condition as linked to the actions of powerful states. The aggrieved group is not part of the citizenry of the powerful states, and thus has no say in the policies that it perceives as hurting it. Under such conditions, how is such a group to register its complaints? How is its voice to be heard? It is not unreasonable for the aggrieved group to think it has no other option than to engage in political violence.

It is often assumed by Americans that the United States offers to others a model to be emulated. This assumption perhaps forgets the struggle and violence needed to make the United States into something worth emulating. The high quality of life in the US was gained, in significant measure, by the struggles of poor and oppressed peoples against the power elite. The end of slavery, the end of segregation, the extension of the franchise to women, the 8-hour workday, retirement benefits, healthcare benefits, unemployment insurance, non-toxic workplaces – none of these were given freely by the elite, each of these was won after long struggle. These struggles frequently included violence, on both sides, a violence either started by the elite or made likely by their intransigence in the face of just demands. No one can question the worth of these improvements for the quality of life in the First World. Indeed, it is precisely these things that make First World societies models for poorer countries to aspire to. These very improvements were brought about, in many cases, by violence. The violence did not win the improvements outright, it did not overthrow the elite and put into power a new, people's regime that instituted popular reform. Rather, the violence got the attention of the elite and convinced them that it was in their own long-term interest to grant the popular reforms. If the global elite does not work on behalf of the establishment of a just global system, they are inviting the poor of the world to undertake violence in the same way in which the First World poor undertook it: to convince the elite that it is in their long-term interest to allow the demanded reforms to go through.

Conclusions

A. Our Dangerous World: Two Factors.

It is all too obvious that we live in an increasingly dangerous world. Two factors, in particular, are relevant to the argument for the necessity of movement towards a democratic supranational political regime. The first factor contributing today to the dangerous potential for large-scale violence has to do with thc increasingly easy availability of the means to produce violence on such a scale. One of the lessons to be drawn from the tragic events of September 11 has become known as the "democratization of violence." The 9/11 attacks show that technological advances have brought about a new situation in which the tremendous kill-power that was heretofore monopolized by national armies is now obtainable with relative ease by small groups. This kill-power is available both in the form of loosely controlled weapons of mass destruction,[25] and under the guise of ordinary materials (like airplanes, or fertilizer and diesel fuel) needed by ordinary folks for ordinary activities.

The second factor contributing to the perilous state in which the world finds itself might be called the "condition of desperation." If we assume for the sake of argument that Osama bin Laden is an evil person, that alone does not explain the power he has amassed that has enabled him to kill thousands of people. Alone, he cannot kill very many. What he needs, and what those who are interested in disrupting his power must be concerned with, are the large number of people who find him inspiring and form a pool of people from which emerge those smaller groups of people who are willing to take extreme measures.[26] These are the people who are driven by desperation beyond the limits of normal political action into terrorist action, even to the point of suicidal terrorist action. There are many things that can drive a person to desperation. Certainly material want, especially for the most basic needs, can create the condition of desperation. But other things can also move a person to that kind of desperation, e.g., a perception of the world as extremely unjust and rigidly resistant to any attempts to rectify the situation.

The combination of these two factors – the democratization of violence and the condition of desperation – has produced a large pool of desperate people who can obtain with relative ease tremendous kill-power. This constitutes a truly dangerous world. It is incumbent upon us to remove the motivation for turning to super-violence; thus, we must address the argument, put forth in the previous section, suggesting a prima facie justification available to terrorists.[27] Unless and until we move beyond the structures fashioned by colonialism, the fight against terrorism will be hamstrung by the appearance of hypocrisy, an appearance perceived ever more clearly by the people living under the enduring colonial structures. Moving beyond the structures of colonialism entails enabling the emergence of non-colonial democratic supranational structures.

B. A Democratic Global Political Regime.

Some words of clarification must be said here about the democratic aspect of the proposed global political regime. It has become accepted truth that the world, since the demise of the Soviet Union, has become more democratic, and it is taken for granted that the promotion of democracy is both a good thing and the guiding rationality of international actions of powerful countries like the U.S. Indeed, one of the reasons put forth as justification for the US invasion of Iraq was to end tyranny and establish democracy. However, proponents of this reason typically intend not democracy *tout court*, but neo-liberal democracy, i.e., democracy combined with neo-liberal capitalism so that a) Iraqis can choose their leaders, while b) transnational corporations can have access to Iraqi resources (principally, of course, oil) under "free-trade" conditions, i.e., without the Iraqi state being able to impose conditions for that access. In the neo-liberal view of the world that guides this policy, a) and b) should coincide. However, experience has shown that, for the U.S., when they do not coincide, or if the voters in newly democratic states elect leaders who want to impose conditions on the access to their countries' resources, neo-liberal capitalism takes precedence over democracy.[28] When I speak of democracy, I do not intend this neo-liberal variant. Rather, I mean a decision-making process wherein each member of the relevant community has a say, equal to all other individual members, in determining the regimes under which she lives. Thus, the extent to which a government enters into the economic realm with regulations meant to promote social ends[29] would be determined by the sovereign citizens who put that government in power.

How this emerging global democratic regime is to be structured is an open question, but conceivably it could be approached in a graduated fashion. For example, the permanent, veto-wielding members of the United Nation Security Council could be reconfigured to consist of all countries with a population greater than 100 million (eleven countries),[30] later to include all countries with a population greater than 40 million (bringing the total to twenty-nine countries),[31] with each country, at least initially, having one vote. Later still, this could be revised into a voting procedure in which each country's vote is weighted according to its population, and finally all countries admitted to the Security Council, effectively instituting a kind of international democracy.[32] Similar arrangements would have to be gradually put in place in connection with all the regimes that govern international life (e.g., the World Bank, IMF, WTO, International Court, ILO, etc.). Such arrangements are obviously to be resisted by the powerful countries because the increased democracy dilutes their power. One of the purposes of my paper is to argue that without taking such steps the powerful countries leave themselves increasingly open to terrorist attacks.

The U.S. today has the greatest accumulation of power the world has ever known. Certainly much of that power is due to the hard work and allegiance unleashed by the novel and important structures of democratic freedoms put in place here. But in our history, therefore in reality, the positive values of "liberty and justice *for all*" have frequently been intertwined with the negative values of exploitation and oppression. The negative values are definitively overcome only through the realization of the universality (explicit, but ignored in practice) in the positive values, the real universality of that phrase, "for all." This universality requires the creation of a democratic supranational regime.

C. Ur-Akte and End-Akt

The history of injustices that produced the current distribution of power in the world must be recognized because the injustices of the past live on in the political structures of the present: there, in those structures, power still resides where the unjust placed it. The structures brought about by those past injustices result in an unjust international situation in which a few states are able to dominate all others. The overcoming of this injustice, thus, entails the creation of democratic supranational structures. The failure to move towards the creation of such a regime a) contributes to the rule of might-makes-right in which the struggle against terrorism is hamstrung, b) fosters the growth of desperation and cynicism, both of which promote terrorism, and c) provides a *prima facie* legitimation for terrorism. Thus, the failure of the powerful states to give up some of their power to a democratic supranational regime makes the citizens of the powerful states less secure than they otherwise could be.

The heinous acts (genocide, slavery, etc.) that accompanied the West's rise to power, and were to some significant degree responsible for that rise, must certainly be counted as acts of terror. It is vitally important for the powerful to recognize, as part of that most primary philosophical exercise of knowing thyself, coming to knowledge through self-examination, that the primal acts of the powerful, *die Ur-Akte*, the ones that gained them their power, were terrorist.

Terrorist acts by the oppressed, too, can be self-perceived as primal acts whose extreme nature can be self-excused as once-only. Of course, this is the basest kind of "end justifies the means" thinking and it cannot serve as a blanket justification for all means. But while this justification may be obviously wrong in an academic setting, it may be far more appealing in the heat of struggle, especially when there is available to the oppressed a well-documented history of the powerful engaging, with *gargantuan* profit to themselves, in precisely the means that they, the powerful, are now criticizing. What's more, while the primal acts of the West, the terrorism (genocide, slavery) by which they gained their power, were carried out against weaker and relatively peaceful Others (Native Americans and Africans), today's oppressed get to exercise their terror against the most powerful empire in history: their turn to terror can thus seem all the more appealing for being principled.

Failure by the powerful to redress the advantage gained by unjust *Ur-Akte necessarily* amounts to an implicit claim that these primal acts were justified. The unavoidable implicit claim by the powerful is that what they have today was worth it, that the means used to obtain it were justified by the end that exists today. The only way to vitiate this implicit claim is to make explicit redress for the ill-gotten gains. What was gained? Power. The currency in which the debt must be paid is the same: power.

The powerful move sincerely to condemn the justification of "end justifies means" *only* when they act to share the end which was gained through unjust means; *only* the powerful can make this move. Failure to make this move leaves intact the appearance that the justification of "end justifies means" is legitimate, an appearance that benefits all terrorists. The unjust *primal act* must now be answered; the *Ur-Akt* calls for an *End-Akt*, an end-act that restores balance. Failure to do so leaves the world unbalanced, fundamentally and essentially unjust, a world in which those with the power to act – powerful countries and terrorists alike – understand that anything goes. Only the powerful can perform the end-act: such is the real burden of power.

Political "realists," as opposed to the social contractarians, assume that, in the absence of an overarching authority, the final arbiter is violence. They justify the use of force by the powerful by noting the lack of an overarching authority.[33] But now it turns out, if my arguments are accepted, that the powerful are assuring the continuation of the dog-eat-dog reality that they assume is natural. Regardless of how one views the question of whether such a reality was indeed natural in the past, it can no longer be seen to be so: once humanity has realized that there is a way out of the dog-eat-dog scenario, failure to move in that direction makes the continuation of the dog-eat-dog reality not natural but man-made.

Note, the claim that only the powerful can perform the end-act, is not a claim that only the powerful can move to create a just world; but the end-act *is* the only way that the *powerful* can move to create a just world. It is also the only path towards a just world that does not involve the external overthrow and destruction of the powerful. And it is the only path towards a just world on which the powerful maintain some agency, even as (and after) they sacrifice some agency by empowering others. Fundamentally, there are only two paths towards a just world: one on which the powerful act to establish justice, and one on which the oppressed act to overthrow the powerful, seize the reins of history and take their turn at the attempt to create a just world. If the powerful fail to use their power to move towards a world in which power is shared democratically and, thus, one in which the powerless are empowered, the powerless will organize, sooner or later, to seize power. Either way the powerless gain power. The difference is the extent to which the powerful maintain a fair, equal agency (as opposed to the surfeit of agency they currently enjoy). When the powerless gain power, another cycle of history begins. It can repeat the pattern of the past in which the newcomers to power act to maximize and maintain power to the exclusion of all others, or it can look to end that cycle by building structures that gravitate towards a democratic sharing of power. If the first option is chosen, the cycles will continue, with the newly oppressed eventually organizing to take power. At some point, the powerful – whether it be a long-entrenched power elite or a newly victorious, formerly oppressed insurgency – will have to perform the end-act or the inherently unstable situation of "end justifies means" in which anything (with the proper spin) goes will continue. The cycle continues until the end-act, the creation of truly democratic means of exercising power.

D. A New Social Contract

To the extent that I am arguing that it is in the interest of the powerful to sacrifice some of their power, my argument is a reiteration, at the international level, of the social contract arguments which have been used at the national level. Countries should give up some sovereignty in exchange for more security.[34] But not only is such a move *reasonable* in an enlightened, self-interested way, it is *just* because it is the redress for the fact that the current distribution of power was obtained unjustly. We, the citizens of the powerful countries, should be motivated to move in the direction of democratic supranational political regimes that will infringe on our power and privilege, for reasons of enlightened self-interest and for reasons of justice. As Peter Singer notes, "[f]or the rich nations not to take a global ethical viewpoint has long been seriously morally wrong. Now it is also, in the long term, a danger to their security."[35] If concern for morality and justice is not enough to get us moving towards a redistribution of power, terrorism, as the quintessential weapon of the weak, may act as the goad that will move us in that direction. This is not to justify terrorism, any more than the crimes committed in the state of nature are justified because they prompt people into the social contract. But just as the insecurity of the state of nature is understandable, with no overarching authority to which those who considered themselves aggrieved may appeal, so too are the terroristic outbursts of an immiserated world understandable, if not justified. There is a tremendous pool of people who feel themselves aggrieved by the current structures of power. There is no court of appeal to which they may turn; that is an anarchic, violent, dangerous situation that should prompt nations into a society of nations, creating the international governing structures to which the aggrieved parties can submit their claims.

E. Hegemonic Elimination

It is often argued, against the emergence of supranational structures, that the diversity of the world=s cultures and political forms means that no one form will be found under which all would be content to live. However, that uncomfortable diversity is precisely why it is in the interest of today's hegemon to promote supranational structures under which it would be content to live when it is no longer the hegemon. *Now* is the US's chance to shape those structures, to get them in place before its time as the hegemon is over. At the end of the Nineteenth century, the US surpassed the UK as the largest economy in the world, and within a half-century the US had also replaced the UK as the dominant political and military power in the world. China's economy is currently the second largest in the world; it is about 65% the size of the US economy but is growing far more rapidly than the US's and, if current trends continue, could become the world=s largest economy in little more than a decade, and will probably do so well before the middle of the century.[36] China has already surpassed the US in consumption of grain, meat, coal and steel; and while its consumption of oil is currently only a third that of the US, China's need for oil is growing three-to-four times faster than that of the US. At that rate, China will become the world's largest consumer of oil well before mid-century. At the current level of economic expansion, China's population will achieve by 2030 the same per capita income that the US population enjoyed in 2005. Assuming that the Chinese will consume that income in a manner similar to the consumption patterns developed by Americans, they will be generating pollution at the same per capita rate Americans did in 2005. Thus, China as a whole will be generating, in 2030, five times the pollution (including green house gases) as the US produced in 2005. And by 2030, China will not even be the world's most populous nation! India will have surpassed it.[37] If the US wants to live in a world that is not drowning in its own waste, now is the time for it to be setting an example and working to put in place the global environmental regimes that will guide the emerging super-economies in a way that makes it possible for the rest of the world to live with them.

None of this is to suggest that there is some sort of looming peril to fear if the Chinese or Indians supplant the US as the world's hegemon. The supranational structures a new hegemon might attempt to create could well be better than the anemic regime the US has fostered. But if the US wants to shape supranational structures that will outlive its time as the world's largest economy, it must do so now. In effect, the US is now faced with a kind of Rawlsian original position: as the world=s sole superpower it can play the leading role in structuring the regime under which it will have to live when it is no longer the sole superpower, a regime that, if strong enough, will constrain future superpowers and thus, in effect, eliminate the phenomenon of superpower. The only real choice for a hegemon is whether to move in the direction of eliminating the phenomenon of hegemony, whether to perform the end-act. Anything less amounts to being on hegemonic autopilot, simply doing what hegemons do. And continuing on hegemonic autopilot makes it more likely that future hegemons will do the same. Again, it is thus in the long-term interest of the current hegemon to move in the direction of democratic supranational governance.

In sum, the creation of a more just world requires that we find a way to definitively overcome the colonial structures that still govern the world. Colonialism sought, successfully, to hoard power for a few, and the only way to overcome the structures bequeathed to the present by colonialism is to share that power. This can only happen through the creation of a supranational democratic regime of governance. The powerful countries of today, most especially the United States, should be interested in moving in this direction for reasons of justice and efficacy, as well as for reasons of self-interest.

Notes

---

[1] The ideas presented here were first worked out in my course, "The Ethics of Globalization," at Furman University. I am greatly indebted to my students whose enthusiasm and feedback have continually helped in the maturation of these ideas. I am also indebted to my colleagues at Furman University, in particular: Dr. Erik Anderson, for insightful comments on an early draft of this paper; and Dr. Carmela Epright for the opportunity to present my work for extensive and helpful discussion in a faculty seminar (Piper Seminar) which she organizes. Early versions of parts of the paper were presented at meetings of the North American Society for Social Philosophy and the Society for Philosophy in the Contemporary World; comments and discussion at each venue greatly helped in the development of the ideas presented here.

One of the theses presented here (in the section on "The Logic of Colonialism"), as well as some of the related supporting material in the "Introduction," is developed more fully in Gandolfo, "The Ethical Threshold: Democratic Supranational Governance As A Necessary Condition for Non-Neocolonial Globalization," *Philosophy in the Contemporary World*, Vol. 15, no. 1 (Spring 2008).

[2] Even Kant, one of the earliest theorists to consider the feasibility and desirability of a global political regime, counseled that the implementation of the rules that would govern such a regime should not be seen as an opportunity to redress past injustices. Cf., *To Perpetual Peace: A Philosophical Sketch* (Indianapolis: Hackett, 2003 [1795]).

[3] "Terrorism" is notoriously difficult to define. I will use it in the following sense: the use of violence against a random section of a population for the purpose of sowing fear among that population, seeking thereby to influence the policy of its leaders; I do not restrict it to non-state actors, i.e., I hold open the possibility of state terrorism. It is important for the definition of terrorism not to preclude from the start the possibility of its justification. In this, I follow Virginia Held's remarks on violence: "It is sometimes suggested that violence is by definition wrong, but to maintain this is not a satisfactory position. It is easy enough to think of examples of acts of violence of which it is meaningful to ask whether they were wrong or not. One of the clearest examples would be the 1944 bomb plot against Hitler. To answer questions about the justifiability of acts of violence requires that the issues not be construed as ones which can be settled merely by appealing to a definition." (Virginia Held, "Violence, Terrorism, and Moral Inquiry," *Monist* 1984, pp. 605-626; here p. 605.) Held's further remarks are also relevant: "Terrorism is sometimes defined as 'the systematic use of murder, injury, and destruction' to create terror and despair through 'indiscriminate' attacks in which 'no distinction' is made that might exempt the innocent from being targets of such attacks [Paul Wilkinson, "The Laws of War and Terrorism," in *The Morality of Terrorism*, eds. David C. Rapoport and Yonah Alexander (New York: Pergamon Press, 1982) pp. 310-311]. Terrorists are sometimes said to 'sacrifice all moral and humanitarian considerations for the sake of some political end' [Paul Wilkinson, *Political Terrorism* (London: Macmillan, 1974) p. 17]. If terrorism is defined this way, we may be unable even to raise the question of whether it could be justifiable. . . . [T]he question should be open, not shut by definition. Any adequate definition of terrorism must be able to include terrorism carried out by a government as well as by its opponents. If, as some report, terrorist acts 'are often viewed in many Third World countries as noble acts of "freedom fighters"' [John Drugard, "International Terrorism and Just War," *Stanford Journal of International Studies* XII, 21-37, p. 77], we should be able to examine the reasons *without having precluded them by definitional fiat*." (Virginia Held, *op. cit.*, p. 619, emphasis added.)

[4] The payment of reparations may appear to be a second option, but such payment is, at best, a means to structural change – and given the gargantuan size of accurate reparations (see footnote 12), not a very likely option. Moreover, if reparations were to be paid out in such a way that their only effect was to enrich some individual descendents of those who were wronged in the past – in other words, if the payments did not result in structural change – then the world would still remain colonial and, therefore, unjust.

[5] I am using this term according to its original meaning, "on its face," i.e., "at first glance," and not according to the more specialized meaning it has acquired in contemporary ethical theory. What I am concerned with is whether a potential justification makes sense to "the person in the street," the average person who is not going to engage in a rigorous critico-philosophical analysis of his/her position. The struggle against terrorism, like struggles against insurgency, needs to take the positions of this person seriously since a failure to win her/his heart and mind is a

failure to make progress against terrorism.

[6] The approach presented here is based on the work of Ibero-Salvadoran philosopher, Ignacio Ellacuría (1930-1989). His work, in turn, is heavily indebted to Basque philosopher, Xavier Zubiri (1898-1983). Zubiri developed a systematic philosophy which argues that human reality is fundamentally social and historical, and Ellacuría developed this into a philosophy of liberation. I trace the development of Ellacuría's thought out of Zubiri's, and give a far fuller development of the material presented here in Part I of the paper, in *Human Essence, History and Liberation: Karl Marx and Ignacio Ellacuría on Being Human* (doctoral dissertation, Loyola University Chicago, 2003), especially pp. 222-360. See also, Ignacio Ellacuría, *Filosofía de la Realidad Histórica* (San Salvador: UCA Editores, 1990, 1999), and Héctor Samour, *Voluntad de Liberación: El Pensamiento Filosófico de Ignacio Ellacuría* (San Salvador: UCA Editores, 2002), which is the single best source for a comprehensive overview of Ellacuría's philosophical thought. Helpful overviews in English of Ellacuría's thought can be found in Kevin F. Burke and Robert Lassalle-Klein, eds., *Love that Produces Hope: The Thought of Ignacio Ellacuría* (Collegeville, MN: Liturgical Press, 2006); and Kevin Burke, *The Ground Beneath the Cross: The Theology of Ignacio Ellacuría* (Washington, DC: Georgetown University Press, 2000), especially chs. 2-3, which treat the philosophical underpinnings of Ellacuría's theological work. An excellent intellectual biography of Ellacuría, which helpfully places his thought in the context of the political and ecclesial changes taking place in the world (Cold War, Cuban revolution, Vatican II, liberation theology, etc.), is Theresa Whitfield's *Paying the Price: Ignacio Ellacuría and the Murdered Jesuits of El Salvador* (Philadelphia: Temple, 1995).

The upshot of this part of the paper is that the structures built by humans are social and historical, and that these structures, thus, embed past actions. Therefore, past injustices stay with us until they are actively addressed, either by undoing them (reparations) or by overcoming them. Other thinkers have made similar claims, notably Marx. What I prefer about Ellacuría's approach is the emphasis on history as the accretion of praxis; this makes it easy to see that humans are responsible for the creation, development, improvement and/or razing of the controlling structures of reality. In other words, Ellacuría resolves the controversy between dialectical materialism and historical materialism in favor of the latter: history is material but it is not determined or deterministic because it is driven forward by free human action.

[7] Ellacuría uses the term "history" to refer to that time period, in the development of reality, that is under the sway of praxis. Thus, the billions of years in which reality developed solely according to the logics of physics and evolution, i.e., up to the arrival of human beings, do not count, speaking technically, as history. I will follow their usage, and reserve the term "history" for the progression of human attempts to effect reality.

[8] The social and historical character of human reality is explored in much greater depth in my doctoral dissertation, *Human Essence, History and Liberation: Karl Marx and Ignacio Ellacuría on Being Human*, *op. cit.*, especially chs. 2,4,5. See also, Ellacuría, *Filosofía de la Realidad Histórica*, op. cit., and Héctor Samour, *Voluntad*

---

de Liberación: El Pensamiento Filosófico de Ignacio Ellacuría, op., cit.

[9] Consider the narrative of Manifest Destiny. By using it, the United States convinced itself that wars of aggression, theft of land, and genocide were acceptable. The rest of the world knows this; they know how that narrative turned out for Native Americans. There is a strong prima facie case in favor of resisting, strongly, any American policy that resembles, and/or attempts to continue, this narrative. It should not be surprising that there are those who resist, with every means at his disposal, the continued expansion of American power.

[10] For example, the value of the labor stolen from Africans enslaved in the 13 British colonies and, later, the United States, is variously estimated between $1 and $10 trillion dollars. (Cf., Stephen Kershnar, *Justice for the Past* [New York: SUNY, 2004], p. 143, n. 3.) This figure is on a par with the national debt of the United States. Service on the national debt (i.e., just the interest payments) – which does nothing to reduce the principal – runs about $300 billion annually, and will continue to do so for as many decades into the future as one can see. A focus on reparations, which is not my point in this paper, could argue that a similar sum of money should go to the descendents of those whose labor was not recompensed. Note that the comparison to *interest* on the national debt is particularly appropriate since unrecompensed labor represents principal that was never allowed to accrue the interest, financial and social, that one's labor typically does accrue.

[11] The geographic scope of the exploitation of the world by Europeans and North Americans is truly staggering. In every one of the areas listed (which together account for over 95% of the world's inhabitable surface) labor, land and other natural resources were stolen; and in many of the areas listed, genocide occurred.

[12] The work of dependency theorists has not been surpassed. Cf., Andre Gunder Frank, *Capitalism and Underdevelopment in Latin America* (New York: Monthly Review Press 1967, revised ed. 1969); Frank, "The Development of Underdevelopment," in James D. Cockcroft, Andre Gunder Frank, and Dale Johnson, eds., *Dependence and Underdevelopment* (Garden City, New York: Anchor Books, 1972); Immanuel Wallerstein, *The Modern World-System, vol. I: Capitalist Agriculture and the Origins of the European World-Economy in the Sixteenth Century* (New York/London: Academic Press, 1974); Wallerstein, *The Modern World-System, vol. II: Mercantilism and the Consolidation of the European World-Economy, 1600-1750* (New York: Academic Press, 1980); Wallerstein, *The Modern World-System, vol. III: The Second Great Expansion of the Capitalist World-Economy, 1730-1840's* (San Diego: Academic Press, 1989).

[13] Peter Singer argues that the moral preference shown to one's immediate kin (parents, children, and, to a lesser extent, siblings) is not valid at the level of race or nation; within and between these larger groups, moral impartiality is the only defensible morality. *One World* (Yale, 2002), ch. 5, especially pp. 167-180.

Iris Marion Young acknowledges that group membership is an important source of the self, and that there is some value to a preference for other members of the group to which one belongs. But the group extension is stronger the more local it is, and the further one moves from kin the more manufactured is the group identity; thus, one can manufacture a global group identity instead of a nationalist one. This leads her to propose a federated system of democratic world government wherein local autonomy is promoted and everyone has an equal say in electing global leaders. See her "Self-Determination and Global Democracy," *Inclusion and Democracy* (Oxford, 2000), ch. 7.

[14] The rule of power can be dressed up with narratives about religious, racial, cultural superiority, but the bottom line is still power.

[15] Theoretically, the claim of the oligarchy that it is more deserving to rule could be grounded in merit. But for this to be legitimate, society would have to have genuine equality of opportunity for all children (starting with, e.g., truly equal educational opportunities and truly equal access to healthcare). Inherited membership in the oligarchy is based in power, not merit.

[16] Peter Singer, in his recent book, *One World* (Yale, 2002), pp. 151 ff., makes a similar point to the one presented here. However, I first encountered the argument on the bulletin boards of the theology department at the Universidad Centroamericana, in El Salvador. There, within days of September 11, posters began to appear reminding people of *all* the innocent ones who had died on September 11.

[17] Thomas Pogge argues that those with superabundance are especially culpable: with the arrival of more closely integrated economies, the wealthy countries now actively contribute to the deaths of the poor. Cf., *World Poverty and Human Rights* (Polity, 2002), pp. 1-26. See also John Harris' suggestion that "the moment we realize that harm to human beings could be prevented, we are entitled to see the failure to prevent it as a cause of harm." (John Harris, "The Marxist Conception of Violence," *Philosophy and Public Affairs* [Winter 1974] vol. 3, no. 4, pp. 204-205, cited in Virginia Held, "Violence, Terrorism, and Moral Inquiry," *Monist,* vol. 68 [1984] p. 625, n. 4.)

[18] Cf., the remark by Madeleine Albright, then Secretary of State under President Clinton, in 1996. When asked if the toll of some half-million dead Iraqi children caused by the economic sanctions then in effect was an acceptable price to pay for the policy, she responded, "I think this is a very hard choice, but the price--we think the price is worth it" (*CBS 60 Minutes*, May 12, 1996). The idea that the deaths of thousands of innocent victims is an acceptable price for achieving one's political goal is an idea that bin Laden would probably agree with. (The figure of a half-million dead Iraqi children resulting from the policy of sanctions comes from the U.N. Food and Agriculture Organization, and was later verified through an in-depth investigation conducted by UNICEF. An excellent discussion of the determination of this figure can be found at FAIR, http://www.fair.org/extra/0111/iraq.html)

This kind of imperial hubris plays badly in the rest of the world, especially when Muslims in the Middle East consider how differently the US might react if the half-million dead children were white or Christian.

[19] Bat-Ami Bar On, "Terrorism, Evil, and the Everyday Depravity," *Hypatia*, vol. 18 (Winter 2003), p. 157 ff.

[20] Ibid.

[21] For instance, Virginia Held's canonical piece, *op. cit.*

[22] Joseph Stiglitz, *Globalization and Its Discontents* (New York: W.W. Norton, 2002), p. 21, emphasis added.
[23] Lewis A. Coser, "Some Social Functions of Violence," *The Annals of the American Academy of Political and Social Science*, vol. 364 (March 1966), p. 14; cited in Virginia Held, *op. cit.*, p. 609.
[24] Virgina Held, *op.cit.,* p. 611.
[25] There is a large array of super-powerful weapons available to the truly desperate, some of which are more controllable than others. Graham Allison argues that, unlike biological and chemical weapons, nuclear weapons are completely controllable under a strict international regime of inspections, a regime that is yet to be created but one that could be easily realized if the US were to take the lead. *Nuclear Terrorism: The Ultimate Preventable Catastrophe* (NY: Henry Holt, 2004).
[26] Michael Scheuer, at the time a senior U.S. intelligence analyst, characterized bin Laden as "the most popular anti-American leader in the world today." Scheuer ("Anonymous"), *Imperial Hubris: Why the West Is Losing the War on Terror* (Washington, DC: Brassey's Inc., 2004).
[27] The struggle against terrorism should also address the other two factors: the democratization of violence and the increasing pool of desperate people. The first of these, the democratization of violence, is a change brought about by technology and will be very hard to change: a) weapons of mass destruction can be catalogued and safe-guarded effectively only so long as the people doing that work are not themselves ideologically or materially desperate; b) the list of everyday items that can be used to inflict massive casualties is probably a lot longer than airplanes and fertilizers.

The second factor, the growing pool of desperate people, is more amenable to change, and would be positively impacted by movement towards power-structures that take into account the interests of all people, not just the interests of the powerful.
[28] Three historical examples, and a current one, should suffice to make the case: The overthrow of Mossadeq in Iran (1953), Arbenz in Guatemala (1954), and Allende in Chile (1973): in each instance, the US worked for the violent overthrow of a democratically elected leader because this leader had moved against the interests of American corporations. More recently, the democratically elected and re-elected government of Hugo Chavez in Venezuela has earned the ire of the US for, among other reasons, seeking to collect back taxes from international oil companies. The US was very quick to recognize a coup against this democratically elected leader in 2005.
[29] For example, a Third World country may decide that strengthening its economy and promoting its security requires the imposition of tariffs that a) keep out a segment of First World industrial goods so that its own nascent industries can grow strong to the point of being able to compete with First World industry; and b) keep out the highly subsidized First World foodstuffs so that its own agricultural sector can move away from export-oriented mono-cropping (e.g., coffee, cotton, bananas) and grow the country's own food, thereby achieving the important goal of food security.

Of course, the large subsidies received by First World agricultural sectors (which enable these sectors to overwhelm and destroy Third World agricultural producers) contradict the free-trade policies of neo-liberalism. Add to this the history of industrial development in the First World, where *every* country used tariff barriers to protect its developing industries, and one sees another aspect of the First World's policies towards the Third World that can be easily interpreted as hypocritical.

[30] China, India, the US, Indonesia, Brazil, Pakistan, Bangladesh, Russia, Nigeria, Japan, and Mexico. Collectively, these eleven countries with populations over 100 million account for 61% of the world's population, and 57% of the world's economic activity. Figures are based on the 2007 estimates for population and GDP from the *CIA World Factbook*, available online at: www.cia.gov/cia/publications/factbook.

[31] In addition to the eleven countries already listed, this would include the Philippines, Vietnam, Germany, Egypt, Ethiopia, Turkey, Democratic Republic of the Congo, Iran, Thailand, France, United Kingdom, Italy, South Korea, Burma, Ukraine, Columbia, South Africa, Spain and Argentina. Together, these 30 countries with population over 40 million account for 79% of the world's population and 81% of its economic activity. Figures are based on the 2007 estimates for population and GDP from the *CIA World Factbook*, available online at: www.cia.gov/cia/publications/factbook.

[32] This arrangement, based on preserving the votes of *nations*, is still a step towards genuine supranational democracy, which would entail the world's people, one-person-one-vote, directly electing representatives to a world parliament.

Many of the philosophers currently working on the topic of globalization have focused on reforms to the UN Security Council as an evolutionary step towards a more just world. Iris Marion Young, *Inclusion and Democracy* (Oxford, 2000), pp. 271 ff.; David Held, *Democracy and the Global Order: From the Modern State to Cosmopolitan Governance* (Stanford: Stanford University Press, 1995), pp. 87 ff., and *passim*; Peter Singer, *One World, op.cit.*, pp. 144-146; Thomas Pogge, *World Poverty and Human Rights* (Cambridge [UK]: Polity, 2002). Pogge does not address the Security Council directly, but many of the reforms he discusses, for example, the Democracy Panel (pp. 156-164), would have implications for the current make-up of the Council.

[33] For a good summary of the realist position and the assumptions it relies upon – and an argument for why those assumptions no longer hold true in a complexly interdependent world – see Robert Keohane and Joseph Nye, "Realism and Complex Interdependence," *The Globalization Reader*, Frank Lechner, Joseph Boli, eds. (Oxford: Blackwell, 2000), pp. 77-83.

[34] According to many of the interviews broadcast in the wake of the London transit bombings (July 7, 2005), which themselves came after both 9/11 and the Madrid train bombings (March 11, 2004), the people responsible for security in most large cities concede that attacks like those in London are now inevitable, that there is little to be done to stop them. What is interesting is the assumption that the citizens of the powerful countries are now to take it as a fact of life that they and their loved ones can now disappear, from one day to the next, while going about their daily routine. It is a sad commentary on the Western imagination that no other way can be envisioned, that so few look beyond the logistical nightmare of searching every package of the

---

tens of millions of people who use public transportation daily, to examine what perceived injustices may be motivating the bombers. It is, indeed, considered taboo to examine the possible motivation of the bombers.

[35] Peter Singer, *One World*, *op. cit.*, p. 13.

[36] Economic data comes from the *CIA World Factbook*, estimates for 2007, available online at: www.cia.gov/cia/publications/factbook.

[37] The consumption and pollution data comes from Lester Brown, *Plan B 2.0: Rescuing a Planet Under Stress and a Civilization in Trouble* (New York: W.W. Norton, 2006), pp. 3-11.

How to be Properly Unnatural: Nature, Essences, and the Metaphysics of Heterosexual Normativity[1]

Jeremy Barris, Marshall University

Heterosexual normativity, like any way of dealing with reality, can only exist given particular ideas about what can make sense and about the ultimate nature of reality. In other words, heteronormativity, as I shall call it, is based on a logic and a metaphysics. (As I shall argue, it is important for the sake of queer theory itself to note that this *is* true of all ways of dealing with reality. Even if, as in the case of many sexuality theorists, the "metaphysics" is a view that there is no, or no constructive, metaphysics, this is still a view about the ultimate truth of reality, and that is what a metaphysics *is*. The "no metaphysics" view, then, really only rejects *competing* metaphysics, which take reality to include something beyond historical, social, material reality.) One dimension of the heteronormative metaphysics and logic that I would like to explore is its widely recognized understanding of homosexuality (in particular, though not uniquely) as "unnatural," as not belonging to the way things truly, unquestionably, and inescapably are.

Over the last few decades, sexuality and gender theorists have increasingly responded to this heteronormative view by rejecting the idea of a "nature," of an inescapable way that things are, independent of historical change and social construction. This has been the gist of much of the debate between constructionism and essentialism. And even though there have been substantial attempts in that debate to make room for natures or essences, this has been done, I shall argue, in ways that really subordinate natures or essences thoroughly to construction. Against these responses, what I want to show is that, on the one hand, this thoroughgoing ultimate rejection of a "nature" of things cedes too much to the victimizers: too much that is of value, and in fact that is more than just valuable, but essential (if you will pardon the term) to our lives. And I want to show, on the other hand, that this thoroughgoing rejection requires too little of us who reject heterosexism, makes us too liable to repeating related kinds of injustice ourselves.

I shall approach this discussion by revisiting the essentialism versus constructionism debate. In recent years many theorists have come to dismiss this debate as irrelevant, largely because of the widely familiar attempts to reconcile the two views.[2] But I want to argue, first, that these attempts have not in fact succeeded, and, second, that there is still a great deal of politically relevant insight to be gained from these views in their specifically antagonistic forms.

I shall begin by sketching the logic of the metaphysics of "natures" and its close connections with the logic of essences. I shall then argue that the essentialist/constructionist debate, in working with and against that logic, has been caught up in unrecognized and insoluble contradictions. I shall argue that these contradictions are another way of expressing the problem of ceding too much and taking too little responsibility that I mentioned above. I shall then try to show that the solution to both these forms of the problem lies precisely *in those unresolved and unresolvable* contradictions.

I shall propose an alternative logic to both those of heterosexism and those so far relied on, as it seems to me, by sexuality and gender theorists. This will be a contradictory logic, and will underpin a contradictory metaphysics. I shall try to show that these particular kinds of contradiction make viable sense, and so are capable of being helpful in the ways I claim for them. I shall also discuss some dimensions of what this logic concretely requires of us in practice.

While a lot of feminist work, especially some versions of "French feminism," has already developed logics of contradiction, these logics, as I shall discuss, only go so far. They remain consistently – non-contradictorily – contradictory. As a result they still really preclude the sense of a nature or essence, which is characterized by being entirely without contradiction, by being simply and changelessly what it is. In fact they themselves (contradictorily, as one would expect from standpoints that consist in contradiction), in pursuing contradictions that are *only* or non-contradictorily contradictions, are still too committed to the idea of an unwavering self-consistency in the case of contradiction itself. That is, they are still committed to the idea of a "nature" or unvarying essence *of contradiction*. (This remains true even if they acknowledge *other, separate* aspects of things that are not contradictory).

Since the logic I want to explore violates the logic that belongs to thinking of things (and logics) as having natures, as being simply self-identically what they are and are meant to be, I think of it as a logic of "the unnatural." My hope is that this "unnatural" logic will contribute to resolving some of the more recalcitrant problems encountered by sexuality theorists (and of course their readers) in dealing with heteronormativity.

The Logics of Nature, Essence, and Construction

The heterosexist reaction to homosexuality as unnatural is an especially extreme form of normativity. For this reaction, there are things that are not merely statistically normal, not merely conveniently or comfortably standard and so, by default, preferable for the (by definition) standard majority, but are *natural*, are the way that belongs to them without any possible or conceivable question, the only way they can conceivably be. As a result, anything that conflicts with what is natural is literally inconceivable, contradicting sense and the only way that things can be.

Roland Barthes, for example, notes about the role of the "myth" of nature, in the case of bourgeois ideology, that it "transforms . . . History into Nature . . . man as represented by it is universal, eternal . . . bourgeois ideology yields an unchangeable nature" (1972, 141-142). Similarly, Rosalind Coward and John Ellis write that this kind of ideology is "effective precisely for the reason that it appears as 'natural,' 'the way things are . . .'": so, "for example the existing relations of power are . . . perceived precisely as the way things are, ought to be and will be" (1977, 67). Because the concept of nature is that of things as the only way they can be, it makes the idea of accounting for "natural" things literally meaningless. If something cannot be conceived to be otherwise, there is no meaning to asking how it got to be that way. The question contrasts its present way of being with some other, and no other way of being is conceivable for it. In Barthes' words, this concept of nature "refuses explanations," and, in the case of human reality, "produces the . . . image of an unchanging humanity, characterized by an indefinite repetition of its identity" (142).

The politically relevant result, of course, is that those things that are understood as natural, like heterosexuality, have no conceivable alternatives. They are the unique and unquestionable standard by which all related things are measured, and the idea that things might be different from what they legislate is not merely false but utterly incoherent. As Barthes, again, puts it, "ideology is . . . constituted by the loss of the historical quality of things: in it, things lose the memory that they once were made" (142). In fact, they (in this case, heterosexuality as a "natural" norm) lose the sense that they are the kinds of things that could even be thought of as having been made, and so of course also the sense that they could even be thought about with a view to being re-made.

Closer to home, however, as Coward and Ellis argue, "what is produced in ideology is the very basis of the [human] subject's activity, . . . and the coherency of that subject. . ." (1977, 67-68, my insertion). This implies two things that are important here. The less radical one is that one's sense of being a person is subject to the concept of the natural. As a result, if one does not conform to what is usually taken to be part of being a person, one is unnatural: and it is clear that this now means that one is inconceivable, without an identity (that is, without logical coherence, without sameness with oneself), and so not part of reality at all. As Judith Butler writes, "The cultural matrix through which gender identity has become intelligible requires that certain kinds of 'identities' cannot 'exist' -- that is, those in which gender does not follow from sex and those in which the practices of desire do not 'follow' from either sex or gender. . . . Indeed, precisely because certain kinds of 'gender identities' fail to conform to those norms of cultural intelligibility, they appear only as developmental failures or logical impossibilities from within that domain" (1990, 17). More simply, Michael Warner refers to "the assumption that this group [queers] . . . does not or should not exist" (1993, xxv, my insertion).

The second, more radical implication of the idea that "the coherency of the subject" is produced by the ideology of the natural is that *the very idea* of being a person, a human subjectivity, *at all*, is born out of this concept. And this means that *any* sense of being a person is subject to the extreme normativity that it involves. As a result, many gender and sexuality theorists have argued that if we want to avoid being entrapped by politically motivated normativities, we need to reject being persons, identities, subjects, at all. Butler, for example, is troubled by putting herself forward under *any* category: "To write or speak *as a lesbian* . . . is . . . to come out or write in the name of an identity which, once produced, sometimes functions as a politically efficacious phantasm." For, she argues, "identity categories tend to be instruments of regulatory regimes," even when they are "the rallying points for a liberatory contestation of . . . oppression" (1991, 13-14). Similarly, Denise Riley notes that "Feminism has intermittently been as vexed with the urgency of disengaging from the category 'women' as it has with laying claim to it" (1988, 3-4). And John Champagne (1995) follows Foucault in arguing that although "one cannot *not* be a subject," we need to "resist the continuing practices of subject formation and . . . work strategically towards a 'freeing' of the subject from subjectivity" (xxvii).

The result of this kind of response has often been the articulation and endorsement of a kind of "unnaturalness" as a sort of "anything but nature," as the opposite, and only the opposite, of what is natural, of what is simply given as what the thing simply is. Mark Blasius, for instance, discusses how "Lesbians and gay men virtually invent a way of life through which they create and re-create the self continually" in ways that "have, of course, nothing to do with any intrinsic qualities of homosexuals" (1994, 192). Eve Sedgwick writes that one value of the term "queer," in contrast with the "univocal whole" that "sexual identity" refers to, is that it can name "the open mesh of possibilities, gaps, overlaps, dissonances and resonances, lapses and excesses of meaning when the constituent elements of anyone's gender, of anyone's sexuality aren't made (or *can't be* made) to signify monolithically" (1993, 8). Similarly, Steven Seidman embraces postmodernism as a "standpoint that aims to decenter or destabilize unitary concepts of the human subject, foundationalist and objectivist views of knowledge, and totalizing perspectives on society and history" (1997, 109). Leo Bersani, again, argues for a "'self-shattering' . . . anti-identitarian identity" (1995, 101). Reflecting on Jean Genet's celebration of being an "outlaw," an outcast from all norms, a status that Bersani takes as one fruitful model of this kind of "identity," he notes that "the question becomes: how do you get rid of an essence . . . ?" (173). And in an extreme but by no means unique formulation, Gregory Bredbeck asserts that even "'sense' itself is form of cultural fascism that seeks to pin down, label, constrain, control, and dismiss in a way that is undermined by history itself" (1991, xii).

And the theorists of subjectivity (or anti-subjectivity) mentioned above certainly do not want to settle for any form of unquestioned or unchallenged subjectivity or "having a nature." As Cathy Griggers, for example, notes, "In the lesbian cultural landscape of postmodernity, essentialist arguments about feminine identity are more defunct than ever" (1993, 184).

But there are problems with this purely anti-natural or anti-essentialist stance, problems in fact often recognized by these same theorists in connection with the conflict between "essence" and "construction."

The Incompatibility but Necessity of Both Essence and Construction

While, as we have just seen, many sexuality and gender theorists now completely reject the concept of a nature or essence, many others have come to see a need for something like this concept in a viable sexual politics, and have developed a variety of ways of accommodating it to the alternative idea of social construction. In either case, the respective theorists have largely come to regard the debate between essence and construction as settled, and so no longer relevant. In this section, however, I want to show *both* that we cannot dispense with either the concept of an essence or nature *or* that of construction, *and* that the familiar ways of accommodating them to each other have not succeeded, and logically *could not* have succeeded. The problem, then, is still very much with us.

As the discussion has already indicated, there are close connections between the assumptions that underlie the visceral reaction to the "unnaturalness" of homosexuality, and the theoretical language of essences that has played such a large role in analyses of homophobia and the ways to fight it. The concept of an essence in fact neatly translates the concept of a nature. It too is the final and fixed answer to the question of what something is, beyond which there are no questions to be asked. And as a result it is inconceivable here as well that anything with an essence could have genuinely different variations, or that it could (and still less should) change in any fundamental way. As Barthes makes this connection between "nature" and "essence," in his discussion of the "myth" of the natural, "The world enters language as a dialectical relation between activities, between human actions; it comes out of myth as a harmonious display of essences" (1972, 142).

Because these concepts are closely related and also play a closely related political role, the reasons for fighting the concept of essence are identical to those for fighting the concept of nature. They both belong to a logic and metaphysics of a given, exclusive sense and identity of things. Butler (1990, 12ff.) and Diana Fuss (1989, 2ff.), among others, have elaborated some of the politically relevant problems with this logic and metaphysics. Essences, being the ultimate answer to what things are, and constituting their fixed identity, allow for no fundamental change, development, or deep differences between people who share an identity understood as an essence. The idea of essences also denies social responsibility for how groups are categorized. And beyond these problems, this idea puts an unjustified and unjustifiable end to explanations and analysis, so that the standpoints based on this kind of concept are ultimately arbitrary.

The alternative concept is, of course, social construction, or the production of what things are by specific historical circumstances. But, as I mentioned, it has become increasingly apparent to many in these debates that we cannot do without either concept. This has emerged as the case not only because both are necessary in order to allow a viable politics, but, more fundamentally, because both are also *logically* (and in fact also metaphysically) necessary. That is, both concepts are also necessary to sense or meaning itself (not, I think, in Bredbeck's sense of a "fascistic," controlling "making sense of things," but) in the sense of *having* meanings, and articulable connections between them, *at all* (for an extended discussion of this literature, see Fuss 1989; see also Bredbeck 1991, 237-238; Butler 1990; Riley 1988, e.g., 99ff.).

With respect to political concerns, essences without construction present the problems I have mentioned just above. And, with respect to sense or meaning itself, without construction, that is, without genuine historical production and change, there would be no escape or separation from the absolutely unchanging given that would make it possible to put it in relation to anything else, and so even to refer to it, let alone reflect on it. If each thing were really an eternally self-same essence, one could not alter one's state (oneself also being an essence) to relate oneself to it, and more generally there could be no "relating" of anything "to" anything else, only simply being the thing or simply not being the thing, always in exactly the same way. There could be no transformations of anything, no processes, including the shifts or movements of consciousness involved in making statements, still less modifiable statements, about anything.

But, on the other hand, constructions without essence would be continuous production and transformation. With respect to sense or meaning, this would allow nothing to be graspable *at all*, nothing to be *that specific thing that is* constructed or *those specific things that are* constructed *from*, or anyone in particular for whose sake one is thinking about these issues in the first place. It would allow us to have no specific meanings, and so to say nothing specific – not even to mean anything in particular when we deny that "essences" exist. Neither the words and ideas one would use in discussing this process nor the actions one would take in participating in it would have any coherence, would *be* any particular words or any particular actions.

We need to recognize that the essences required here are essences *entirely unqualified* by construction, what I shall call pure essences. It is incoherent to think of construction *itself* without something *simply given, not-to-be-explained and so ahistorical*, in some form, that the construction can work *on* and that the process of construction can already *be*. Otherwise every part and aspect of the process and materials of construction must be conceived as being constructed before any construction can begin. That is, construction must take place in order to make it possible for it to take place: it must happen before it is possible for it to happen.

In fact, as Fuss points out, social constructionist explanation as it exists already relies on a pure essence: the idea of the "social," itself not requiring, and insusceptible of, explanation (1989, 6). Because construction is performed by the social conditions, the "social" is what is doing the explaining. It is consequently *presupposed* by this kind of explanation, and so necessarily remains unexplained by it. And that at least something that is doing the explaining must necessarily remain unexplained is another way of arguing the inescapable reliance of sense or meaning in general on pure essences, on a simply given starting point.

Butler makes another kind of argument for the reliance of "non-essential" thought on essences or simple identities, noting, for one example, that when Kristeva adopts the (obviously tempting) strategy of developing an opposition "between the principle of multiplicity that escapes the charge of non-contradiction and a principle of identity based on the suppression of that multiplicity. . . . that very principle of multiplicity . . . operates in much the same manner as a principle of identity" (1990, 89). Contradictory multiplicity, by being stably opposed to and contrasted with identity and singleness, gains a self-same, unified consistency: a simple identity. The same problem, I suggest, applies to the consistent kind of logic of contradiction explored by thinkers like Luce Irigaray, who writes, for example, that "woman . . . enters into a ceaseless exchange of herself with the other without any possibility of identifying either" (1985, 31). The idea of contradiction itself is usable only because it *has a given, self-same sense*. (And if there is genuinely no essence here, the problem I discussed above applies: because there is *only* contradiction, we are no longer saying anything identifiable at all.)

On the political side, as Fuss puts it, in the course of a general argument that constructionism and essentialism depend on each other, politics itself is unthinkable without some sense of a self-identical phenomenon in its own right (1989, xii). One cannot mobilize on behalf of "homosexuals" or "women" without a sense that these categories refer to something sharing stable traits with others of its kind (24ff.). And for the same reasons that sense requires something simply given, it is not enough to regard these categories as historically assembled, temporary stabilities. (As Butler, for example, argues we should, proposing "the reconceptualization of identity as an *effect*, that is, as *produced* or *generated*" (1990, 147); or as Alison Stone (2004) has more recently argued along different lines, in the course of proposing that we should reject even the concessions that have so far been made to essence in these debates.) Again, what these categories were assembled *out of*, and something about the process *by which* they were assembled, needs to be *simply given* in some form if the process of assembly can be coherently conceived at all. Otherwise, again, neither the words one uses in discussing this process nor the actions one takes in participating in it have any coherence, *are* any particular words or actions.

As I shall discuss in the next section, the concept of essence in fact has positive value in its own independent right. Here I am restricting myself to the ways in which it and construction are both simply necessary, in order to show the nature of the logical problem they present.

Lately, as I mentioned above, many theorists have taken these developments to show that the debate is now pointless. Seidman (who in fact only sees a point in constructionism, and not in essentialism at all) makes this point forcefully: "the arcane polemics between constructionists and essentialists has evolved into a sterile metatheoretical debate increasingly devoid of moral and political import" (1997, 109). But, while both concepts are necessary, as the history of this debate *has* succeeded in showing, they are also, as I am about to argue, incompatible, and in fact irreconcilably contradictory. Consequently, we are caught in a real contradiction to which we so far have no solution.

The theorists who have attempted to reconcile these concepts do not of course see them as incompatible in this way. Fuss, for example, refers to "a largely artificial (albeit powerful) antagonism between them" (1989, 119). But the idea of construction as a basic explanation denies the possibility, or any sense to the very idea, of being simply *given*, without a history of being produced, which partly defines an essence. And the idea of essence, as the related concept of nature brings sharply into relief, denies any sense to its being constructed *in any way*. What counts as an explanation for the one simply is not an explanation, is not even coherent as a statement about the matter, for the other. As a result the attempts so far made to reconcile them have failed, I believe, and necessarily so.

Both Fuss and Butler, for example, while explaining the necessity for both views, in the end do not, it seems to me, give them both equal weight. While clearly trying to make a place for essentialisms, they nonetheless still think about how to combine them with constructionist insights from within what is really an entirely constructionist perspective. Fuss, for her part, writes that "we need both to theorize essentialist spaces from which to speak and, simultaneously, to deconstruct those spaces to keep them from solidifying. Such a double gesture involves once again the responsibility to historicize, to examine each deployment of essence . . . in the complicated contextual frame in which it is made" (1989, 118). But this does not really do justice to the concept of an essence. From a genuinely essentialist standpoint, essences are *not historical at all*. Consequently, they are also not the kind of thing that can be "deployed" –

they just *are*, they are just given as the core of what is real, not strategically selected from among alternative possibilities of thought. And, as I argued above along the lines introduced by these theorists themselves, it is just *this* sense of "essence" – that it just *is*, that it is simply given – that we need if either politics or sense itself are to be possible.

Butler, similarly, proposes to understand identity as, exactly, an historically constructed effect, and notes that this view "opens up possibilities of 'agency' that are insidiously foreclosed by positions that take identity categories as foundational and fixed. . . . Construction is not opposed to agency: it is the necessary scene of agency." As a result, "The critical task for feminism is not to establish a point of view outside of constructed identities" but rather to participate in "those practices of repetition that constitute identity and, therefore, present the immanent possibility of contesting them" (1990, 147). This preferential reliance on constructionism is easy to understand: a view of social reality as deeply historical, that is, as deeply changeable and therefore full of contrasts, seems readily to account not only for phases of history that continuously or pervasively undergo fundamental change, but also for phases that contrast with those by having become temporarily stable, circumstantially constellating something like an essence or identity or nature. But, again, in the essentialist view "social" reality is *not ultimately historical, or ultimately social, at all.* And essences are not the kind of thing one contests. They are the basis of reality and sense, and so are that which gives sense to contestation, that on the basis of which one contests. If one were to try to contest them, one would be relying on them entirely in doing so, and contestation would lose its meaning.

To the degree that theorists who want to retain constructionism also want be logically coherent, then, they cannot accommodate the concept of essentialism. Despite this kind of attempt at harmonizing the two views, they remain irreconcilably contradictory.

And this is where, I believe, a logic of the unnatural can help us: a logic that is incompatible with itself, contradictory, not self-identical, and in these specific ways not coherently conceivable. As I shall discuss, because it is *genuinely* contradictory, contradicting even itself *as contradiction*, it can make legitimate room for what it (also) excludes, for what is *absolutely not contradictory* but is simply and unquestionably what it is: essences and natures.

The Character and Value of a Logic of the Unnatural

In this section I shall first sketch the character of a logic of the unnatural -- its basic elements and how they fit together. Then, in the light of the discussion above of essences, I shall discuss the problems that, at the start of the paper, I suggested arise from abandoning the concept of nature to heteronormativity. I shall then outline some of the ways in which this unnatural logic responds to those problems. The problems involve not only the issue of contradiction between necessary concepts that I have just discussed, but also positive dimensions of "nature" or "essence" that, I claimed, we have ceded at our own political and moral cost. (In the next section I shall try to show in more depth that this logic makes viable sense, and discuss some aspects of what it concretely requires of us in practice.)

I suggest that the logic that we need is one that can work with a certain kind of unmitigated contradiction, work with it not only as a flaw that needs to be resolved, but (also) as part of how sense, and so reality, work. That is, we need to be able to work with a particular kind of breakdown of sense itself, a specific kind of incoherence or inconceivability, without eliminating it. And this is exactly what a thoroughgoing concept of the "unnatural" involves. As I have discussed, the idea of a nature involves the inconceivability of any alternatives to the sense that things have in its context. Consequently, the idea of the unnatural, in *this* context, is exactly an idea of what is inconceivable, what is beyond the boundaries of sense.

But this is not the unnatural as "anything but nature" or "anything but stable sense." These ideas, as I have argued, are defined by a stable contrast with "nature" and stable sense, and therefore really have a "nature" and sense of their own. Instead, this is the unnatural as *genuinely* contradictory and genuinely without a nature: an *also self*-contradictory alternative to nature and sense. Because it is properly self-contradictory, it can *also* make room, paradoxically, for what it *excludes*: that is, for the concept of a self-identical nature. This is an unnatural that contradicts itself *even as contradiction*, to make room for natures, that is, for sense that is entirely independent of it and entirely unqualified and unchallenged by it. Differently expressed, it makes room for sense to which it is simply meaningless and irrelevant.

This is why it can (contradictorily) allow us to work with the contradiction between standpoints without either simply eliminating the sense of one or both of the standpoints altogether, or evading the force of the contradiction.

In the case of essentialism and constructionism, each of these, as I have argued, depends on the other *as the other is entirely independently of it*, completely unqualified by it. We need *pure* essences (otherwise, again, we would have nothing that we could grasp), for which change is simply not conceivable. And we also need to think of *real* change as built into things (otherwise, again, we could not even have the shifts of consciousness and relation necessary to refer to anything), and for this the idea of something whose nature excludes the very sense of change is simply incoherent. That is, what each of these standpoints depends on, in the other, is an understanding of things for which the alternatives it itself presents are inconceivable, literally have no sense. And this is the idea of a nature.

We have, then, two incompatible ideas of what is natural, and the need for both. A logic of the unnatural, if it is possible at all, makes room for the sense of both and so for the contradiction between them, *and* for their simple, independent inconceivability or meaninglessness to each other. That is, it makes room both for the contradiction between them and for the meaninglessness or irrelevance of the contradiction to each of them. It connects them and it keeps them disconnected in the same act.

Now, if we *can* have both construction and essence, as we have established we *must* (meaning and sense-making themselves require it, and consequently logic requires it), then we *can* think both together while accepting each one's understanding of reality as entirely excluding the very sense of the other's understanding of reality. That is, more generally, we can think two or more incompatible "natures," *and* the literal non-sense that each is to the other. We can consider and maintain incompatible views together, as simultaneously *both* of them *exclusively and entirely* true (and false).

This is not an idea of relative truths, but rather an idea of *more than one absolute* truth. That is, this is an idea of more than one truth each of which excludes the possibility of any other truth.

In short, then, as human beings, whatever our politics, we *need* to take certain things for granted (though not necessarily the same things as others do); we *do* take certain things for granted; and we are *right* to do so. In different words, because we are human -- that is, not out of self-indulgence, but because of what is *true* about being human -- with our human limitations, including limitations on our responsibilities for reality, we are entitled to be sometimes deeply at ease, to relax, to be at peace with ourselves.

Let me stress here that my main thesis is that we can, unnaturally, have more than one such unquestioning sense of the nature of things. So in arguing for the validity of our own sense of nature, I am not implying that we should or are entitled to subject everyone to our own normativity. I am only arguing that we are wrong to make *no* room for our own sense of nature. And, as I shall argue below, where there *is* more than one such nature to consider, this unnatural logic allows us *also* to *question* our unquestionable "natural" meanings and practices.

We also need the concept of what is natural to give genuine respect, to do justice, to ourselves and our sense of our own reality, and also to others' senses of their own realities. For example, part of the problem with the vocabulary of "sexual preference" or "choice of one's sexuality" is that it ignores the ways in which, in being false to oneself, one betrays oneself, is untrue to *who one really is*. And that experience of self-betrayal or, alternatively, of being true to oneself, is surely not sufficiently expressed by saying, "in another social formation I could have been otherwise." *This* "I," one could reasonably argue, could not have been otherwise without simply being some other person, and not myself at all.

Again, if one really treats oneself or others as living in a constructed reality, one does not give what they (or oneself) take to be reality the status of reality, but rather the status of a *version* of reality, a sort of "almost the real thing." But surely it is insincere or false to treat someone's reaction to the death of their lover, or to the legal exclusion (or, by contrast, recognition) of their own personhood, as having only a restricted claim to reality, as being just one version of the reality of what they are feeling and of what they are responding to, among other ultimately equivalent alternatives. Surely this disrespects, trivializes, evades, is false to, their experience, part of whose force *is*, precisely, that it is an unquestionably real confrontation with something unquestionably real.

And, finally, this kind of un-self-critical unfairness directly harms our own lives, in itself. It is a form of deep dishonesty, not only with respect to our immediate thinking and activities, but also with respect to our status as epistemically and morally fallible human beings. In this way it divides us from our own reality, that is, from ourselves, and as a result deprives us of full presence and participation in our own lives. And it cuts us off from the possibilities of growing beyond our current depth of insight, and developing in new and unanticipated directions. (I shall discuss these possibilities further below in connection with the unnatural logic.)

The possibility of fundamental difference between "natures" is important not only for confrontations between bigotry and liberatory perspectives, but also for dealing fairly and with fidelity to truth with deep differences among liberatory perspectives themselves. In the context of an "unnatural" logic, various deeply conflicting liberatory frameworks can *all* be valid without resolving any of the conflicts.

This does not mean that the debates between them lose their point. Each still needs to uphold its own sense of things, to come to understand the perspectives of the others, and to question itself in the light of the insights of the others (while *also*, in this contradictory context, recognizing the *irrelevance* of the others). And all of this requires the mutual struggle of justifications and explanations. But it does mean that one can recognize and respect why another standpoint, given its ways of sense-making, thinks one's own standpoint is clearly wrong, while still having no doubt, given one's own ways of sense-making, that it is the other one that is clearly wrong.

In the bigger picture, I think we need to recognize that being in a situation predominantly structured by ideologies that distort sense and reality – and this is what requires a theorized struggle for justice in the first place – means that we are already in a situation predominantly characterized by contradiction. (And this is the kind of contradiction that is *simply* opposed to what is "natural.") Consequently, if we are to fight all of what is wrong in this situation, we can only do so by adopting a variety of contradictory stances. Given that an "unnatural" logic allows us to see how this is approach is viable, it follows that it is appropriate and constructive that we have a variety of unresolvedly contradictory standpoints.

(In a still bigger picture, it is arguable that just being human is contradictory in the "unnatural" sense, so that we need this logic among ourselves even where there are no political concerns at issue. But that is not a line of thought I shall pursue here.)

A logic of the unnatural, then, gives us the means of satisfactorily and completely *justifying* our general standpoints (if not particular issues within them) without committing the injustice of reserving that complete justification for ourselves, and without the self-disservice of preventing growth and change in our general sense of things.

Because this logic validates concepts of *nature*, that is, ways of sense-making to which there are no meaningful alternatives, it validates bases of thinking that cannot be meaningfully questioned. Questions *within* a natural order presuppose those bases to make sense at all, to be the questions they are, while questions *outside* it are literally senseless. This logic, then, allows the possibility that there are things we can *legitimately* take for granted. It justifies our having a sense of simple reality.

And because this logic, in being a logic of contradiction, *also* makes room for us to consider a nature *outside* its boundaries of sense, in (contradictory) relation to another or others, it enables our moving outside its bases altogether, to the entirely different bases of a different sense of "nature." As a result it also allows radical criticism of a position as a whole, including our own, and so allows for deep responsibility, and for deep social and personal growth.

Finally, since this logic justifies the concept of the natural, it allows us, again, to deal with heterosexism in a way that does not repeat the constitutionally un-self-critical and so constitutionally unjust exclusions made by the heterosexist version of the natural. Instead it lets us find ways of acknowledging heterosexism's own sense of itself, while also fully endorsing our own. And, as I have suggested, it allows the same in our attitudes to and dealings with each other, within the field of attempts to oppose heterosexism.

In the next section I shall try to show in a little more depth how the type of contradiction in this unnatural logic makes viable sense, and I shall discuss some dimensions of what this logic concretely requires of us in practice.

The Sense and Some Practical Dimensions of an Unnatural Logic

One line of thought that helps, despite itself, to show the sense of this concept of the unnatural occurs in Richard Rorty's discussion of relativism. Part of Rorty's argument is that we cannot coherently conceive a way of making sense that is completely inaccessible to our own ways of making sense, a way that is inconceivable for us. That idea itself, if it makes sense to us, can only be part of our own way of making sense. Consequently it cannot to refer to something excluded, by definition, from our way of making sense (1991, 25ff.). The result is something like what I have discussed as the concept of what is natural: there is no conceivable alternative to our way of construing things.

But this argument only works if one *starts* – so far arbitrarily, as I shall discuss further shortly below – with the assumption that only a self-identical, never-contradictory logic or way of making sense is possible. This is what makes it simply inconceivable that we could step outside our way of making sense, that there could be alternative ways of making sense that contradict our own. We could, instead, begin (so far no more arbitrarily, though also no less so) with the assumption that sense itself is not always self-identical, that there are contexts in which the senselessness of contradiction has a place in the structure of sense itself. On this assumption, that sense does not always coincide with itself, we sometimes *start* in two logically incompatible places at once: we are sometimes *already* simultaneously inside and outside our way(s) of making sense. In that case we can and often do simultaneously work with contradictory ways of making sense, and we can come to learn an entirely new way of making sense (as we all in fact did as infants in learning our present ones).

It would remain true that, as Rorty argues, and as I have maintained in the context of unnatural logic, each of our ways of making sense would be inconceivable to (would fall outside the boundaries of sense of) the others. But, on the assumption of this contradictory logic, there would be no problem granting *both* that we cannot conceive one way of sense-making from within another, *and* that we can inhabit and come to inhabit more than one such sense-making framework.

Now this, of course, is just to start with the assumption that I am supposed to be justifying, the possibility of a contradictory, "unnatural" logic, and so is uselessly circular. But Rorty's kind of argument *does exactly the same thing*. It only works on the *assumption* that this kind of contradiction (conceiving what is beyond what we can conceive) is *not* possible: but that is exactly what it is supposed to be showing. His argument depends equally uselessly on the "natural" logic it is supposed to be justifying, as mine depends on the "unnatural" logic *it* is supposed to be showing. As a result, there is no logical reason to begin with one of these assumptions rather than another.

It follows that there is nothing to prevent our legitimately *exploring* a logic of the unnatural. And, in exploring that logic, we have seen a variety of reasons why it is necessary. And even more than this, an unnatural logic can recognize and deal with exactly *this* situation, the illegitimacy of making a general decision between logics, which natural logic cannot do.

In fact, as I have argued, unnatural logic, which allows for its *own* contradiction and so for its own simple senselessness, can *justify and endorse* beginning with the assumptions of natural logic, in contexts where one is already working within a particular standpoint. *Within* a standpoint, that is, considering that standpoint on its own, one can only make sense by pursuing its ways of sense-making. If one does not, one is simply not making sense, with nothing further to be said about it. Here only the logic of the natural has a claim to meaning.

But, when claims to a different way of making sense enter the picture, there *is* good reason to make room for at least the possibility of moving beyond one's current boundaries of sense, and so for the senselessness and inconceivability of self-contradiction. And here the logic of the unnatural is the appropriate starting point.

The logic of the unnatural, then, legitimates contradiction, or senselessness, but only does so in specific and limited contexts, when one is making room for the possibility of alternative ways of making sense.

When, for whatever reasons, this possibility is no longer relevant (a satisfactory outcome has been negotiated; an existential decision as to life-choice has been made; some other non-conflictual issue is now the issue under consideration; one has done the best one can and no longer has the resources to pursue negotiations), natural logic and non-contradiction, that is, sense, are the only legitimate possibilities.

But it is also *only* when unnatural logic *is* relevant, when we *do* need to take into account contrasting "natures," that we can justify, through this logic's legitimating its own irrelevance, our resting on a standpoint's *natural* logic.

All of this really expresses the not very strange insights that, first, we need to be open to the possibility of learning new ways of making sense, which means learning what for us, now, is inconceivable. And that, second, we can legitimately require that others, equally, be open to the possibility of our own present ways of making sense, however unassimilable they may be to those others. And, third, that all parties should be open to the possibility of the simple, unavoidable reality of their own and others' experience.

And being prepared to succeed in grasping new ways of making sense means being prepared to be surprised by sense-making possibilities we could not have foreseen, including unforeseeable possible ways of negotiating our own standards of sense with these conflicting ones, and of finding resolutions in those negotiations.[3]

In experiential terms, encountering ways of making sense that are currently inconceivable for us, and working towards grasping them, necessarily means dealing with periods of confusion, of being unable to make sense of what or whom we encounter, being unable to find our bearings, stumbling blindly about, not seeing clearly what does and does not make sense. These are experiences that we need to learn to welcome, and actively develop our receptivity to, as part of coming to recognize and understand unfamiliar ways of making sense. For that matter, we also need them as part of acquiring perspective, through now having these other standpoints for comparison, on our *own* general standpoints. As I have argued, without that comparison, we have no way of knowing if our *own* standpoints really make sense, or are justified, or do for us what we think they do.

The other side of this confusion and surprise, then, is that this process is what allows us legitimately and genuinely to have *clear sight*, and legitimately to rely on the simple coherence and consistency of sense, *within* any framework. As a result of undergoing this process we have not simply assumed and so arbitrarily imposed the claims of our "natural sense," given in our framework, as the only relevant "natural" claims, but we have also not simply eliminated the "natural" character of our sense-making. Here, then, we have simple sense and clear sight that we can rely on as genuine. We have established that they are not also blind injustice to other positions, or to the tentativeness that, when other "natures" have claims, is part of the only way we can honestly approach ultimate or foundational truths. (And the need for this tentativeness holds even if the ultimate truth we claim is that there are no foundational truths. This too is a particular view among other possibilities, and so must be open to question and further thought.)

Certainly, there will be truths that we have never had occasion to notice have alternatives in other frameworks of what is natural, that we have not "achieved" a perspective on. But here our willingness to *come* to notice that we might have to make room for a conflicting version of sense allows others the possibility of justice from us, and allows us the possibility of learning better. This willingness, then, is the moral equivalent of the legitimating achieved perspective.

Conclusion

In the spirit of opposition to heterosexual normativity and the metaphysics of which it is one expression, let me suggest what I think of as, and I think genuinely is, a rightly perverted principle of knowledge and truth. Our uncomprehending struggle with a new sense-making framework leads us to the surprise of a sense we can necessarily only discover well after it was already being made. If we can recognize it, we must already, before we came to be aware of it in that way, have been initiated into it to some substantial degree, otherwise its sense could not yet *be* sense to us. As a result, we might say, revising the norms in whose context we think of truth and enquiry, that it is in the nature of truth often to take us from behind.

In this light, we need a new sense of what dignity, empowerment, and insightful conduct can involve.

As Emerson, for one example, wrote about our relation to the nature of things, all the more fittingly because it was in his essay "Self-Reliance": "Who has more obedience than I masters me . . ." (1941, 134).

Works Cited

Barris, Jeremy. 2003. *Paradox and the Possibility of Knowledge: The Example of Psychoanalysis*. Selinsgrove, Pa.: Susquehanna University Press.

—. 2006. The problem of comparing different cultural or theoretical frameworks: Davidson, Rorty, and the nature of truth. *Method and Theory in the Study of Religion* 18 (2): 124-143.

—. Forthcoming. *The Crane's Walk; Plato, Pluralism, and the Inconstancy of Truth*. New York: Fordham University Press.

Barthes, Roland. 1972. *Mythologies*, trans. Annette Lavers. London: Granada.

Bersani, Leo. 1995. *Homos*. Cambridge: Harvard University Press.

Blasius, Mark. 1994. *Gay and lesbian politics: Sexuality and the emergence of a new ethic*. Philadelphia: Temple University Press.

Bredbeck, Gregory W. 1991. *Sodomy and interpretation: Marlowe to Milton*. Ithaca: Cornell University Press.

Butler, Judith. 1990. *Gender trouble: Feminism and the subversion of identity*. New York: Routledge.

—. 1991. Imitation and gender insubordination. In *Inside/out: Lesbian theories, gay theories*, ed. Diana Fuss. New York: Routledge.

Champagne, John. 1995. *The ethics of marginality: A new approach to gay studies*. Minneapolis: University of Minnesota Press.

Coward, Rosalind, and John Ellis. 1977. *Language and materialism: Developments in semiology and the theory of the subject*. London: Routledge and Kegan Paul.

Emerson, Ralph Waldo. 1941. *The best of Ralph Waldo Emerson: Essays, poems, addresses*, ed. Gordon S. Haight. New York: Walter J. Black.

Fuss, Diana. 1989. *Essentially speaking: Feminism, nature and difference*. New York: Routledge.

—. ed. 1991. *Inside/out: Lesbian theories, gay theories*. New York: Routledge.

Griggers. Cathy. 1993. Lesbian bodies in the age of (post)mechanical reproduction. In *Fear of a queer planet: Queer politics and social theory*, ed. Michael Warner. Minneapolis: University of Minnesota Press.

Irigaray, Luce. 1985. *This sex which is not one*, trans. Catherine Porter. Ithaca: Cornell University Press.

Riley, Denise. 1988. *"Am I that name?" Feminism and the category of "women" in history*. Minneapolis: University of Minnesota Press.

Rorty, Richard. 1991. *Objectivity, Relativism, and Truth*. New York:

Cambridge University Press.
Sedgwick, Eve Kosofsky. 1993. *Tendencies*. Durham: Duke University Press.
Seidman, Steven. 1997. *Difference troubles: Queering social theory and sexual politics*. New York: Cambridge University Press.
Stone, Alison. 2004. Essentialism and anti-essentialism in feminist philosophy. *Journal of Moral Philosophy* 1 (2): 135-53.
Warner, Michael, ed. 1993. *Fear of a queer planet: Queer politics and social theory*. Minneapolis: University of Minnesota Press.

Notes

[1] I would like to thank the journal's anonymous reviewer for her or his encouraging comments and helpful suggestions.
[2] I shall quote some of these below (for example, Seidman 1997).
[3] I have explored the possibility and nature of these kinds of negotiation in detail elsewhere. See, for example, Barris 2003, 2006, and forthcoming.

THE METAPHYSICS OF DEATH IN BATAILLE AND BAUDRILLARD

APPLE ZEFELIUS IGREK, SEATTLE UNIVERSITY

By risking ourselves at the limit of death, by assenting to life to the point of death, even in death, we transgress ourselves in a moment of expenditure and communication which "cannot proceed from one full and intact individual to another. It requires individuals whose separate existence in themselves is *risked*, placed at the limit of death and nothingness."[1] Hence, for Georges Bataille, risk taking and the nothingness of death converge. In some ways this is reminiscent of Georg W. F. Hegel's life-and-death struggle in the *Phenomenology of Spirit*, for in each case the putting at stake of life is bound up with the development of human awareness. Paul Hegarty is right, though, to point out that Bataille's notion of death is the "empty version" of Hegel's;[2] it is the version of negativity which participates in a release of energy, a negation of self, without thereby incorporating the results into absolute knowledge. So while it seems that loss, chance, and death are vital aspects of Bataille's theory of expenditure, it nonetheless remains to be seen how they help us to demarcate the realms of containment and transgression. It will be necessary to show that even while work, language, and subjectivity participate in the otherness which they exclude and marginalize, it is still possible for each of these categories, as well as taboo and self-preservation, to exceed themselves in a play of antitheses which cannot be reduced to any given terms or conditions. This, in turn, will presuppose a metaphysical distinction between primary and secondary expenditure. Jean Baudrillard has critiqued the former notion as detrimental to Bataille's thinking on death, exchange, and communication. Explicating the role of death in Bataille's communication will therefore bring us closer not only to answering questions surrounding the distinction between self-interest and self-abandon, but also the meaning of giving death outside of reciprocal obligations.

Bataille has written that all communication is criminal, transgressive, an act of suicide.[3] It is transgressive, I believe, in the sense that it presupposes the negation of individual and collective projects. Our projects are typically associated with the acquisition of goods, the preservation of life, and the calculated pursuit of the Good. It might therefore be said that communication is a gift of death, or a violent blow. This certainly accords with Bataille's view that communication stems from uncontrollable desire, the kind of desire that ultimately destroys us. It is only on the condition that we are fragmented, and born of chance, that we are capable of existing outside of ourselves, in what Bataille calls "mutual penetration."[4] The reason why this seems to accord with communication qua violence is because, if we look at the irreducible difference of heterogeneity, it is evident that from one mortal to another it is impossible to achieve a fixed, complete synthesis. Because we are separated by an infinite gulf, I cannot die in your place, I cannot offer you hope or salvation, but I can give you my life, which is essentially all that I *can* give to you. Reflecting on Heidegger's apprehension of death, being-towards-death, Derrida puts forth, "I know on absolute grounds and in an absolutely certain manner that I will never deliver the other from his death, from the death that affects his whole being.... Only a mortal can give... and that mortal can only give to what is mortal since he can give everything except immortality, everything except salvation as immortality."[5] What exactly is everything? What am I capable of giving if not the completion of being, the immortality of the soul, or the full integrity of the subject? An image? A sign? A part of myself? If we cannot trade places, if we are each irreplaceable, then at most I can sacrifice myself and give to you my heterogeneous existence. I can, that is to say, separate myself from myself, become an image or specter of my "true identity," which is exactly how Roland Barthes describes the Photograph: "In terms of the image-repetoire, the Photograph (the one I *intend*) represents the very subtle moment when, to tell the truth, I am neither subject nor object but a subject who feels he is becoming an object: I then experience a micro-version of death (of parenthesis): I am truly becoming a specter."[6] This is comparable to how Bataille elaborates on the catastrophic object, the same object which embodies death as a non-dialectical waste of energy. In both cases what is communicated is a cut, something that is pensive, thought-provoking,[7] and something which opens up a wound, discloses the infinite nothingness which I am to the desire of another who is affected by this "orifice of filth."[8]

At the same time, it should be recognized that it is not nothingness *in itself* which is desired, given, or communicated. Nothingness, as such, cannot be risked. Nor can it be destroyed, not, at least, in the way that a fellow creature is destroyed: I am attracted to the sacrifice of the Other, to the universal aspect of the Other which is nothingness, but this nothingness has no value for me outside of death and risk taking.[9] The modification of an object, the negation of a thing-in-itself which is nature, or in this context, pure and simple nothingness (that is, primary expenditure), is the infinity which never dies. But since desire has for its object the desire of another, it is, in the words of Alexandre Kojève, "directed toward a non-natural object."[10] Bataille is faithful to this Kojèvian line of thought when he writes, "Compared to the person I love, the universe seems poor and empty. This universe isn't 'risked' since it's not 'perishable'."[11] The distinction here is a complicated and nuanced one. It is, paradoxically, what allows Bataille to circumvent Baudrillard's claim that there exists an ahistorical longing in his theory of exchange, death, and symbolic return.[12] Ultimately, the charge is that Bataille misreads French sociology, in particular Marcel Mauss, and reintroduces an aspect of naturalized expenditure in his account of potlatch and sacrifice. Before directly taking on Baudrillard's criticism, it may be helpful to consider a specific, historical example in which Bataille observes the overlapping of death and communication.

The example is the Crucifixion. Because the Crucifixion is a sacrifice, a gift of death to humanity, it is a crime. It is the summit of evil by means of which God communicates to his creatures. Many theoretical factors informing Bataille's notion of expenditure converge in this one tragic moment of Christianity. There is a Nietzschean reversal of values in which it is learned, in Bataille's version of genealogy, that universal salvation, the promise of redemption, is based upon, necessarily, an immeasurable crime. The exuberance of the crime is studied with Mauss and Emile Durkheim in mind, while the dialectics of desire and suffering bring together, in a bizarre way, Kojève and the Marquis de Sade. Perhaps most striking of all, and this is what provokes Baudrillard and Mark C. Taylor to assert that Bataille has reified expenditure, there is a mystical "beyond" expressed in the killing of Christ and the torment of his followers. This beyond will be elucidated in my next article, but for now it can be said that it is related to the shattering of limits which allows God to communicate with those who are guilty, the sinners who comprise the entire human race: "If human beings had kept their own integrity and hadn't sinned, God on one hand and human beings on the other would have persevered in their respective isolation. A night of death wherein Creator and creatures bled together and lacerated each other, and on all sides were challenged at the extreme limits of shame: that is what was required for their communion."[13] The death of Christ is madness and murder, yet it is also a revelation of the beyond which is the negation of all projects, the salvation of humankind.[14] Without a doubt, there lurks here an extraordinary ambiguity. The beyond is revealed, and to the extent that it is revealed it is *something*; it is a summit motivated by the sublimation and transcendence of time. In this regard, the mystical experience depends upon an affirmation of a project that negates projects only on the condition that they themselves are temporary. It does not, that is to say, negate every project, for it does not negate itself. The experience preserves itself in everlasting life: the absolute, perpetual beyond. Nevertheless, the beyond is revealed by the corpse of God, by the presence of God which is no longer distinct from his absence.[15] The Christian therefore lives in torment, in the agony of guilt for having killed Christ, for being responsible for the greatest sin ever committed.[16] But the laceration of God in the form of Christ, the bodily injury to the infinity of God who is the absence of light, the reality of nothingness,[17] is itself the affliction of guilt which culminates in the excess of God which surpasses God, and not only God, but likewise the worshippers who lose themselves in agony, torment, and giving death to God.[18] This is why, even though the beyond is *revealed* in a bloody sacrifice, the beyond is also that which can never be revealed: "The sacrifice is madness, the renunciation of all knowledge, the fall into the void, and nothing, neither in the fall nor in the void, is revealed, for the revelation of the void is but a means of falling further into absence."[19] For Bataille, then, nothingness is indeed the object of desire, the moment of sacrifice which destroys itself as an object, as something intelligible, revealed, or seen; and thus, it will be argued, it is not equivalent to an abstract entity or an ideal form which is nothingness in and of itself.

Like Friedrich Nietzsche before him, Bataille's work is ever shifting among the ruins of high and low. In his trademark provocative manner he writes: "My true church is a whorehouse --- the only one that gives me true satisfaction."[20] This satisfaction, however, is never far from a hellish torment of the senses. In describing one of his many orgies, he uses words like "depression," "disgust," "horrible," and "unsatisfied" to give us a personal account of erotic licentiousness.[21] Clearly, for Bataille, the meaning of "true satisfaction" has to be qualified. The ideal, the truly satisfying, is deeply and tragically infected by its other: the base. We have already seen this in his characterization of the Crucifixion: the salvation of the soul, the redemptive power of sacrifice, is contingent upon the communication of death. In addition, it is the death of God, the inviolable One, which overtakes the "meaning" of his gift: "The *absence of God* is no longer a closure: it is the opening up to the infinite. The absence of God is greater, and more divine, than God."[22] The glory of God cannot be found in the supreme self-satisfaction of a necessary and unchanging substance: it is essential that we lacerate ourselves *and* our gods. In this way, every ideal is transformed and carried away by its shadow.[23] For Bataille, this includes a wide range of historical data that exceeds the confines of any given religion. The same logic, for instance, bears upon the architecture of monuments, obelisks, and the royal tombs of Egypt. The tombs represent greed and power, a naked lust for immortality.[24] Raised up against the unlimited sky, they serve as a constant reminder of the *will to be*: "The existing pyramids still bear witness to this calm triumph of an unwavering and hallucinating resolve."[25] Vast monuments dedicated to the god-kings, to the Egyptian pharaohs, the pyramids were built as a counter-movement to the drifting away of time. They were constructed at the center of human existence, or what was taken to be the center, and it is by virtue of their endurance, by their very success, that we are today haunted by empty shadows of timelessness: "In their imperishable unity, the pyramids -- endlessly -- continue to crystallize the mobile succession of the various ages; alongside the Nile, they rise up like the totality of centuries, taking on the immobility of stone and watching all men die, one after the other."[26] Because of the ideal, death is reflected back to us. As long as the pyramids continue to stand, we will see ourselves transcended by an endless sea of change. Perhaps we have here one reason why it is so difficult to categorize Bataille's work. He speaks of a center, he speaks of God, the ineffable, and the ineluctable dialectic, but the center explodes and the bottom falls out from beneath us.[27] If we are shades of nothingness, it is still true that we exist only to the extent that we idealize ourselves in the presence of gods and the erection of great monuments. In this manner, everything which is captured by the apex of life and community, everything which is pure, symbolic, and true, emanates from a "double movement of attraction and repulsion."[28]

The last quote is taken from a lecture given during the late 1930s, during which time Bataille's thinking remained, for the most part, within the confines of psychoanalysis and French sociology. It is true that as early as "Sacrificial Mutilation," first published in the art review *Documents*,[29] Bataille comments on a certain lacuna in Mauss's theory of sacrifice. It would be some time, however, before he would flesh out his own theory of economy and distinguish himself, in a more systematic way, from his many influences.[30] When he writes that the central nucleus of a human society is both attractive and repulsive, that it entails a transformation of the left sacred into the right sacred, it is difficult to see how this diverges, in a fundamental way, from the ambivalence detected by Henri Hubert and Mauss in the religious and social mechanism of sacrifice.[31] Bataille's ambivalence is undecidable: The horror of the eye, particularly in the film *Andalusian Dog*, which Bataille distinguishes from "banal avant-garde productions,"[32] is highly seductive. The sun is elevated and beautiful so long as we don't look at it.[33] A closed mouth is safe, perhaps even human or cultivated, but it is still a threat to neighboring animals.[34] In all cases the high and the low are bound together. If it is right to say, for Bataille, that expenditure is a release of energy that obscures the difference between these two sides of social reality, then how exactly does this depart from Hubert and Mauss, in terms of general economy, without incorporating the very idealism which he seemingly deconstructs?

Bataille's expenditure, according to Baudrillard, falls into the trap of an ideal economy. This is precisely the kind of economy which Bataille thought he had overcome. Hence, as Baudrillard writes, death is no longer the regulator of tensions in Bataille's anti-productivism, but instead "there is a vision of death as a principle of excess and an anti-economy."[35] It is therefore Bataille's "anti-economy" which inspires Baudrillard. The problem is simple: Bataille unwittingly reinscribes this principle of excess in the progressive, naturalized principle of science and truth. Objectivity wins. And Baudrillard brings us back to a point in which the myth of death is once again realized as a human construction, as a total social phenomenon. Baudrillard, it might be said, is more Bataille than Georges Bataille himself. At any rate, it is somewhat of a caricature to think of Bataille as anti-production or anti-economy. It is certainly not the case that he condemned the ideal economy in order to be, once and for all, free from it. There is no politics of liberation in Georges Bataille. But then again, this is the exact same point which Baudrillard claims for himself: "If we can speak of a society with neither repression nor unconscious, it is not in order to rediscover some miraculous innocence where the 'flows' of desire roam freely and the primary processes are realized without prohibition."[36] This quote tells us that Baudrillard has a very different conception of innocence and freedom than either Bataille or Sigmund Freud. The primary processes, in Freud, and primary expenditure, in Bataille, are the imaginary complements to rationalized prohibition. Likewise, death is only a phantasm of idealized desire.[37] While, at least in Bataille's theory, it *is* the imaginary which is crucial. The absence of myth, the absence of an incorporated, rationalized economy, is itself innocence, freedom, and pure, unequivocal myth. It was, indeed, the erosion of myth in modern civilization which added urgency to Bataille's contacts with Michel Leiris, Roger Caillois, Pierre Klossowski, and many of the surrealists. To understand how Bataille navigates the difference between myth and the destruction of myth, it may be helpful to take up Marcel Mauss once again. In this way, perhaps, it will be seen that Bataille's "misreading" of Mauss's gift-economy was in fact a critical, and all-important, *re*reading.

After Mauss we have an entirely new way of looking at the foundations of political and social economy. His theory of the gift, *kula*, potlatch, and "total services" have reoriented the premises of classical economy away from bargaining and barter to the extravagance and rivalry of exchanging gifts. The most highly developed and purest form of potlatch, or what Mauss also refers to as a "system of total services," can be found in the regions of the American Northwest, Melanesia, and Papua.[38] Because the potlatch is a total social phenomenon, all aspects of tribal life are bound together in the institution of giving: marriage, hierarchy, alliances, religion, festivals, banquets, law, and, of course, the economy. Along the Pacific Northwest coast, during the winter months, a continual state of excitement is generated by the give and take of potlatches. They occur everywhere and often: when a seal has been killed, a promotion celebrated, or in response to a rival's challenge. If a challenge is not accepted, or if it is not reciprocated, there is a loss of honor: "The obligation to reciprocate worthily is imperative. One loses face for ever if one does not reciprocate, or if one does not carry out destruction of equivalent value."[39] Unlike commodities which are bought and sold in predominantly capitalistic societies, a thing given to another, for the Haïda, Tsimshian, Kwakiutl, and Tlingit, is not merely a thing, but expresses the animating principle of the person who gives it.[40] The gift is always a gift of oneself and one's community. It is a sign of wealth and honor, and it is also a sign which is humiliating for the recipient of the gift, potlatch, or service. Hence, on the part of the recipient, an obligation to reciprocate is unavoidable. To remove the humiliation that has been forced upon him, and which is expressed by the spirit of the thing, it is essential to give back with interest. As Mauss notes, if a subject receives a blanket from a chief, he will give back two in return on the occasion of a marriage, enthronement, and so forth.[41] In this manner, a threefold cycle of obligations is perpetually maintained: to give, to accept, to reciprocate. The sacrifice of wealth, which is deeply connected to the prestige of a person, family, or tribe, is to be contrasted with the accumulation and calculative reasoning which motivates the merchant and banker.[42] It is true that self-interest plays a role for both modern and pre-capitalistic societies, but in the latter, Mauss observes, rank and social status are directly linked to giving. What is at stake is the struggle of wealth, to humiliate a rival by giving or destroying, and this often includes the murder of slaves, breaking valuable copper objects, burning houses and thousands of blankets, as well as providing benefits, services, and feasts for the opposing clans.

In chapter three of his monograph, Mauss traces the development of modern law and economy from the reciprocating structures found in earlier societies. Modern experience, based on the division of social life into isolated categories of private and public, interested and disinterested, retains vestiges of the gift-exchange morality. Nevertheless, Mauss would like to see a return, if not to the outright violence and slavery of the Northwest Pacific, then at least to a system of total services in which the concepts of liberty and obligation are once again mixed. The ambivalence which I spoke of toward the end of the last section, in terms of dynamic social relations, can now be ascertained. Mauss, in response to the political climate of his time, set forth a position which was neither over-generous nor individualistic.[43] Self-interest and self-destruction are brought together in a form of exchange which is defined by its convergence of the moral, aesthetic, and religious, as opposed to the modern fragmentation which now prevails. Insofar as utility and luxury are fused in a single act of destruction, in the circulation of wealth by dint of services and counter-services, the pleasure described in the following passage will be seen as having more affinity to Baudrillard's notion of giving than Bataille's: "Even pure destruction of wealth does not signify that complete detachment that one might believe to be found in it. Even these acts of greatness are not without egoism. The purely sumptuary form of consumption... in which considerable amounts of goods that have taken a long time to amass are suddenly given away or even destroyed, particularly in the case of the potlatch, give such institutions the appearance of representing purely lavish expenditure and childish prodigality. In effect, and in reality, not only are useful things given away and rich foods consumed to excess, but one even destroys for the pleasure of destroying."[44] Pleasure is derived from a destructive act only to the extent that it is witnessed, insofar as it has value in the symbolic realm.[45] The ambivalence of egoism and social obligation is thus resolved: the acquisition of rank satisfies both personal interest and the institution of symbolic interaction.

A principle of agonistic rivalry captures the essence of Mauss's ambivalence. The transference of wealth by means of reciprocating exchange, or relations of giving, stimulates the process of recognition which is concomitantly social and self-interested. Recognition arises from the symbolic act of giving which humiliates the beneficiary. To overcome the humiliation, it is essential to return gifts and services to the one who initiated the exchange. The reciprocating movement, which is a total social phenomenon, is known as either a counter-gift or counter-service. Baudrillard and Bataille are equally enamored by the intense display of wealth and destruction in the American Northwest, even if Baudrillard would like to see it as a purely symbolic function. Julian Pefanis articulates this difference in economic terms: "Like Bataille, Baudrillard privileges the destructive consumption of the potlatch against the homeostatic kula --- whilst rejecting the former's inclination to turn its negating potential into a positive economic principle; refusing not only the distinction between the general/restricted economies as theorized by Bataille, but also any discussion of the economic at all."[46] The difference, then, is that Baudrillard rejects Bataille's metaphysical, objective, naturalized expenditure. The pleasure of death, the pleasure of self-destruction in Mauss's theory, is entirely social. Extrapolating beyond the social only returns us to an economy of prohibition, interior existence, and the belief in value (abstracted from the equivalence of life and death). Taboos are social in Bataille, but they also presume a general economy of energy which transcends the limited ends of both individual and collective identity. The strange, unhappy turn that Baudrillard observes in Bataille, as he reads Bataille against Bataille, is that the excess of primary expenditure, the inherent prodigality of nature, is itself an idealized economy.

There is no psychical domain for Baudrillard. Every individual act belongs to the symbolic circulation of signs. In this regard he is very close to Mauss who mediates the ambivalence of egoism and self-destruction in purely symbolic terms: recognition, agonistic rivalry, signs of wealth, and the obligation of return. There is no outside and there is no inside. There is only exchange. Baudrillard eliminates the bar; he eliminates the divide which separates us from an outside world which is either natural, inanimate, or constantly changing. We are only separated from death, and from the general economy of waste, by a single, all-penetrating illusion: *value*. Value is an expression of power: to produce, abstract, economize, oppose, discriminate, and rationalize. Baudrillard's conception of value, while associated with repression and the interiority of self-consciousness, is still connected to many of Bataille's concerns. For example, Bataille understands the role of immediacy, or what he also calls "lived experience," as affirming the interconnectedness, the profound ambivalence, of life and death. In this regard we are always bound to something horrible and disgusting. Social life magnifies the very thing which it denies: embodied absence. In Baudrillard, the symbolic overturns the prohibition on death which is, in our society, omnipresent, or nearly so.

This is why, despite his reservations, Baudrillard borrows the phrase "accursed share" from Bataille's magnum opus: excess and prodigality are at odds with a systematic, dominant exchange that suppresses the continuity of life and death, pleasure and pain.[47] Culture is the real, death is the imaginary, and symbolic circulation defies both: "The symbolic is neither a concept, an agency, a category, nor a 'structure', but an act of exchange and *a social relation which puts an end to the real*, which resolves the real, and, at the same time, puts an end to the opposition between the real and imaginary."[48] Bataille, needless to say, would never agree that useless expenditure "puts an end" to the dualisms which are prevalent in all societies. And Baudrillard, for his part, would take issue with the idea that all cultures introduce imaginary constructs: it is *our* Western society, overdetermined by the Law, the Father, and liberal individualism, which divides the real and the unreal into separate categories.

Negativity, in the final analysis, is what pushes Baudrillard away from Bataille. Without a doubt, for Baudrillard as much as for Bataille, the rationality of the human is based upon the irrationality of the inhuman: doubles, spawned and multiplied, create the outside as an excess form. Baudrillard calls the human a "structural double" in the sense that it incorporates the outside at the very moment of its rational, normalizing extradition. The reality of the human, from its advent,[49] is an expression of language. Language, in turn, is a manifestation of power. When the dead cease to exist, when power creates a division between life and death, the reality of the human is born. Power, on this model, exists without negativity: it is purely social. Language and power converge in a social act which is repressive without presupposing the existence of energy, libido, death drives, or unconscious pulsions.[50] There is no reality on the other side of repression: its contents are mythic, produced, socialized. There is only the process and principle of the collective. Negation, on the other hand, presupposes something else entirely: in Bataille's case, a general movement of waste. Negation is a movement within a movement, a movement that resists its own irreducibility. This is *too much* for Baudrillard. The movement that exceeds itself, that cannot be contained by social categories, postulates, according to Baudrillard, something natural, something outside of symbolic exchange. It does not allow for an extreme reversibility of life and death. There is ambivalence, but there is also an inexpugnable, one-sided finality: death. Baudrillard, in relation to Freud, applies death against death.[51] By its very hypothesis, the death drive can be applied to its own mythic reality. The same is true of Bataille: his interpretation of Mauss's gift-economy seems to forget that expenditure can always be reversed, can always be challenged and reassessed. Outside of reciprocal obligation, there is neither gift nor sacrifice: "This is not the law of the universe. He who has so well explored the human sacrifice of the Aztecs should have known as they did that the sun gives nothing; it is necessary to nourish it continually with human blood in order that it shine. It is necessary to challenge the gods through sacrifice in order that they respond with profusion. In other words, the root of sacrifice and general economy is never pure and simple expenditure -- or whatever drive of excess that supposedly comes to us from nature -- but is an incessant process of challenge."[52] Nature is the imaginary of a repressed society. It is a product of the fundamental disjunction of life and death.[53] Baudrillard's critique can therefore be summed up in the following manner: Bataille, misreading Mauss,[54] reads into nature an ideal circulation and prodigality.[55] The result of this, invariably and in the particular case of Bataille, is that nature serves as a paradigm for unilateral giving, in which case the emergence of rank, the acquisition of power that adulterates the unlimited nature of giving, is reduced to a kind of functional, positive magnanimity.

This logic needs to be challenged. The first point to make is that Bataille constantly rejects untainted, unmixed expenditure. No release is devoid of limited ends. The fundamental object of general economy, to be sure, is the consumption of wealth.[56] But in the *Accursed Share*'s preface, Bataille qualifies his terms by suggesting that consumption as well as labor are always contaminated. In the domain of social life pure loss and pure profit are nonexistent.[57] Baudrillard is right about one thing: Bataille posits an extra-social principle. We see this most vividly in *Erotism*: "Man has built up the rational world by his own efforts, but there remains within him an undercurrent of violence. Nature herself is violent, and however reasonable we may grow we may be mastered anew by a violence no longer that of nature but that of a rational being who tries to obey but who succumbs to stirrings within himself which he cannot bring to heel."[58] This is an extremely complex line of thought. There is no return to nature in the sense of an asocial expenditure. There is no ahistorical longing; but there is an extra-social principle insofar as the violence of rationality, history, and culture cannot be separated from a release of energy irreducible to the categories of thought employed by human society. Nature is violent only to the extent that we fail, and must fail, to understand it. Our misrecognition of nature is not an objective, inherent property of nature, but it suggests that we are very limited creatures, overcome by that which is infinite change. Baudrillard's mistake is to assume that this indicates an idealistic economy. We can show otherwise by looking at Bataille's interpretation of the potlatch.

As already stated, Bataille rejects the notion that expenditure, as a moment of sacrifice or gift-giving, is free from the constraints of social reality. This means, contrary to Baudrillard, that he does not affirm unilateral giving.[59] This is reflected by his study of Mauss. He writes that the paradox of the potlatch is that the acquisition of limited ends, such as the rank and glory derived from giving, is necessarily intermixed with a movement of energy that otherwise exceeds us: "Gift-giving has the virtue of a surpassing of the subject who gives, but in exchange for the object given, the subject appropriates the surpassing: He regards his virtue, that which he had the capacity for, as an asset, as a *power* that he now possesses. He enriches himself with a contempt for riches, and what he proves to be miserly of is in fact his generosity."[60] Taken by itself, this one quote alleviates any doubts that Bataille misreads the anthropology of Mauss. Socially speaking, in the eyes of the recipient and others, rank is conferred upon the one who gives and destroys. As Kelly Oliver argues, an act of recognition is bound up with a dialectics of mastery that cannot be understood apart from abuse, power, and self-interest.[61] It is no different in the case of potlatch: the person who gives a potlatch is seeking the recognition of the other and desires to gain that recognition by the humiliation intrinsic to receiving gifts.[62] Bataille's chapter "The Gift of Rivalry," in his first volume of the *Accursed Share*, provides us with an accurate, compelling picture of this institutionalized antagonism. But he goes further in his assessment of rank than either Mauss or Baudrillard. It is primary expenditure, the violence of nature which "masters us anew" in the form of rivalry, social exchange, and sacrifice, that draws criticism from Baudrillard. The criticism, however, should be turned back upon itself. Baudrillard claims that the infinity of nature, the extra-social element which he construes as an ahistorical *truth*, reinvests nature with an idealistic, self-satisfying economy.[63] Once again the human is projected to the outside, to an imaginary, anthropomorphic nature which is always already the mirror of the self: the absolute, actualized human. The inhuman serves the interest of the human, the real, and the species.[64] In this manner nature is not merely reinvested; it is in fact produced and reproduced. It is created as "other" to magnify the same. In his critique of repression, Baudrillard neglects the obvious. Although Bataille posits an outside, this should not be construed as an outside which reifies a possession, a negative, or an ideal cause. Doubtlessly, *rank is one such cause*. When we possess rank we belong to an economy of signs that cannot but add to our own interest, at least when we are successful at the game. In some fashion or another we all play the game: we lie to ourselves, we create myths, we believe in our self-identity and our limited gains. But the game is no less imaginary. Rank and social status, in any game (whether one of greed or glorious destruction), are short-lived to the extent that every condensation of force is limited, that is to say, socio-historically situated. Bataille writes, "In the end, with the possibility of growth or of acquisition reaching its limit at a certain point, *energy*, the object of greed of every isolated individual, is necessarily liberated --- truly liberated under the cover of lies. Definitively, men lie; they do their best to relate this liberation to interest, but this liberation carries them further.... As a rule the individual accumulation of resources is doomed to destruction. The individuals who carry out this destruction do not truly possess this wealth, *this rank*."[65] Baudrillard laments the principle of rationality that today dominates our lives. We live in a culture of simulacra, totalizing codes, and the universality of death: an illusory death that accompanies the construction of life according to value.[66] But rank too is a value. It may be derived from an exchange of gifts, but it still belongs to an economy of riches and wealth that are only given to the extent that they buttress the standing of the participants. Baudrillard attacks idealism, but he also affirms the closed system of exchange in which rank is a fundamental sign. We cannot escape our myths, there is no return to innocence, as long as we are alive. But the release of energy which cannot be reduced to any particular economy opens up to the outside and ensures, contrary to the idealistic, closed systems of reciprocity, that rank (or any other limited end, achievement, or social status) is never fully recognized.[67]

I began this article with a highly contestable assertion, namely, that expenditure is an unconditional loss. This is only possible if we assume that there is an extra-social release of energy which cannot be dissociated from the primary violence of nature. This is why, in the third volume of the *Accursed Share*, Bataille is careful to theoretically separate the natural given from the sacred, even though the sacred (for example, the experience of loss) is itself, in a sense, the natural given.[68] It is probable, as Judith Butler argues, that there are no desires which exist prior to the act of prohibition. Desire, in short, is a socially produced phenomenon. But this proposition does not necessarily imply that desire, or the objects of repression, are absolutely and thoroughly social. The same holds true for Baudrillard. Simply because every expenditure is limited in some fashion, it does not automatically follow that expenditure, even while limited, conditioned, or socialized, is *absolutely* and *thoroughly* defined by those terms. In the last section Baudrillard's objections against naturalized expenditure were taken into account. He obviously thinks that the contamination of sacred, symbolic exchange by an extra-social element, by a movement of energy which cannot be fully recognized, is irreconcilable with his anti-economic stance. It was pointed out, in response, that a system of mutual obligations is in fact a closed economy, and therefore an idealistic economy. In this way the idealistic charge is turned against itself. And insofar as rank is an illusory category, one that is necessarily contaminated by primary expenditure, there are ramifications for Bataille's theory of transgression.[69]

Ultimately, transgression is a secondary expenditure. It presupposes that nature is a movement of energy that cannot be contained, but which is nonetheless repressed, resisted, and transfigured. Hence, for Bataille, every transgression is socially delimited. Every transgression is both limited and unlimited, which helps to explain the extreme, paradoxical nature of certain pleasures: "Man differs from animal in that he is able to experience certain sensations that wound and melt him to the core.... If there is nothing that surpasses our powers and our understanding, if we do not acknowledge something greater than ourselves, greater than we are *despite ourselves*, something which *at all costs must* not be, then we do not reach the *insensate* moment towards which we strive with all that is in our power and which at the same time we exert all our power to stave off."[70] The insensate moment would therefore be, simultaneously, extreme agony and extreme pleasure. It is not so much the collapse of values as it is the accentuation of the self as it opens up to that which it is not: *infinite nothingness*. Transgression, accordingly, is neither anti-culture nor anti-economy. It is the affirmation of economy, even a restricted economy, as necessarily open to the outside.[71] In a previous article I noted that taboos are already in themselves identifiable as transgressive. In this article some of the aspects of secondary expenditure were elaborated further. In Bataille's work, expenditure is typically determined by an irretrievable loss, the play of non-identity, the suffering of death, the abjection of life, and a form of exchange which cannot be fully recognized or reciprocated. But since all of these aspects of transgression can also be used to describe the workings of prohibition, that which is otherwise opposed to suffering and loss, it would seem that we are still lacking a perspective on transgression that would set it apart, however tenuously, from a mode of prohibition which is stagnate, reactionary, and oppressive. We can nonetheless, based upon what has been indicated many times throughout this article, give an abstract characterization of that which exceeds the bounds of social rank, subjectivity, and the interiority of self which Baudrillard rejects. Bataille, in his lecture "Attraction and Repulsion II," maintains that the transgression of socially determined boundaries and limitations takes place at the very heart of social existence: "[T]he central nucleus of primitive agglomerations seems to be no less a place of license than a place of prohibition. The prohibition is obviously the primitive phenomenon that stands there in the way of expending forces, but, if it is at this particular spot that it stands in the way, it is because that is precisely where expenditure can take place."[72] It would appear that transgression is the unleashing of force which is itself an accumulation of force. Bataille sees prohibition as an accumulation of force and power which invariably resists its own destruction. But to the extent that every isolated system, and thus every prohibition, depends upon a movement of energy which is unlimited and unconditional, it can be argued that the inexorable movement of change can either be affirmed or disavowed. In the case of a transgressive affirmation, all of the above stipulated aspects of secondary expenditure would have to be met. My next article will provide a more concrete footing to this abstract formulation. To do so, it will be essential to distinguish expenditure from its containment in specific cases, namely, those which involve capitalistic risk, Sadean apathy, teleological dialectics, mysticism, and the animalistic display of excess vitality.

Notes

[1] Georges Bataille, *On Nietzsche*, trans. B. Boone (St. Paul: Paragon House, 1992), p. 19; *Oeuvres complètes* VI (Paris: Gallimard, 1970-88), p. 44.

[2] Paul Hegarty, *Georges Bataille: Core Cultural Theorist* (London: Sage Publications, 2000), p. 55.

[3] Bataille, *On Nietzsche*, p. 26; *Oeuvres Complètes* VI, p. 49.

[4] Bataille, *On Nietzsche*, p. 25; *Oeuvres Complètes* VI, p. 48.

[5] Jacques Derrida, *The Gift of Death*, trans. D. Wills (Chicago: University of Chicago Press, 1995), p. 43.

[6] Roland Barthes, *Camera Lucida: Reflections on Photography*, trans. R. Howard (New York: Farrar, Straus, and Giroux), p. 14.

[7] Barthes, *Camera Lucida*, p. 38.

[8] Bataille, *On Nietzsche*, p. 22; *Oeuvres complètes* VI, p. 45.

[9] Bataille, *On Nietzsche*, p. 70; *Oeuvres complètes* VI, p.85.

[10] Kojève, *Introduction to the Reading of Hegel*, trans. J. Nichols (Ithica: Cornell University Press, 1969), p. 5; *Introduction à la lecture de Hegel* (Paris: Gallimard, 1947), p. 12.

[11] Bataille, *On Nietzsche*, p. 69; *Oeuvres complètes* VI, p. 84.

[12] It may not seem like much of a paradox, since it was just stated that the object of desire turns on something "non-natural"; but it is still true that the desire of another

embodies death, infinity, and nothingness, all of which hint at the overlapping of primary and secondary *dépense*. There is, in other words, an element of the ahistorical in Bataille's sacrificial economy which, undoubtedly, Baudrillard would eliminate altogether.

[13] Bataille, *On Nietzsche*, p. 18; *Oeuvres complètes* VI, p. 43.

[14] Bataille, *Inner Experience*, trans. L. Boldt (Albany: State University of New York, 1988), p. 47; *Oeuvres complètes* V, p. 60.

[15] Bataille, *Inner Experience*, p. 5; *Oeuvres complètes* V, p. 17.

[16] Bataille, *On Nietzsche*, p. 17; *Oeuvres complètes* VI, p. 42.

[17] Bataille, *Inner Experience*, p. 103; *Oeuvres complètes* V, p. 121.

[18] Bataille, *Inner Experience*, p. 51; *Oeuvres complètes* V, p. 65.

[19] Bataille, *Inner Experience*, pp. 51-2; *Oeuvres complètes* V, p. 65-6.

[20] Bataille, *Guilty*, trans. B. Boone (Venice, California: The Lapis Press, 1988), p. 12; *Oeuvres complètes* V, p. 247.

[21] Bataille, *Guilty*, p. 13; *Oeuvres complètes* V, p. 247.

[22] Bataille, *The Absence of Myth: Writings on Surrealism*, trans. M. Richardson (London: Verso, 1994), p. 48.

[23] The black sky which fell upon the earth at the final instant of God's sacrifice has not, to this day, returned from whence it came.

[24] Bataille, *Visions of Excess*, ed. A. Stoekl (Minneapolis: University of Minnesota Press, 1985), p. 215; *Oeuvres complètes* I, p. 504.

[25] Ibid., 216; *OC*, I: 504-05.

[26] Ibid.; *OC*, I: 505.

[27] Ibid., 222; *OC*, I: 513.

[28] Ibid., "Attraction and Repulsion II," 122.

[29] It is germane to point out that Bataille, joined by the likes of Dalí, Picasso, and Miró, used the journal, which he edited as general secretariat, to counter the moral idealism of Breton (Surya, *Georges Bataille: An Intellectual Biography*, p.118).

[30] Bataille seems to indicate as much in footnote 25, p.193, *The Accursed Share* vol. I. The ambiguity that he refers to was a "recent" development, thus intimating that earlier versions of ambivalence in Bataille were not fully worked out in accord with general economics.

[31] Hubert and Mauss, *Sacrifice*, 60.

[32] Bataille, "Eye," 19n1; *OC*, I: 187n1.

[33] Ibid., "Rotten Sun," 57; *OC*, I: 231.

[34] Ibid., "Mouth," 59-60; *OC*, I: 237-38.

[35] Baudrillard, "Death in Bataille," 140.

[36] Ibid., *Symbolic Exchange and Death*, 137.

[37] This is Baudrillard's version of Bataille and Freud.

[38] Mauss, *The Gift*, 7.

[39] Ibid., 42.

[40] For the Polynesians this would be connected to *mana* (p. 8); and for the Melanesians, the inhabitants of the Trobriand Islands, it is captured by the word *hau* (pp. 11-12).

[41] Ibid., 42.

[42] Ibid., 75.
[43] As compared, respectively, with Communism and Capitalism (p. 69).
[44] Ibid., 74.
[45] Ergo Mauss's version of Hegelian recognition: "The potlatch, the distribution of goods, is the basic act of 'recognition'.... One 'recognizes' the chief or his son and becomes 'grateful' to him (p. 40)."
[46] Pefanis, *Heterology and the Postmodern*, 29.
[47] The wording of the following quote indicates, however, that Baudrillard's appropriation of Bataille's 'accursed share' is less Bataillean than Maussian: "Always the accursed share... the fragment which is the whole secret of symbolic exchange, because it is given, received and returned, and cannot therefore *be breached* by the dominant exchange, remaining irreducible to its law and fatal to it: its only real adversary, the only one it must exterminate (*Symbolic Exchange*, p. 180)."
[48] Baudrillard, *Symbolic Exchange*, 133.
[49] Ibid., 125.
[50] Ibid., 130.
[51] Ibid., 150.
[52] Ibid., "When Bataille Attacked the Metaphysical Principle of Economy," 193.
[53] Ibid., *Symbolic Exchange*, 133. Interestingly, even while Baudrillard adamantly opposes any objective or natural explanation of things, he posits an originary bifurcation upon which man/ nature, human/inhuman, and masculine/feminine partitions are established.
[54] Ibid., "When Bataille Attacked the Metaphysical Principle of Economy," 193.
[55] Ibid., *Symbolic Exchange*, 157.
[56] This sense of consumption is used interchangeably with dépense, waste, sacrifice.
[57] Bataille, *The Accursed Share: Consumption*, 12; *OC*, VII: 22.
[58] Ibid., *Erotism*, 40; *OC*, X: 43.
[59] When he speaks of the violence or sacrifice of nature, he speaks poetically.
[60] Ibid., *The Accursed Share: Consumption*, 69; *OC*, VII: 72.
[61] See her book *Witnessing: Beyond Recognition.*
[62] Humiliation can also be seen as essential to gift-giving in psychoanalysis. A gift to a child from a parent or guardian suggests that a substitution has taken place. The gift is a mediation that stands in for the loss of protection and love as afforded by the caretakers. It is both an expression of love as well as a sign, a metonymic function, that facilitates the recognition that love is no longer immediate, but instead divided, disjointed, and painful.
[63] I am using the term "extra-social" as an alternative to "asocial": while nature surpasses us in its wildness, the term nonetheless reminds us that the movements which surpass us can only be comprehended as a going-beyond, as opposed to something objective. The *extra*-social exceeds us even as it accentuates the social, lived, transgressive experience.
[64] Baudrillard, *Symbolic Exchange*, 158.
[65] Bataille, *The Accursed Share: Consumption*, 74-75; *OC*, VII: 77.

[66] I am using the term "value," in the context of this debate, in the way that Baudrillard tends to use it: as an expression of something instrumental, useful, or productive.[2]
[67] In other words, far from falling into the trap of idealism, Bataille's primary expenditure is that movement which explodes every closed system. Secondary expenditure is never free from mediation, regulation, or self-interest, but it is nonetheless open to an endless change of events which overturns every sign and every accumulation of force, including Baudrillard's "rank."
[68] Ibid., *The Accursed Share: Sovereignty*, 215; *OC*, VIII: 264.
[69] Although Bataille's notion of expenditure can be used to describe all forms of release, even those which are static, reactionary, and oppressive, he also uses the notion as interchangeable with a kind of transgression which affirms life. This last paragraph, then, is an explication of expenditure qua transgression.
[70] Ibid., *Madame Edwarda*, 141.
[71] Affirmation, as I understand it, gives secondary expenditure an extreme intensity which cannot be reduced to pure and simple change. It is true that the accumulation of force embodied, say, by a particular person, can be disavowed until the end, but in that case the ineluctable release of energy will not be experienced transgressively. It will, instead, look much more like the pure and simple change which was initially transformed in the formation of subjectivity.
[72] Ibid., "Attraction and Repulsion II," 123.

TOWARDS A MORE EMPIRICALLY INFORMED ETHICS[1]

STEPHEN MORRIS,
MISSOURI WESTERN STATE UNIVERSITY

I. Introduction

Until recently, the study of ethics was relegated to the domain of abstract reasoning, having little in the way of input from the empirical realm—save for philosophers' introspections and perhaps a very rudimentary understanding of human psychology. Today, however, the traditional approach of addressing morality from a more or less strictly theoretical standpoint has given way to approaches that incorporate a more empirical perspective. As empirical disciplines continue to provide insights into the human mind, philosophers have been forced to reassess their views about morality in light of this new information. Our current understanding of how we come to form our moral beliefs and execute our moral judgments surpasses by leaps and bounds any such information that we had just a decade earlier. Evolutionary theory has traced the rudimentary origins of our moral concepts to our primate relatives. Modern psychology continues to reveal the subtle components that figure heavily in the formation of our moral attitudes. And perhaps most significant of all, neuroscience is beginning to identify the physiological underpinnings of our moral experiences. The benefits of such knowledge, however, may come with a significant cost. For an increasing number of philosophers, the picture of the mind revealed by science provides reason for denying the existence of moral truths.[2] For these philosophers, the belief in moral truths is a peculiarity of human psychology that has no connection to anything real. The moral truths that most of us take to be obvious turn out to be deceptions played out unwittingly by our own minds. In this paper I consider whether a skeptical attitude towards moral realism is justified by our current understanding of both how the human mind works and the nature of our moral experiences. Drawing from evolutionary theory and contemporary neuroscience, I argue that an anti-realist position on morality is more compatible with empirical findings than the realist position. I end by considering the shape that the study of ethics should take in light of abandoning the belief in moral realism.

II. The Empirical Case against Moral Realism

Before discussing reasons for rejecting moral realism, I should clarify the sense in which I will be using the term "moral realism". Following the lead of Geoffrey Sayre-McCord, I consider moral realism to consist of the following two theses: (1) Moral claims are either literally true or false, and (2) Some moral claims are literally true.[3] The anti-realist position that I argue for rejects only the second thesis. In other words, I do not deny, a la the noncognitivist, that statements making moral claims (e.g., Agent *A* ought morally to do *X*) have truth values.[4] Rather, I will argue that all such statements are false. Strictly speaking, the kind of anti-realism that I subscribe to is known as an error theory. An error theorist believes that while we can meaningfully engage in discussions about moral concepts, all normative moral claims—such as "Lying is wrong"—are false. The error theorist denies the existence of the property of wrongness that is needed to make the preceding statement true. In this sense, the property *wrongness* has the same ontological status as the property *phlogiston.* Since the term "phlogiston" fails to designate anything real in the actual world, any assertion that an object has the property of *containing phlogiston* is false. Likewise, the error theorist holds that any assertion that a particular act has the property of *being morally wrong* or *morally right*—or that anyone is *morally obligated* to either do or refrain from doing a particular act—is false. In as much as my attack on moral realism is based on denying the existence of moral properties that would substantiate moral claims, the case that I build against moral realism will rely on metaphysical, rather than on linguistic or semantic, arguments.[5]

It may help to clarify the type of moral anti-realism that I am defending in this essay by pointing out how such a view undercuts the notion of moral desert and other related concepts—such as retributivist justice—that are founded upon it. If the kind of moral realism that I am considering is correct, then it makes sense to believe that it is sometimes appropriate to reward or punish people on strictly retributivist grounds—i.e., that people *deserve* a certain type of treatment when what they do is either morally good or morally bad. If the type of moral realism that I am concerned with is false, however, then there would appear to be no rational basis for either rewarding or punishing people for their acts (or omissions) on purely retributivist grounds. Of course, this does not imply that there are not other justifiable reasons for doling out reward or punishment that may be grounded, for instance, on prudential considerations (such as ensuring the safety of one's community).

In the course of providing arguments against the kind of moral realism sketched above, I will not spend any significant time distinguishing between objectivist and relativist accounts of moral realism. For the purposes of this paper, it does not matter whether a particular account of moral realism maintains that moral truths hold for all people in all situations or whether it takes such truths to be relative to personal circumstances. What matters is whether the particular account of moral realism in question asserts the existence of moral properties that, in turn, ground the propriety of the retributivist model of reward and punishment. Since I will argue that science provides reason for doubting the existence of any such moral properties, the issue of whether or not such properties might be influenced by one's culture, particular moral perspective, etc., is a moot point.

From what has preceded, it should be apparent that there are different versions of moral realism in the philosophical literature and this paper aims only at rejecting one of these. Nonetheless, the version of moral realism that I deny is of particular importance. As I have discussed, it is the kind that grounds the retributivist model of justice. This kind of moral realism is important since it reflects common sense views about morality. The fact that so many of us believe that possessing a particular moral status renders one deserving of particular types of treatment is a testament to how the kind of moral realism that I am attacking is an integral part of our value systems.[6] Since retributive justice plays such a fundamental role in both our commonsense moral beliefs and in our social institutions (e.g., in a court of law), it is of high philosophical importance to address whether the kind of moral realism that is required to legitimize the retributivist model of justice is true.

Beyond its relevance to ordinary attitudes about morality, the account of moral realism that grounds retributivist justice is notable in that it reflects how many prominent philosophers conceive of morality. J.S. Mill, for instance, claims that the distinction between "deserving and not deserving punishment…lies at the bottom of the notions of right and wrong."[7] To say that moral realism is true is to say that beings can be morally responsible. Yet, what does it mean to say that one is "morally responsible" for an action *A* if not that one is in some sense deserving of a particular type of treatment for having performed *A*? Such is the opinion of Galen Strawson, who puts the matter as follows:

> As I understand it, true moral responsibility is responsibility of such a kind that, if we have it, then it *makes sense*, at least, to suppose that it could be just to punish some of us with (eternal) torment in hell and reward others with (eternal) bliss in heaven.[8]

I am in agreement with Mill and Strawson (and, presumably, with many non-philosophers as well) that the very concept of morality includes the idea that people ought to be punished or rewarded according to whether or not they have behaved properly. Operating under this view, I will assume for the purposes of this paper that being a moral realist requires that one believe that people sometimes deserve—*on strictly retributivist grounds*—to be punished (when they behave immorally) and rewarded (when they behave morally). Given that this understanding of moral realism appears to resonate with the views of both philosophers and non-philosophers alike, I believe that the burden is on anyone who rejects this account to explain why it is that we should adopt an alternative conception of moral realism. At any rate, even if one were to provide a convincing argument for why we should not view the moral realist as being committed to advocating the retributivist model of justice, this would not undermine the philosophical relevance of this paper. The question of whether the retributivist model of justice is defensible for human beings would still be an important philosophical issue for reasons discussed earlier. Hence, I would think that even ethicists who disagree with my conception of moral realism would take an interest in my arguments against the propriety of retributivist justice.

As a final preliminary point, I should mention that in denying the existence of moral properties, I am not thereby asserting the falseness of *all* normative claims. While I believe that there is reason for rejecting all claims consisting of moral "ought" statements, I am nonetheless willing to grant that there are non-moral properties that ground the truth of some non-moral "ought" statements. For instance, there are prudential "oughts" that place normative restrictions on us. If you desire to keep living, are on the brink of starvation, and have no desire that would be furthered by refraining to eat the steak that is in front of you, I am willing to say that you *ought* to eat the steak. Along the same lines, a mouse that desires to live *ought* to avoid the cat that is waiting to eat him just outside of his mouse hole. In both of these examples, one can coherently say that the individuals in question "ought to"—from considerations of self-interest—act in a particular way, while denying that it would be immoral not to do so.

A. The Evolutionary Challenge to Moral Realism

Traditionally, philosophers have rarely questioned the existence of moral truths. Differences in moral philosophy were focused not on whether moral truths exist—since their existence was usually taken as a given—but rather on what these truths are. Metaethical discussions about whether moral truths exist became more widespread in the twentieth century, thanks in large part to the noncognitivist arguments of philosophers like A.J. Ayer. Following on the heels of the logical positivist movement that was in vogue during the early part of that century, the noncognitivists believed that moral claims held no truth value. Falling prey to persuasive objections, noncognitivist attacks on moral realism began to fall out of favor towards the latter half of the twentieth century, giving way to more sophisticated anti-realist arguments. One of the better known of these was the evolutionary argument put forth by Michael Ruse and E.O. Wilson (1984). According to this view, our moral beliefs are the product of natural selection, and their existence is owed to the fact that they served our survival needs by fostering cooperation among our evolutionary ancestors. For Ruse and Wilson, the fact that natural selection is responsible for our having moral beliefs is reason in itself for rejecting the notion that our moral beliefs correspond to any moral truths. As Ruse puts it in a more recent work:

> ...normative ethics is a biological adaptation, and I would argue that as such it can be seen to have no being or reality beyond this. We believe normative ethics for our own (biological good), and that is that.[9]

As many philosophers commenting on this argument have pointed out, the fact that a faculty owes its existence to evolutionary causes does not necessarily justify rejecting the truth of all beliefs that are generated by way of this faculty. In support of this view, Zachary Ernst (2007) correctly points out that the fact that our visual faculties were crafted by natural selection does not warrant the rejection of our beliefs about the existence of the things that we see. Ernst acknowledges, however, that there is an important difference between our evolutionarily-caused judgments about the things that we perceive visually and our evolutionarily-caused moral judgments. Namely, that the former judgments are open to empirical verification while the latter are not. In addition to the fact that our vision has been known to provide us with accurate information in the past, the visual input that we get can be verified through our other senses. In the case of our moral judgments, however, there seems to be no way, empirical or otherwise, of verifying whether or not they are correct. As Ernst puts it, "For if we are unsure about the correct moral theory, then we do not know what facts the moral faculty should track."[10] Since there is nothing close to certainty about the correct moral theory, we are apparently without the means to verify whether our moral beliefs are true.

It seems reasonable to maintain that we should withhold asserting the truth of any belief unless the truth of the belief can be confirmed (or at least strongly supported) either *a priori* (e.g., mathematical truths) or through empirical verification (e.g., the external reality of the objects we see).[11] And yet if evolutionary theorists like Ruse are right, there is no reason to believe that any such confirmation or support of our moral beliefs is possible. According to Ruse, our moral beliefs exist because they provided a survival advantage, *not because* they effectively picked out anything real. In contrast, our visual faculty provided a survival advantage *precisely because* it effectively tracked actual objects in the world. Given that our capacity to make moral judgments was not selected for its ability to apprehend facts, it is difficult to justify the claim that moral facts exist. After all, there seems to be no reason for asserting the existence of moral truths beyond the intuition that tells us that they are out there. But merely having this intuition—the origin of which, according to the evolutionary account of morality, is unrelated to any moral truths that might actually exist—does not seem to be adequate grounds for positing the existence of moral truths. Ernst puts the idea succinctly:

> Specifically, if the mechanism by which the belief is formed bears no relationship to the facts that would make the belief true, then the belief does not have any evidential value. This is a sort of genetic argument, but not a fallacious one.[12]

In arguing that there is an evolutionary basis for rejecting moral realism, my point is not that the fact that natural selection has provided us with the propensity to make moral judgments warrants, by itself, the rejection of all moral judgments. If this was the case, then we should also reject all of our mathematical and empirical judgments, since the mechanisms by which we come to make such judgments (brains, eyes, etc.) are themselves products of evolution. Nor have I argued that the evolutionary case against moral realism rests merely on the notion that our moral beliefs are *contingent* (upon our having a particular evolutionary history, etc.). Given that our beliefs about mathematics are also contingent upon, for instance, the fact that we have had a particular kind of schooling, such an argument would commit me to rejecting mathematical truths along with moral truths.

What I *have* argued for is that unlike our scientific and mathematical beliefs, our moral beliefs are apparently not subject to any type of verification—be it empirical, analytic, or otherwise. This being the case, it is difficult to find a plausible reason for asserting the truth of moral claims like *stealing is wrong*.[13] The evolutionary explanation of our moral beliefs helps to explain the strong feeling most of us have that there are moral truths, despite the fact that there is apparently nothing we can point to that could confirm whether or not such feelings track anything real. This evolutionary explanation lends support to the moral anti-realist by highlighting how it would be a mistake to place undue emphasis on the intuition that moral truths exist. And yet, this intuition seems to be the only evidence that we have in favor of moral realism. But if the evolutionary account of morality favored by Ruse and Wilson is correct, we would have this intuition even if no moral truths existed. Thus, the mere fact that we believe that we perceive morality in the world does not seem to warrant the assertion of moral truths. In order to justify the belief in moral truths, we seem to require some evidence more than the feeling that such truths exist. Unfortunately for the moral realist, such evidence appears to be beyond our grasp.

In responding to the aforementioned evolutionary-based attack on moral realism, one might counter that some moral assertions—e.g., murder is wrong—are conceptual truths that are immune to empirical falsification. In response to this, I would point out that the debate between the moral realist and his opponent is not whether it is possible to construct a tautology that includes moral language, like "murder (i.e., wrongful killing) is wrong". The point at issue is whether there *actually are* such things as wrongful killings that would make a statement like "Sue's act of killing Janet was morally wrong" true. This is the point on which the moral realist and his opponent disagree—at least it is for the kind of moral realism that I am addressing—and the question will not be settled by affirming the truth of a tautology. Perhaps this point can be made more salient by considering a fictitious argument between a proponent of the phlogiston theory and an opponent. Suppose that after hearing his opponent's reasons for why all statements making assertions about phlogiston are false, the defender of phlogiston responds by asserting the truth of the following statement: *All phlogisticated substances contain phlogiston.* Since "phlogisticated" means "containing phlogiston", this sentence is trivially true. However, this in no way counters the main claim of the phlogiston anti-realist, which is that phlogiston does not actually exist. Likewise, the moral realist's position is not strengthened by appealing to the truth of a tautology like "murder is wrong".

To this point, I have argued that the evolutionary origins of our moral beliefs, when combined with the apparent inability to verify any such beliefs, serve to undermine the moral realist's position. Of course, one might reasonably ask why we should accept the idea that our moral beliefs are a product of evolution. Though providing a thorough defense of this is beyond the scope of the paper, I will discuss, albeit briefly, compelling evidence for this position.[14] The first kind of evidence comes from recent studies done on monkeys that display behavior suggesting that they possess a sense of *fairness*—a concept that is central to the moral attitudes of humans. In a 2003 study, researchers Sarah Brosnan and Frans de Waal allowed capuchin monkeys to trade in tokens for prizes—in this case food. When a monkey was given a prize that was 'inferior' (a cucumber) to the prize that another monkey received (a grape), the monkey with the inferior prize took offense, and either refused to accept the cucumber or, in some cases, even hurled it in disgust back at the researcher. Such behavior led Brosnan to conclude, "notions of justice extend beyond humans,"[15] adding that, "It looks like this behavior is evolved ... it is not simply a cultural construct".[16]

The main idea behind evolutionary ethics is that our moral faculties were created and developed by natural selection because of their propensity to engage us in cooperative behaviors that improved our chances of passing on our genes to subsequent generations. If this were true, we should expect to find the same kind of emotional catalyst for our moral beliefs—which are crucial in motivating cooperative behavior—that we find for other behaviors that serve our fitness needs (e.g., eating, mating, avoiding danger). This is exactly what we find. The idea that emotions play a central role in the formation of our moral beliefs goes at least as far back as the philosopher David Hume, who maintained that the origins of our moral distinctions are to be found in the emotions (or "sentiments" as he called them) rather than in reason. Subsequent research has confirmed the hypothesis that Hume put forward. Drawing from a large collection of psychological and neurological research, the psychologist Joshua Greene concludes that, "Our moral intuitions...appear to depend crucially on our emotional capacities...one might even go so far as to say that, as a general rule, moral intuitions *are* emotional responses."[17] Among the studies that led Greene to draw this conclusion are fMRI studies showing activity in the emotional centers of the brain during moral judgments (Greene et al. 2001, Greene et al. 2004). The studies of Greene and his colleagues showed that emotional centers of the brain were activated for all types of moral judgments, even those involving abstract reasoning. One particularly interesting finding of Greene and his associates is that in addition to their apparent necessary role in generating moral judgments, emotions appear to determine the particular *type* of moral judgments that we make. According to Greene and his colleagues, the level of emotional involvement in our moral judgments is the source of the conflict between the utilitarian and the deontological moral perspectives. Drawing from their experiments, Greene et al. conclude that:

> First, we have seen evidence of increased social-emotional processing in cases in which deontological intuitions are prominent. Second, we have seen greater activity in brain regions associated with cognitive control when utilitarian judgments prevail.[18]

Furthermore, Greene et al. discuss what they take to be the evolutionary origins of the distinct roles that emotions and abstract reasoning (which is captured here under the term "cognitive") play in generating moral judgments:

> We propose that the tension between the utilitarian and deontological perspectives in moral philosophy reflect a more fundamental tension arising from the structure of the human brain. The socio-emotional responses that we've inherited from our primate ancestors…shaped and refined by culture bound experience, undergird the absolute prohibitions that are central to deontology. In contrast, the "moral calculus" that defines utilitarianism is made possible by more recently evolved structures in the frontal lobes that support abstract thinking and high-level cognitive control.[19]

The view that emotions play a critical role in making moral judgments gains additional support from studies conducted on subjects with emotional deficiencies. Commenting on what would count as evidence in support of the notion that our moral beliefs depend more upon emotion than on reason, Greene says that, "If…moral judgment and behavior are primarily the products of emotional response, then we should expect those with diminished emotional capacities (of the relevant kind) to exhibit the most morally abysmal behavior.".[20] The consequent of the foregoing statement is rendered true by what we find in the case of psychopaths. Several studies conducted on psychopaths—who are not typically lacking in their reasoning capabilities—have shown that they display less emotional responsiveness than do non-psychopaths to various kinds of stimuli, including images of people in distress (Hare and Quinn 1971, Blair et al. 1997).

In pressing the view that our moral judgments have an emotional basis, my aim has not been to argue that this emotional basis is itself reason for rejecting the judgments that follow from them. In other words, I do not claim that any judgment with emotional origins should be construed as necessarily false. After all, certain judgments based on emotional responses—e.g., that the rattlesnake in my path is dangerous—appear to be truth-tracking. Rather, my purpose in discussing the emotional aspects of our moral judgments has been to lend support to the evolutionary account of morality which does, I have argued, lend support to moral anti-realism. Given, however, that certain emotional responses (fear) seem to form the basis of judgments that are fairly reliable (e.g., that rattlesnakes are dangerous), one might attempt to defend moral realism by asserting that the emotions that give rise to our moral judgments are themselves reliably truth-tracking. My response to this follows a similar line of reasoning that I employed earlier when distinguishing between our visual and moral faculties. Recall my assertion that while our visual judgments are (at least generally speaking) empirically verifiable, our moral judgments do not appear to be verifiable in any way. Furthermore, I mentioned how, under a plausible evolutionary account of morality, our moral judgments—unlike our judgments about what we see—were not selected for their ability to track anything real.

The distinction between emotionally-based judgments about dangerous things and emotionally-based moral judgments can be understood in much the same way as the distinction between our visual judgments and our moral judgments. In regards to our emotionally-based judgments about dangerous things, we can often determine whether they are accurate. If we find out that the rattlesnake in front of us is made out of rubber, the judgment that it was dangerous was false; if it bites us and causes excruciating pain, it was true. As I pointed out earlier, however, there seems to be no way of verifying our moral judgments. The point is not, therefore, that our moral judgments should be rejected as false in virtue of their emotional origins. The point is that unlike our judgments stemming from either what we see or from what we are led by fear to categorize as "dangerous", our moral judgments were not forged by nature for the purpose of tracking actual properties in the world. Seen in an evolutionary light, our moral judgments are, in some sense, by-products of a system aimed at fostering human cooperation. To achieve this end, it was not necessary—evolutionarily speaking—for humans to apprehend *actual* moral facts. In contrast, the evolutionary fitness of our ancestors depended upon our visual faculty detecting *actual* objects in the world and upon our fears compelling us to avoid *actual* dangers.

Given the important role that cooperation played in allowing our ancestors to thrive (by providing better access to basic necessities, allowing for better group defense against outside threats, etc.), one might be willing to grant the need for natural selection to provide us with behavioral dispositions to refrain from activities that foster conflict with other human beings—the very activities that we often call "immoral." Yet, one might wonder why it was necessary for nature to instill in us the propensity not merely to view certain activities negatively and others positively, but to attach a metaphysical status to behaviors whereby we see them as possessing *real* qualities like being moral or immoral. From an evolutionary perspective, how can we explain the origins of our *concepts* of moral and immoral? Michael Ruse provides one plausible explanation. Ruse rejects the view of the emotivists, who believe that our moral judgments are nothing more than an expression of our emotions and, as such, hold no truth value. Under the emotivist view, a judgment like 'Killing is wrong!' is to be interpreted as 'Killing-boo!'. Ruse's criticism of this position is that it leaves out a component that is crucial to our moral judgments—namely, that our judgments express what we take to be *facts*. A person who affirms that killing is wrong is not merely expressing her opinion. She is pointing out what in her eyes is a fact; of the same variety, more or less, as a mathematical truth. For Ruse, our tendency to believe in moral truths is an adaptation that was necessary for allowing us to overcome our selfish impulses that impede cooperation. In his view, merely feeling an aversion to certain behaviors was not enough—we needed morality. Ruse puts the point this way:

> For someone like the emotivist, normative ethics has to be translated as a report on feelings...For me, this is simply not strong enough...if emotivism were the complete answer, genes for cheating would soon make a spectacular appearance in the human species, or rather, those genes already existing would make an immediate gain. The way in which biology avoids this happening is by making moral claims seem *as if they were objective.*[21]

For evolutionary theorists like Ruse, the brains of human beings are, to use his terminology, "hard-wired" for morality in the same way that certain computers are hard-wired to play chess. Recent studies in neuroscience lend support for this view. Of particular note is the increasingly popular view among neuroscientists that moral judgments are often made by automatic processes that bypass any reasoning on the part of the individual. According to this view—called the *social intuitionist model* of moral judgment—many, if not most, of our moral judgments are the product of quick (or "automatic") intuitive responses to stimuli. For these kinds of judgments, the model claims, reasoning comes into play *after* the judgment has been made, and serves to construct *ad hoc* justifications for the decision that was made. Support for the social intuitionist model has come from studies in which subjects failed to provide a legitimate reason to justify their moral decisions about particular cases. In one study in which subjects were asked to assess an instance of consensual incest among adults, for example, subjects tended to stick by their initial judgment that the incest was wrong despite being aware that their attempts to provide a sound reasoned basis for their decision was lacking. After suggesting a series of flawed justifications for their judgments, subjects fell back on claims like "It's just wrong".[22] If the moral judgments in this particular case were the products of reasoning, so the social intuitionist interpretation goes, we should expect subjects to retract their initial judgments once they abandon the reasons that they originally offered in support of them. The fact that they do not indicates that an emotive, intuitive process—as opposed to a rational one—is the source of the moral judgment. Viewed in this light, moral judgments of this type appear to be *unconscious* in the sense that reasoning appears to play essentially no role in producing them. This notion of moral judgments arising from unconscious processes is consistent with growing empirical evidence indicating that much, if not most or even all, of our behavior is produced by processes in the brain that occur prior to any conscious decision to act. Hence, we have psychologist Jon Haidt acknowledging that, "The emerging view in social cognition is that most of our behaviors and judgments are in fact made automatically (i.e., without intention, effort, or awareness of process)."[23]

B. Neuroscience and Moral Judgments

If the social intuitionist model of moral judgment is correct, it would provide strong evidence for the view that evolutionary forces have hard-wired our brains for making moral judgments. The idea that automatic unconscious brain processes are responsible for producing the majority, if not all, of our actions and decisions is quickly developing into something approaching a consensus among neuroscientists. Much recent attention has focused on experiments carried out by Benjamin Libet (1985), which indicate that the brain activity that initiates actions occurs *prior* to any conscious decision to act. The evidence for this is so persuasive, in fact, that according to neuroscientists Michael S. Gazzaniga and Megan S. Steven, the view that "the brain carries out its work before one becomes consciously aware of a thought" is accepted by most neuroscientists.[24] What Libet found was that the moment at which subjects became aware of consciously willing an action (in this case, moving one's finger) is preceded by brain activity (which Libet called the "readiness potential") that appears to be the initiating cause of the action that is ultimately taken. The causal account of human behavior that Libet provides is consistent with the account of moral judgments offered by Greene and others along the lines of the social intuitionist model. Recapping this view, it holds that the bulk of our moral judgments are the result of automatic processes that are based in the emotions, and which occur unconsciously in the sense that reasoning plays virtually no role in the formation of these judgments.

In what has preceded, I have attempted to show how neuroscience provides evidence against moral realism by lending strong credence to the view that our moral beliefs are the product of evolutionary processes and are not based on an ability to discern actual (moral) properties in the world. Research conducted by Greene and others indicates that our brains are structured to have physiological reactions to certain types of stimuli which, in turn, result in our making moral judgments. Such research provides strong empirical support for the evolutionary account of our moral experiences offered by moral anti-realists like Michael Ruse. Even so, this may not be the biggest threat to moral realism posed by contemporary neuroscience.

A more significant threat may be looming that derives from how neuroscience seems to cast doubt on the possibility that human beings are capable of *free will*. Since philosophers take free will as being a necessary condition for moral responsibility, it seems that without free will, it would be impossible for human beings to act genuinely moral or immoral. This would render as false the whole of our moral judgments—at least in as much as they pertain to people.[25] At this point, a few comments about the term "free will" are in order. While philosophers differ as to what "free will" means, it is fair to say that there are certain core properties of the concept that they virtually all agree on. One is that free will is necessary for moral responsibility, and hence, for moral rightness and wrongness. Another is that having acted of one's own free will requires that one exert *control* over the action in question. Though the question of what exactly constitutes *control* is a contentious one, we can say, at the very least, that control over an action requires that the action is in some way the result of a *conscious decision*.[26] Yet recent discoveries in neuroscience, like those made by Libet, call into question whether our conscious decisions *ever* play a role in instigating our behavior. The studies of Libet have led psychologist Daniel Wegner (2002) to conclude that conscious will is an illusion. According to Wegner, our belief in conscious will arises when we perceive a correlation between our decision to act in a particular way and the subsequent performance of an action that is consistent with the decision. Despite this correlation, however, Wegner maintains that conscious decision-making plays *no causal role* in generating behavior. I should reiterate that Wegner's view fits well with the accepted position among neuroscientists (Gazzaniga and Stevens 2005, Pinker 2007, Greene and Cohen 2004). If Wegner is correct, the implications for free will are pretty straightforward—no conscious will equals no free will. Even if one remains unconvinced that neuroscience has conclusively demonstrated the impossibility of free will for human beings, it is likely that as our understanding of the brain and the physiological underpinnings of mental phenomena continues to grow, it will become increasingly difficult to defend mystical notions like free will.

D. Moral Realism and the Color Analogy

Notwithstanding the foregoing arguments against moral realism, one might counter that there is one version of moral realism that is impervious to my previous attacks. This is the version put forth by John McDowell, who maintains that moral properties are "secondary qualities" that have the same kind of objective reality as colors.[27] For McDowell, values and moral truths are objectively real even though they cannot be understood without reference to the subjective states of observers. According to him, the reality of secondary qualities like values and color derives from their "dispositions to give rise to subjective states."[28] Although McDowell believes that the reality of moral properties derive from their propensities to generate perceptive states, he denies the projectivist account of morality provided by error theorists like John Mackie, according to which moral properties are merely the fabrications of our subjective states that we (mistakenly) project onto real objects in the world. The important point for McDowell is that secondary qualities have a sort of mind-independence in the sense that they exist independently of any particular experience of them. This mind-independent characteristic consists in the disposition to cause a subjective experience of a particular sort, and this disposition might still exist even if it did not influence a particular individual's subjective experiences in a given instance. According to this view, the projectivist's position is flawed because it fails to acknowledge the inherent property possessed by things that give rise to our perceptions of qualities like redness and moral wrongness. Whereas the projectivist views moral judgments as being based on nothing inherent to the object of the judgment, McDowell believes that such judgments are at least sometimes owed to something inherent (i.e., objective) in the object of the moral judgment—namely, the disposition to give rise to this type of judgment.

The question to ask at this point is whether McDowell's arguments can preserve the type of moral realism under discussion. Assuming that moral properties have the same ontological status as colors, would this be enough to justify the kind of moral realism that grounds the retributivist model of justice?[29] To see why it would not, consider McDowell's explanation about how the property of redness is to be construed according to his view: "Thus an object's being red is understood as something that obtains in virtue of the object's being such as (in certain circumstances) to look, precisely, red."[30] In using the qualifier "in certain circumstances", McDowell is allowing that not all things one might consider to be red will appear as such to all others. After all, if one is color-blind, she will obviously not perceive the redness of the tomato that I would. Even so, McDowell seems satisfied that the disposition of the tomato to make people *in my circumstances* see red counts as an objective property of the tomato. Let us now consider an act of stealing that some individuals might take to be morally wrong. Following the analogy with color, while some individuals may not perceive the act as being morally wrong, let us assume that others, in certain circumstances, will. Hence, the fact that the act of stealing elicits judgments of moral wrongness under certain circumstances is what makes it correct to say that the act of stealing is morally wrong. But is the fact that certain actions or individuals are of such a nature as to elicit particular types of moral judgments under certain circumstances enough to justify the retributivist model of justice? In what follows, I argue that it is not.

Under the plausible evolutionary explanation of our moral beliefs discussed earlier, our peculiar tendency to make moral judgments—and, hence, our moral judgments themselves—are the products of selection processes that occurred over millions of years. Given this picture, the question typically asked by participants in the moral realism debate is whether the judgments we tend to make correspond to external or "brute" facts about the world. For McDowell, however, this is the wrong question to ask. Rather than asking whether our moral judgments are based on the apprehension of primary (i.e., "brute" or wholly mind-independent) qualities, we need only determine whether our moral judgments correspond to secondary qualities. But is he right? Can the type of moral realism that most people seem to have in mind—i.e., the kind that lends credence to the retributivist model of justices—be salvaged by appealing to secondary rather than to primary qualities? To see why it cannot, consider the following scenario. Suppose that a fascist dictator desired to bring his non-blue-eyed country to war against its blue-eyed neighbors. Knowing that his soldiers would be apprehensive to go to war—after all, the neighbors have not provoked them in any way—he asks his defense minister to create a substance that would make his country's soldiers long for war. After many months, chemists inside the defense ministry come up with a substance that will make any non-blue-eyed individual exposed to it believe that blue-eyed people were immoral to the point of deserving death. This is to say that a non-blue-eyed person exposed to the drug would believe that being in possession of blue eyes is the very apex of immorality. During the testing stages of the drug, an accident occurs whereby the drug escapes the lab and tremendous doses of it infiltrate the air. The pollution occurs to such a degree that all of the non-blue-eyed people in the world are affected by it. Upon becoming exposed to the drug, all non-blue-eyed people decide that all blue-eyed people are immoral and deserve to die. Subsequently, the non-blue-eyed people of the world unite and eventually wage a war that kills all of the blue-eyed people.

Do the blue-eyed people in the foregoing thought experiment truly deserve death or any other sort of punishment? I assume that virtually no one would agree that they do. The reason for this is that the non-blue-eyed people's judgments that the blue-eyed people were immoral and deserving of death did not correspond to anything *real* in the strong sense of the term. Under McDowell's view, however, it seems as though the moral judgments made by the non-blue-eyed people exposed to the drug would be as legitimate as any moral judgment that you or I might make. Given that the blue-eyed people possessed a disposition to produce a subjective state (perceiving blue-eyed people as immoral) in others (non-blue-eyed-people) in certain circumstances (exposure to the drug), the perceived "immorality" of the blue-eyed people by the non-blue-eyed people would seem, under McDowell's view, to correspond to a secondary quality inherent to the blue-eyed people. But if this is true, then McDowell seems forced to concede that possessing blue eyes in the previous case would be objectively immoral. The fact that McDowell seems committed to asserting the immorality of the blue-eyed people in the foregoing scenario provides strong reason for denying that his account of morality can provide an adequate defense of the kind of moral realism under consideration.

One way that McDowell could attempt to avoid being pinned to the conclusion that the blue-eyed people in the previous case were immoral would be to distinguish cases of "normal" moral judgments from the drug-influenced judgments portrayed in the preceding scenario by asserting that while the former type of judgments are based on real properties, the latter type is not. However, this move seems unavailable to McDowell given his account of secondary qualities. To say that an object, action, etc., has a secondary quality is only to say that it has a disposition to cause a particular type of subjective experience in an individual in a particular situation. Whether the particular situation under which one would have an experience of a particular sort is shaped by evolutionary processes or by exposure to a certain drug (in combination with evolutionary processes) is irrelevant. In order to avoid putting the two kinds of moral judgments discussed on the same footing, McDowell would have to explain why judgments of the "normal" variety are more real than the drug-induced moral judgments. It appears that nothing in his discussion about second qualities, however, provides him with the grounding to make this sort of distinction.[31] These considerations demonstrate that McDowell's approach is unable to provide a satisfactory defense of the type of moral realism that is the focus of this paper.

E. The Collapse of Moral Realism

The insights from a variety of scientific and philosophical standpoints are giving us a more complete understanding of the nature of our moral experiences than we have ever had. As these disciplines converge in providing a comprehensive account of the origins of our moral beliefs, it is becoming more and more difficult to justify the belief in moral realism. It is almost beyond question that our tendency to view the world in moral terms is the product of evolution, and that this tendency evolved not for its ability to pick out moral truths, but for its ability to foster the kind of cooperation that was necessary for allowing our ancestors to flourish to the extent that they did. While the evolutionary origin of human morality may provide the strongest reason for rejecting moral realism, I have discussed an additional problem facing moral realism that derives from neuroscience research which casts doubt on the efficacy of conscious will when it comes to causing human behavior. Since, if true, this would appear to be a fatal blow to the idea that people possess free will and, hence, moral responsibility, such information provides an additional reason for believing that our moral judgments—at least insofar as they pertain to human beings—have no basis in reality.

At the very least, one lesson to be learned from a better empirical understanding of moral phenomena is that proponents of moral realism can no longer rely on the intuitive plausibility of their position to carry the day. Any adequate defense of moral realism requires more than merely appealing to the strong feeling we have that moral truths exist. If science shows us anything, it is the fallibility of our intuitions when it comes to understanding the nature of reality. Granting, then, that moral realism is false, what is to become of ethical discourse? Are we simply to dispense altogether with discussing traditional ethical questions such as, "What is the proper way to live?", "Why we should we treat others kindly?", and "What kind of society is best?" Or might it still be possible to carry on a meaningful dialogue on such matters despite abandoning the belief in moral realism? I conclude by reflecting on these questions.

III. Conclusion: Life after Moral Realism

For many people, a general abandonment of the belief in moral realism would threaten civilization by eliminating what in their eyes is perhaps *the* primary motivator for congenial behavior. If the general populace embraced the kind of moral anti-realism argued for in this paper, so the argument goes, we would see a dramatic increase in crime, cruelty, and unseemly activities of all sorts. After all, our behavior often appears restrained by the belief that we are obligated to do what is right and avoid doing what is wrong. If this belief is mistaken, then what is to stop me—or anyone else for that matter—from stealing what we please or hurting whoever displeases us, whenever we feel reasonably certain that we can avoid punishment? Given these serious concerns, one might justifiably ask why the moral anti-realist is attempting to destroy that which makes civil society possible. Why should one seek to promote an idea (moral anti-realism) that has the potential for causing so much damage? One might be surprised to find that many moral anti-realists believe that by promoting their position, they are actually contributing to the *betterment* of society. Joshua Greene, for one, believes that, "An error theory…is a cause for *optimism*. In a world full of practical problems, news of past mistakes is *good news*, the first step toward avoiding them in the future."[32] In Greene's eyes, the belief in moral realism actually creates more problems than it solves. The reason is that believing in moral truths often fosters human conflict, particularly when different people believe that they—rather than their opponents—have exclusive insight into what is morally right. Greene is clearly correct in believing that differing views about right and wrong are the source of some of the vilest episodes in our history.[33] But is doing away with moral realism likely to improve or hurt human relations worldwide? It will be helpful here to consider the form that Greene believes moral discourse will take once we jettison the concept of moral realism.

Once we reject the existence of moral truths, Greene believes that the stage will be set for the emergence of a universal moral outlook, albeit one that has a subjective rather than an objective basis. "Subjective" and "objective" are to be understood here in terms of the justifications people might have for acting morally.[34] Whereas the existence of moral truths would constitute an objective justification for acting in a particular way, subjective justifications are based on the personal inclinations that someone has. Obviously, what counts as a subjective justification for one person may not be so for another. Greene believes that once we reject moral realism, the focus of ethical discourse will veer away from the metaphysical, and towards the pragmatic in the sense that the emphasis will be placed on how to best promote the overall good for human beings. Accordingly, Greene favors "an anti-realist utilitarian framework for discussing moral issues of public concern."[35] Given the truth of moral anti-realism, one might reasonably ask why we should feel compelled to subscribe to any traditional moral framework, utilitarian or otherwise, as the basis for evaluating individual actions or public policies. Greene's answer is that our reason for doing so follows from the idea that virtually everyone agrees with the kind of utilitarian framework that he recommends. As he puts it:

> Nearly everyone is a utilitarian to some extent. Nearly everyone agrees that *all other things being equal* raising someone's level of happiness, either your own or someone else's, is a good thing, and that lowering someone's happiness is a bad thing.[36]

In Greene's view, the justification for adopting a utilitarian standard to assess potential actions and policies is subjective in nature and derives from the fact that people already agree that such a standard is appropriate. This is to say that the justification is internally sanctioned (by our own attitudes) rather than externally imposed (by moral truths). Greene believes that while there is general agreement that serving human interests is a good thing, there is no such consensus regarding, for instance, whether or not property rights (a deontological concept) demand the elimination of some forms of taxation. Since, from an anti-realist standpoint, there is no truth to the matter of whether or not imposing taxes is moral, he believes our differing intuitions on this subject should not influence policy. Instead, he would recommend addressing questions about taxation by considering the extent to which taxation would contribute to the greatest overall happiness. For Greene, the justification for why one ought to promote the general good is prudential—rather than moral—in nature, and derives from one's subjective desire to see the general welfare advanced.

At this point, one might worry that even if we grant that virtually all people agree with the view that, all things being equal, contributing to the greatest overall happiness is a good thing (i.e., they *desire* it to some extent), this in itself is not enough to keep people from infringing on the interests of others when they would appear to benefit by doing so. Put another way, the concern is that once we reject moral realism, there is no real reason to promote the general happiness whenever doing so goes against one's perceived self-interest. "But certainly," Greene's opponent counters, "there will be *many* instances where selfish concerns do not coincide with the interests of others. Without the belief in genuine moral obligations to keep us in line, our relatively flimsy interest in promoting the overall good will be overwhelmed by selfish inclinations." Thus, while Greene may be right that a utilitarian framework may be more appropriate than any other traditional moral framework for addressing public policy issues in light of the truth of moral anti-realism, the concern is that this framework would not be able to adequately curtail the unrestrained pursuit of self-interest that would render civilized society impossible. The problem here is that since Greene acknowledges that there can only be prudential reasons for adopting the kind of quasi-utilitarianism that he recommends, there is no reason to believe that people will seek to contribute to the greatest overall happiness if they believe that doing so would be contrary to their own self-interest.[37]

Thus, we are back to the worry that the acceptance of moral anti-realism would have a devastating impact on society. Greene himself does not believe that such a concern is warranted. While he does not deny that the belief in moral realism plays some role in promoting amiable relations among people, he does not believe that this role is especially significant. In his eyes, the tendency for human beings to get along is less the product of our moral beliefs than it is the result of our social instincts that have been forged by evolution. According to him:

> The human social instincts that undergird our commitment to [promoting and not infringing upon the interests of others] run deep. Our meta-ethical views concerning the truth of moral realism are not without consequences…but their effects are marginal compared to those that flow from our more basic social natures.[38]

Since Greene believes that abandoning the belief in moral realism would not impact our natural social instincts, he denies that rejecting moral realism would render human relations more hostile. To support this view, he mentions an example of a mother and child. He says that even if the mother were to accept the truth of moral anti-realism, there is little reason to think that she would care for her child any less. The reason is that her caring for her child stems not from a feeling of moral obligation, but rather from the natural instinct mothers have to care for their children. For similar reasons, so the argument goes, rejecting the existence of moral truths would not have a negative impact upon human interactions generally. For Greene, human cooperation is not primarily due to rational considerations, but to innate desires that attach us to the good of others. "Fortunately for us and our genes," Greene says, "the emotional dog wags the rational tail."[39]

The problem facing Greene is that he does not put enough weight in the idea that in addition to those instincts which foster human harmony, there are *equally strong* instincts that lead to disharmony. While there is significant scientific evidence to support Greene's claim that natural selection equipped us with innate altruistic tendencies, there is equally as much evidence, if not more so, showing that our tendencies towards violence, jealousy, and greed are legacies of the evolutionary forces that shaped us. It seems overly optimistic for Greene to maintain that the "lighter" side of our nature will automatically prevail over our "darker" side once we cast away moral realism. For one thing, studies have shown that the propensity of our altruistic tendencies to motivate behavior is contingent upon various psychological factors, including a person's affective state. Summing up the research that has been conducted regarding the connection between affective state and altruistic behavior, Bert Moore and Alice Isen conclude that, "In the main happiness promotes altruism, helpfulness, sharing, and sociability, while sadness retards them."[40] A slew of other psychological studies have generated data supporting this view (e.g., Midlarsky 1971, Underwood, et al. 1977, Crandall 1978, Weyant 1978, Batson 1990). The picture we get from psychology casts doubt on the view that altruism will automatically win the day when it comes to human motivation. Research indicates that unless one is in a particular kind of affective state (positive), there is no reason to expect this individual to exhibit cooperative, as opposed to anti-social, behavior. Greene may be right that the emotional dog wags the rational tail, but Greene has yet to provide a reason for denying that the dog will lead the tail astray more times than not.

Despite my misgivings about what I take to be Greene's overly optimistic views about human nature, I agree with much of what he says about both the truth of moral anti-realism and how the general acceptance of anti-realism is likely to improve the human condition. This being said, there is reason to believe that as science continues to build the case against some key elements of the belief systems of industrialized western cultures (e.g., moral realism, mind-body dualism), many individuals will have a difficult time coming to grips with scientific facts, and there may even be a backlash against science from those whose most cherished beliefs are called into question.[41] Though there are likely to be some individuals for whom the inability to come to terms with a more realistic account of human nature may lead them to fall prey to a destructive nihilism, it is difficult to predict whether this will occur on a significant scale (though I doubt that it will).

I agree with Greene that the truth of moral anti-realism (assuming that it is true) gives us reason for being optimistic, though my optimism has a somewhat different basis than his. I agree that in rejecting moral realism, ethicists would likely turn towards answering pragmatic questions about how to best serve the interests of human beings. Beyond this general focus, where specifically might ethicists turn their emphasis? One possible point of emphasis relates to what I mentioned earlier about how cooperative behavior appears to be intimately connected with affective state. To reiterate, the more positive one's mood is, the more likely she is to engage in cooperative behavior. Granting that this is correct, ethicists and public policy makers would appear to have a strong interest in seeking to improve our understanding of what factors contribute to and detract from human happiness. A recent movement in psychology, called *Positive Psychology*, may prove useful towards this end. Rather than placing an emphasis on the causes of psychological maladies—which has been the emphasis of traditional psychology—positive psychology strives to discover the factors that contribute to positive affective states like happiness and self-esteem. If positive psychology can improve our knowledge about the causes of positive mood states, it may hold great promise in contributing to a world in which hostile human behavior would become increasingly scarce. Obviously, a better understanding of the brain's physiology and how it relates to specific mental states would aid us in our attempts to improve human happiness. Given that this area of study falls into the realm of neuroscience, this discipline may prove to be of primary importance in helping to improve human relations. In this way, neuroscience may turn out to hold the somewhat ironic position of being indispensable both for providing a devastating case against moral realism and for bringing about the kinds of behavior that realist moral theories place such a high emphasis on.

In as much as I believe that embracing moral anti-realism should lead ethicists to focus on promoting the general happiness—primarily by means of better understanding the psychological and physiological basis of happiness—my conclusions are not that far off from Greene's.[42] Where he and I differ pertains to the ease with which we foresee the general acceptance of moral anti-realism leading to a better world. Whereas Greene seems to believe that this transition would be relatively quick and painless, I am more guarded. Although it is difficult to predict how the general acceptance of moral anti-realism would effect society, the impact that it would have on our ethical, religious, and socio-political beliefs is likely to be profound. Coming to grips with a more scientifically-informed worldview that differs from one's own is likely to cause a substantial amount of anxiety and perhaps anger. It is for this reason that I believe ethicists, scientists and public policy makers need to think deeply about the consequences that may follow from radically adjusting our view of ourselves in light of new scientific findings. I am optimistic that a better understanding of ourselves will make for a better world. Nonetheless, for those of us willing to preach the moral anti-realist gospel, we may want to prepare for the worst in order to better deal with the existential growing pains that inevitably accompany increased self-knowledge.

Works Cited

Batson, C.D. (1990), "Affect and Altruism," In Moore, B.S. and Alice M. Isen (eds.), *Affect and Social Behavior*, 89-125, Cambridge: Cambridge University Press.

Blair, R.J.R., L. Jones, F. Clark, and M. Smith (1997), "The Psychopathic Individual: A Lack of Responsiveness to Distress Cues?" *Psychophysiology* 34: 192-198.

Crandall, J.E. (1978), "Effects of Threat and Failure on Concern for Others," *Journal of Research in Personality* 12: 350-360.

Ernst, Z. (2007), "The Liberationists' Attack On Moral Intuitions", *American Philosophical Quarterly* 44(2): 129-142.

Gazzaniga, M. and Stevens, M. (2005), "Neuroscience and the Law," *Scientific American Mind Magazine*, April: 43-49.

Greene, J. (forthcoming), *The Terrible, Horrible, No Good, Very Bad Truth about Morality and What to Do About It.* New York: Penguin Group.

Greene, J., R.B. Sommerville, L.E. Nystrom, J.M. Darley, and J.D. Cohen (2001), "An fMRI Investigation of Emotional Engagement in Moral Judgment," *Science* 293: 2105-2108.

Greene, J., L.E. Nystrom, A.D. Engell, J.M. Darley, and J.D. Cohen (2004), "The Neural Bases of Cognitive Conflict and Control in Moral Judgment," *Neuron* 44: 389-400.

Greene, J. and Cohen, J. (2004), "For the law, neuroscience changes nothing and everything," *Philosophical Transactions of the Royal Society of London B* 359: 1775-1785.

Haidt, J. (2001), "The Emotional Dog and Its Rational Tail: A Social Intuitionist Approach to Moral Judgment," *Psychological Review* 108(4): 814-834.

Hare, R.D. and M.J. Quinn (1971), "Psychopathy and Automatic Conditioning," *Journal of Abnormal Psychology* 77(3): 223-235.

Libet, B. (1985), "Unconscious cerebral initiative and the role of conscious will in voluntary action," *The Behavioral and Brain Sciences* 8: 529-566.

Mackie, J. (1977), *Ethics: Inventing Right and Wrong*. London: Penguin Books.

Markey, S. (2003), "Monkeys Show Sense of Fairness, Study Says," *Natural Geographic*, September 17. http://www.primates.com/monkeys/fairness.html (accessed February 28, 2007).

McDowell, J. (1998), *Mind, Value, and Reality*. Cambridge, MA: Harvard University Press.

Midlarsky, E. (1971), "Aiding Under Stress: The Effects of Competence, Dependence, Visibility, and Fatalism," *Journal of Personality* 39: 132-149.

Mill, J.S. (1863), *On Liberty*. Cambridge, MA: Harvard Press.

—. (1863), "Utilitarianism," In Pojman, L.P. (ed.), *Ethical Theory: Classical and Contemporary Readings*, 171-191, Belmont, CA: Wadsworth.

Moore, B. and Isen, A. (1990), "Affect and Social Behavior," In Moore, B.S. and Alice M. Isen (eds.), *Affect and Social Behavior*, 89-125, Cambridge: Cambridge University Press.

Nahmias, E. (2002). When consciousness matters: A critical review of Daniel Wegner's *The Illusion of Conscious Will. Philosophical Psychology,* 15(4), 527-542

Pinker, S. (2007), "The Mystery of Consciousness," *Time Magazine*, January 29: 58-70.

Ruse, M. and Wilson, E.O. (1984), "Moral philosophy as applied science", In Sober, E. (ed.), *Conceptual Issues in Evolutionary Biology*, 555-574, Boston: MIT Press.

Ruse, M. (1995), "Evolution and Ethics: The Sociobiological Approach," In Pojman, L.P. (ed.), *Ethical Theory: Classical and Contemporary Readings*, 91-122, Belmont, CA: Wadsworth.

Sayre-McCord, Geoffrey, ed. (1988), *Essays on Moral Realism*. Ithaca: Cornell University Press.

Sober, E., and Wilson, D.S. (1998), *Unto Others*. Cambridge, MA: Harvard Press.

Strawson, G. (1994). "The Impossibility of Moral Responsibility." *Philosophical Studies*, 75(1-2), 5-24.

Strawson, G. (1995), "Libertarianism, Action, and Self-Determination," In O'Connor, T. (ed.), *Agents, Causes, and Events*, 13-31, Oxford: Oxford University Press.

Underwood, B., J. Berenson, R. Berenson, K. Cheng, D. Wilson, J. Kulik, B. Moore, and G. Wenzel (1977), "Attention, Negative Affect, and Altruism: An Ecological Validation", *Personality and Social Psychology Bulletin* 3: 54-58.

Wegner, D. (2002), *The Illusion of Conscious Will.* Cambridge, MA: MIT Press.

Weyant, J.M. (1978), "Effects of mood states, costs, and benefits on helping," *Journal of Personality and Social Psychology* 36: 1169-1176.

Whitfield, J. (2003), "Monkeys strike for justice," *Nature Magazine*, September 18. http://www.bioedonline.org/news/news.cfm?art=524 (accessed February 28, 2007).

Notes

[1] I would like to thank J. Jeremy Wisnewski, Lacey Sischo and an anonymous referee for providing helpful comments on earlier drafts of this paper.

[2] By "moral truths", I am referring to alleged "facts"—such as "Lying is wrong"—that are believed to be grounded by the existence of moral properties such as wrongness. Denying the existence of such "facts" does not commit one to denying that there are truths (in the broad sense) about statements that employ moral concepts. After all, the sentence, "If killing is immoral then killing is immoral," is trivially true given a cognitivist understanding of statements employing moral terms.

[3] Sayre-McCord 5

[4] The word "ought" as it is used in prescriptive moral statements is to be distinguished from the non-moral variety of "ought" statements, such as those appearing in prudential "ought" statements. I elaborate on this distinction below.

[5] In building a case against moral realism that is metaphysical rather than linguistic in nature, I am following an approach similar to that taken by Mackie (1977).

[6] J.S. Mill agreed that our commonsense views of morality are tied to the idea of retributivist justice. As he says in *Utilitarianism*, "We do not call anything wrong,

unless we mean to imply that a person ought to be *punished* [my emphasis] in some way or another for doing it" (p. 187).
[7] Ibid.
[8] Strawson (1994) 9
[9] Ruse 103-104
[10] Ernst 138
[11] I am simply assuming here that external objects exist. Hence, I am leaving aside skeptical epistemological arguments to the contrary.
[12] Ernst 131
[13] Where this type of claim is taken to imply the kind of moral realism discussed earlier.
[14] For a more comprehensive account seeking to explain the evolution of moral behavior, see Sober and Wilson (1998).
[15] See Whitfield
[16] See Markey
[17] Greene forthcoming
[18] Greene et al. (2004) 398
[19] Ibid.
[20] Greene forthcoming
[21] Ruse 106
[22] Haidt 814
[23] Haidt 819
[24] Gazzaniga and Steven 44
[25] Strictly speaking, showing that human beings lack free will would not, by itself, constitute grounds for rejecting moral realism in the sense that is captured by Sayre-McCord's two theses that I discussed earlier. Although establishing that human beings are incapable of exercising free will would imply that there are no moral truths concerning human beings, this would not establish that there are no moral truths whatsoever. Since it may be possible for some non-human entity to have free will, it may be possible that there are moral facts concerning this hypothetical being. Nonetheless, since I am primarily concerned with moral realism insofar as it grounds our attitudes regarding the propriety of applying the retributivist model of justice to human beings, demonstrating that humans lack free will would suffice to validate my position. Put another way, I would be satisfied if my arguments warranted the rejection of the kind of moral realism which holds that there are moral truths about either human agents (e.g., Bob was an immoral man) or human actions (e.g., Bob's act of stealing is morally wrong).
[26] There is a virtual consensus among philosophers that an action issuing from one's free will requires that a conscious decision play some important causal role in producing the action in question. This holds true among compatibilists—i.e., those who maintain that free will is compatible with the truth of causal determinism—and incompatibilists—i.e., those who reject compatibilism—alike. Such is the view of Eddy Nahmias, a compatibilist, who mentions that philosophers "generally agree…that free will requires that our conscious deliberations make a difference in what we do" (p. 538). From the incompatibilist

perspective, Galen Strawson (1995) asserts that in order to exercise one's free will, it is necessary for one to be self-determining, which in turn requires that "what one does is indeed a result of one's *choices, decisions, and deliberations* [my emphasis]" (p. 14).

I grant that for one who denies that the causal efficacy of the conscious will constitutes a necessary condition for free will, the prospect that conscious decisions do not influence our actions will not be viewed as a threat to free will. Given that this is not the prevailing view among philosophers, however, I will not attempt to argue against it. For those who deny that free will requires an efficacious conscious decision, the case I make for moral anti-realism will depend on how persuasive they take my evolutionary arguments against moral realism to be.

[27] For what it is worth, I am not convinced that this account of moral realism can elude my previous attacks unscathed. In particular, if there is no free will then there seems to be no way to preserve the kind of moral realism that concerns me in any shape or form. At any rate, a proponent of the "secondary quality account" of moral realism would seem obliged to explain how moral truths pertaining to humans and their actions could stand tall in the face of no human freedom. My incredulity aside, I will assume for the sake of argument that the secondary quality account of moral realism can withstand the arguments I have provided to this point.

[28] McDowell 136

[29] For an argument as to why the color-value analogy does not hold, see Greene (forthcoming).

[30] McDowell 133

[31] Putting the concerns I have raised here another way, why should we believe that our actual moral judgments—which are presumably the *accidental* products of evolution—have a better claim to being true than the kind of moral judgments discussed in my thought experiment, which are the *accidental* products of a lab experiment? My suspicion is that any explanation for why "normal" moral judgments are more real than the drug-induced moral judgments would have to appeal to something other than a disposition to give rise to subjective experiences. The only option available for McDowell here would seem to be an appeal to some kind of primary quality inherent to objects that would justify the first type of moral judgments only. Of course, this would undermine the very thing that McDowell has set out to do, which is to establish the existence of moral properties without having to rely on primary qualities.

[32] Greene forthcoming

[33] Thus, we see how fundamental disagreements about right and wrong have sparked many of the global conflicts that we see today. The struggle, for instance, between certain Islamic factions and the United States can be seen as being the result of differing value systems (e.g., religious versus secular) that shape opinions about right and wrong.

[34] From this point on, it is necessary to distinguish between two senses of the term "moral." Given that at this point in the paper I am assuming that moral realism is

false, I will not be using the term "moral" in referring to behavior that is *moral* in the realist sense, unless otherwise indicated. Instead, I will be using this term to refer to behavior that is consistent with the kinds of actions that are encouraged by traditional moral realist standards. In making this distinction, I am essentially following the approach taken by Greene (forthcoming) in which he distinguishes between the terms *moral*[1]--which relates to facts concerning right and wrong—and *moral*[2]--which relates to either promoting or not infringing upon the interests of others. Greene is correct in asserting that a moral anti-realist can consistently believe that there are reasons for behaving in accordance with *morality*[2] even if she rejects the existence of *morality*[1]. I will be using the terms "moral" and "ethical" interchangeably in referring to *moral*[2].

[35] Greene forthcoming. In saying this, Greene is not claiming that utilitarianism is an inherently anti-realist doctrine. He is merely suggesting that in light of an anti-realist world view, it makes sense to employ a kind of utilitarian calculus when deciding among potential actions and policies. As I discuss below, Greene's justification in doing so derives from subjective desires rather than objective moral truths.

[36] Greene forthcoming

[37] At this point, one might claim that skepticism about free will—a position that both Greene and I accept—renders moot any discussion concerning whether the global adoption of moral anti-realism would negatively impact society. I can think of two reasons why one might make this claim. The first is based on the view that an absence of free will for human beings eliminates the possibility that there can be anything of value for people. Thus, the question of what would result from accepting moral-realism loses its import since nothing at all would seem to matter. In response to this nihilistic conclusion, I would simply point out that while the impossibility of free will may very well eliminate the possibility of *moral* value, there are other types of value that seem unaffected one way or another by free will. The subjective value that I attach to eating chocolate, to take a mundane example, would not be diminished one iota if there was no free will in human beings. To argue otherwise would require one to defend an account of value that is highly counterintuitive.

Another reason that could be given for why one might believe that skepticism about free will makes it pointless to consider the impact that moral anti-realism might have on the world is that, without free will, it is simply pointless to worry about how people will behave. The operating assumption here would be the fatalistic view that since people are without free will, their destinies have already been set. This being the case, any attempts to alter people's behavior would be futile. Furthermore, since we can't change that which is inevitable, the argument goes, there is no sense worrying about what will happen.

In responding to this view, I would point out that we clearly *can* influence people's behavior through our actions. While it may be true that the future has already been determined, it is virtually certain that this future will be determined, in part, by what you and I do. Given that this is true, it does not seem futile to discuss what may occur in the future, and how we might shape the future to suit our interests. Going back to the issue of whether the widespread adoption of moral anti-realism would be devastating for the human race, it may be a determined fact that by discussing the variety of scenarios that might occur, we will come upon answers that will prevent the acceptance of moral anti-realism from having a negative impact. The possibility that this might occur is reason to deny that a lack of free will provides reason to refrain from considering future events and how we can influence the behaviors of others.

[38] Greene forthcoming

[39] Ibid.

[40] Moore and Isen 18.

[41] This may be especially true among those whose religious beliefs are threatened by scientific findings.

[42] Nor, one might add, are my assertions that far off from J.S. Mill's version of utilitarianism given our shared emphasis on the general happiness. While this is true to some extent, there is an important distinction between the pragmatic course that I recommend for ethicists and the position put forth by Mill. Whereas the anti-realist position I favor sets out to attach us to the welfare of others via strictly prudential considerations, the language Mill uses indicates that he takes our attachment to others to be of a genuinely moral nature. Remarks he makes in both *On Liberty* and *Utilitarianism* provide strong evidence that he subscribes to the kind of moral realism that I reject (i.e., the kind that is intimately tied to retributive justice). In *On Liberty*, for instance, he states that, "If anyone does an act harmful to others, there is a *prima facie* case for punishing him" (p. 25). The same sentiment is expressed in the quote in *Utilitarianism* mentioned earlier in which Mill states, "We do not call anything wrong, unless we mean to imply that a person ought to be punished in some way or another for doing it" (p. 187). Furthermore, the fact that Mill places an emphasis upon moral as opposed to strictly prudential considerations is apparent when he states in *Utilitarianism*, "As between his own happiness and that of others, utilitarianism requires him to be as strictly impartial as a disinterested and benevolent spectator" (p. 178).

MONTESQUIEU AND THE ENGLISH COMMON LAW

KYLE SCOTT
UNIVERSITY OF NORTH FLORIDA

> But one must not always so exhaust a subject that one leaves nothing for the reader to do. It is not a question of making him read but of making him think.
> —Montesquieu

Montesquieu gives us a text which discusses law, jurisprudence, constitutional design, and government institutions; to name just a few of the topics. What is peculiar about this text is that he neglects to mention the English common law. Since the English constitution takes center stage in *The Spirit of the Laws*, and for those who study the text, it is important to know what Montesquieu says about the English constitution and why he says it.[1] Since he sets out on an examination of the English constitution, and celebrates its protection of liberty, it is not clear why he omits a discussion of the English common law in his discussion of the English constitution given the prominent role the common law plays in defining the constitution. While some have noticed that this omission occurs, and note the importance of investigating further, no one has taken up the task of doing so.[2]

The obvious subject of study for Montesquieu scholars is his treatment of the law and what structure of government is best suited for protecting liberty. The secondary literature on Montesquieu prior to 1960 tended to be a description of his theory in an effort to make a sizeable and complex text more manageable.[3] Later efforts tried to uncover the method of Montesquieu's writing and the plan of his book in order to understand it as a cohesive whole.[4] What these writers found is that Montesquieu had a particular style of writing that left the inattentive reader to conclude that there was no plan to his book, when in actuality, to uncover the plan was to uncover the teaching. These writers taught that one must reconcile the contradictions, understand the silences, and make sense of the order if one was to understand Montesquieu's teaching. While these writers do not fully agree among themselves what Montesquieu's teaching is; they each agree that he had a style of writing that was intended to make the reader think, rather than merely read. It is fair to classify Paul Carrese as a proponent of this method of Montesquieu analysis as he tends to focus on the cloaking of judicial power, and draws our attention to Montesquieu's silence on the common law in the English system.[5] In addition, Isaiah Berlin recognized this omission long before Carrese wrote, and recommended that the reader take note of this silence on the common law.[6] However, Berlin and Carrese each stop their discussion of the absence of the common law in Montesquieu when they make mention of its absence and do not investigate what the absence might mean.

A more recent article on Montesquieu has attributed his silence on the common law to an oversight and thus represents Montesquieu's misunderstanding of the English judiciary and therefore undercuts his entire theory on separation of powers.[7] "Montesquieu did not appreciate the nature of the English common law and the mechanism that its doctrine of precedent established for authoritative judicial exposition of existing laws."[8] Unlike Claus, I do not think Montesquieu made a mistake. But rather, his treatment of the judiciary and silence on the common law gives us insight into his political theory and his ambition to make the judiciary a vehicle for moderate reform.[9] Claus thinks he has uncovered a fatal flaw in Montesquieu and seeks to expose that flaw. I, on the other hand, consider Montesquieu to have been a careful writer whose genius is matched by only a few in the history of Western political thought.[10] While I do not want to make Montesquieu an idol, I do not look to make him a fool either. My project—which is to understand Montesquieu's political philosophy more fully—may be less ambitious than Claus's—who set out to expose Montesquieu and his errors—I do not think the project is less valuable.

The argument made throughout this essay is that Montesquieu's omission can teach us something as the omission must have been intentional as he was made aware of the centrality of the common law to the English constitution during his travels in England and through his association with Bolingbroke.[11] Those who brush aside his silence on the common law by saying that he did not intend to give an exhaustive treatment of England, or that he made a mistake, underestimate the ability of selection bias to convey a message. Silence on a central component of his idealized system should provoke questions, not dismissals. While this paper puts forth explanations for why the silence occurs, I should find it beneficial if all the reader is persuaded by is that Montesquieu's silence was intentionally meaningful.

Most studies of Montesquieu, including the studies already cited, focus on his teaching with regard to the separation of powers, the purpose and meaning of law, or the role of moderation in the creation and maintenance of liberty. Sharon Krause has emerged as one of the preeminent Montesquieu scholars. Krause's work has investigated the nuances of his thought, but most of the work comes back to the separation of powers, its role in maintaining liberty, and the centrality of England in these lessons. Few can object that Book XI.6 has emerged as a favorite of those who study Montesquieu. Krause is one of the few who take the proposition seriously that Montesquieu does not hold England to be the ideal model, but instead, England serves as another example Montesquieu uses to teach his readers.[12] Krause argues that Montesquieu sees English liberty as extreme, and Montesquieu abhors extremism, thus reinforcing the point that liberty is maintained through moderation.[13] England, according to Krause, is a model of the limits of a system of separate powers combined with extreme liberty. This point is not lost on Jacob Levy who also recognizes the limits of the English model as expressed by Montesquieu.[14] An entire volume of collected essays focuses on these themes.[15] Each essay in this volume, in its own way, investigates the connection between institutions, law, and liberty in Montesquieu.[16] Thus, the parameters for a discussion on Montesquieu have been set by those who have come before. Any study of Montesquieu must treat the themes of liberty, law, and institutions, with some eye to the role of moderation as the sinew that binds these concepts.

This paper builds on the work of Isaiah Berlin and Paul Carrese who recognize the omission of the common law in Montesquieu, and also on the work of Sharon Krause who suggests that Montesquieu may not hold England with as much reverence as has been traditionally thought. This paper suggests that the omission of the common law in the *Spirit of the Laws* is an indication of the role he gives to the judiciary in his ideal system. Montesquieu seeks to make the judiciary a vehicle for moderate reform. In order to be effective the method by which this type of reform is to be carried out would have to be out of public sight in order to not disrupt customs and traditions, nor undermine the legitimacy of the law. The English jurist, if removed from his common law restraints but were left to remain in the English institutional arrangement, provided the perfect method for achieving these ends.

Section I: Common Law Reasoning

The common law is grounded in canonical law, natural law, customs, history, parliamentary law and King's Law. The common law courts were charged with the duty of deciding cases in accord with all of these categories. This makes the job of judges quite difficult, and for researchers searching for a clear understanding of its origin and definition the task is equally difficult. Common law scholars, such as Lord Coke, often accept the maxim that the rules of common law have been in existence since time immemorial. Therefore, Lord Coke made the argument that judges were in a unique position to make decisions at common law.

Coke's writings are often considered the embodiment of the common law. His authority was so strong that later commentators have written, "that it is useless to contend that 'he was either misled by his sources or unconsciously misinterpreted them,' for Coke's mistakes, it is said, are the common law."[17]

In one instance of judicial review, Coke came into direct conflict with the king's order. In reaction to Coke's writs of prohibition against ecclesiastical courts from taking equity claims, the Archbishop of Canterbury appealed to the king's authority. Coke denied the Archbishop's claim and in his decision said that judges had the necessary reason to make such decisions. King James replied that he and others had reason, and that reason was not a trait of common law judges alone and therefore the writ of prohibitions should be repealed. In reply to James, Coke wrote in *Prohibitions del Roy*

> His majesty was not learned in the laws of his realm of England, and causes which concern the life, or goods, or fortunes of his subjects, are not to be decided by natural reason, but by the artificial reason and judgment of law, which law is an act which requires long study and experience, before that a man can attain to the cognizance of it.[18]

Needless to say James was not pleased, but at this time Coke escaped reprimand. But, Coke did not stop making comments to this effect, nor was he the only common law jurist to make such statements. Another common jurist said that, "The common law is a reasonable usage throughout the whole realm approved time out of mind in the King's court of record which have jurisdiction over the whole kingdom, to be good and profitable for the commonwealth."[19]

Therefore, one of the reasons judges hold the unique position of being the interpreters of the common law is because they possess the necessary training and knowledge which reflects the artificial reason found in common law. Coke gives support to this argument by saying, "The Law is like a deep well, and he that reacheth deepest sees the amiable and admirable secrets of the Law, wherein the Sages of the Law in ancient Times have had the deepest Reach"[20] In this statement one can see the inductive process which animates common law reasoning. Understanding the common law, and Coke's take on it particularly, requires that one understand the thought process of a common law jurist in order to understand how the common law differs from positive law. The reason of jurists, and the reason of the common law, is artificial reason. That it is artificial does not make it a false kind of reason, but a reason that is unique to common law jurists and the common law. "The law, to Coke, is thus a science in something like the Aristotelian sense of practical science, joining reason and knowledge of particulars, yet contained not in books as a body of knowledge but in the minds of those who can use it."[21] To this, Stoner adds, "the most significant principle in Coke's understanding of the law is his insistence upon the equation of law and reason…"[22] This is a common point found in Stoner, perhaps the most authoritative political theorist on matters of common law in addition to Paul Carrese, who in another instance writes

> The common law proceeds by reason, but by reason that collects and judges particulars—by a sort of Aristotelian practical reason—rather than by reason in the modern, Enlightenment, analytical sense—the reason that breaks apart and reassembles. It stresses continuity rather than novelty, though it demands some reason greater than custom alone, for by common law, unreasonable customs have no legal force.[23]

Because of the process by which judges make their decisions, and the training and experience which they draw upon in making their decisions, the common law is reason. But it is a reason that respects the changing demands and needs of the society in which it serves. Precedents are a guide to show what has been done before, but they are not binding on a judge since facts change and each case deserves its own unique treatment. But, as more opinions are made, and the experience and training of judges culminates in successive opinions, the knowledge of the law improves as it begins to reflect the reason of men who respect law and tradition. On this point Coke writes in Part I of the *Institutes*

> For reason is the life of the Law, nay the Common Law itself is nothing else but reason, which is to be understood of an artificial perfection of reason gotten by long study, observation and experience and not every man's natural reason…This legal reason is the highest reason…And therefore if all the reason that is dispersed into so many several heads were

> united into one, yet could he not make such a Law as the Law of England is, because by many succession of ages it hath been fined and refined by an infinite number of grave and learned men, and by long experience grown to such a perfection for the government of this real, as the old rule may be justly verified of it…No man (out of his own private reason) ought to be wiser than the Law, which is the perfection of reason.[24]

Artificial reason is manufactured by men, but not from first principles, from experience with human affairs. The common law, with its artificial reason, is a fusion of reason and experience in which neither is the final authority. "Reason is not original and comprehensive; rather, it takes what is given and works upon it, improves it. It does this by bringing to bear no logic alone, but logic together with wide learning. The reason Coke appeals to is not a theoretical but a practical faculty. It is certainly not mere discretion, but neither is it logic devoid of experience. It is a trained way of thinking, not arbitrary but also not apodictic."[25]

Even though this complex system seems to defy simple categorization, scholars have not stopped trying to categorize it. The six components of artificial reason as seen by Gerald Postema are: (1) it is *pragmatic* as it focused on practical problem-solving, (2) it has a *public mission* which means it seeks to solve problems with the public in mind, (3) artificial reason is *contextual*, which means judges had knowledge of experience and study, not abstract principles, (4) because it is practical and not theoretic, artificial reason is *non-systematic*, "On this view, the law is to be found in the accumulated experience recorded in the books and memories of common law jurists, not in any theory, or articulation of this experience. Law is practice, not a theoretical representation of it."[26], (5) artificial reason is *discursive*, meaning, arguments were made about the law prior to the facts being introduced which led to a deliberative reasoning and argument about the law, (6) artificial reason, like the common law in general, is *common*, which means "it was the practice of public forensic argument, situated and moving about in a world of recorded experience of 'human affairs and conversation'."[27] Therefore, for Postema—who puts forth a position similar Stoner's—Coke's artificial reason is called artificial not because, "it rests on some special insight or intuition vouchsafed only to those initiated into the professional mysteries, but rather because it is the disciplined practice of argument and disputation in a public forum…It is 'artificial' in the sense of being the product of reflective practical experience, as opposed to untutored individual intuition or a natural capacity for deductive reasoning exercised in abstraction from the concrete details of ordinary life."[28]

To put simply and in more modern terms, common law exists when precedents are used to identify law. This is quite different from the Oliver Wendell Holmes, Jr. formulation. Holmes considers common law to be judge made law—as do most modern American and English textbooks on the subject—therefore precedent creates common law. The more traditional approach says that precedents reveal common law. Precedents are used as a guide to indicate to judges what the previous path has been, as justice demands that similar cases be treated in similar ways. Judges in the common law tradition do not make law; they discover it through a systematic search and application of precedent. The law exists independent of the judiciary.[29] James Stoner, in refutation of the Holmesian definition of the common law, says "Common law emphasizes assent rather than domination, the community rather than the state, moral authority rather than physical power."[30] This is the clearest distinction between traditional common law and the way it is currently adapted in America. Traditional common law cannot be policy-oriented as it is an inductive process. For something to be positivist it must have a specified ends; a common law jurist has no ends beyond resolving the dispute immediately before him. This means that judges in the traditional common law system are not, and cannot, be advocates of reform as their vision does not extend past what is immediately in front of them.

Common law respects custom, tradition, and history. This is understood if one briefly reflects on the principle of precedent. Precedent requires that a judge and jury consult past decisions, and it is those past decisions that embody a community's custom, tradition, and history. A fusion of custom and law is the foundation on which common law was built, "Yet Anglo-Norman records and legislation do not support such a tripartite division. Customs are either more local or notably unvaried... Such was a further step...towards the fusion of various elements into a common law."[31] John Hudson goes on to say later in the same chapter that, "Together with the inheritances of custom and strong kingship from the Anglo-Saxon and Norman periods, these combined to form the common law."[32] Similarly, the reader of Montesquieu sees support the idea of custom in judging and lawmaking when he writes, "The monarch, who knows each of his provinces, can set up various laws or permit different customs. But the despot knows nothing and can attend to nothing; he must approach everything in a general way..."[33] What separates a Montesquieu jurist from a common law jurist is that for Montesquieu the judge ought to be an advocate of reform, albeit moderate reform.

Book XIX of *SL* specifically addresses the need to respect a nation's general spirit, mores, and manners when one aims to reform the laws of a nation. In Chapter 4 Montesquieu says "Many things govern men: climate, religion, laws, the maxims of the government, examples of past things, mores, and manners; a general spirit is formed as a result."[34] Then Chapter 5 goes on to explain "how careful one must be not to change the general spirit of a nation."[35] The rest of Book XIX is the advice of Montesquieu to rulers who seek reform, with the primary lesson being "…when a prince wants to make great changes in his nation, he must reform by laws what is established by laws and change manners what is established by manners…"[36] Montesquieu directly states that custom should be used to supplement the written law, and where written law is silent custom should be the guide. Although, as will be seen, Montesquieu shows how one can reform manners without laws. Therefore, what at first might appear as a respect for manners and mores is simply advice for the would-be reformer that certain things need to be changed in some way other than legislation in order not to upset the local mores and customs and also to preserve moderation.[37]

Montesquieu's agenda includes a lesson on reform. He advocates a new role for judges by making them reformers. This is distinct from the common law tradition. By relying so heavily on the British model, and leaving out the common law, Montesquieu is suggesting that the British model is in need of revision. Common law jurists are too passive for Montesquieu's purposes.

Section II: Potential Meaning of the Silence

For Montesquieu the nucleus of his system is the power of judging and laws. The importance that Montesquieu gives to laws and judging is what makes an omission of the common law in Books XI and XII so mysterious. For Montesquieu reform is to be brought about by the judiciary, a judiciary that also respects history and customs, but not because history and customs have an intrinsic value, but because of their utility in efforts of reform and the potential disruption that could occur if a nation was taken too quickly away from its history and customs. The common law is not discussed by Montesquieu because of his ambivalence to speak directly to the desirability of having the power to reform in the hands of judges and because the common law proper could not be exported to other countries due to its reliance on history and custom.

Sharon Krause boldly explores the possibility that England is not Montesquieu's ideal model, and that Montesquieu has reservations about the extreme liberty of England. There is certainly no disputing the point that Montesquieu abhors extremism, even extreme liberty. I suggest in the following subsections that Montesquieu's commitment to the English model is stronger than Krause recognizes. What is missing in Krause's analysis is a discussion of the common law. It is certainly true that the picture presented in Book XI.6 appears to be extreme, but in fact that is because the judiciary is absent from the discussion.

Section IIA: Reform, Moderation, and Judiciary

Certainly a judge is not intrinsically objectionable, and neither is reform. So why Montesquieu considers reform at the hands of the judiciary to be a teaching that needs to be presented in a discreet fashion is not altogether clear. While I disagree with Berlin's conclusions, his observations on this point are invaluable. Berlin correctly points out that Montesquieu's goal is to create, "unvarying, everlasting rules."[38] But Berlin identifies a tension in Montesquieu which he considers unresolved. Montesquieu seeks the creation of laws that are grounded in history but also adaptable to changing needs or recognition of past errors. For Berlin the two extremes of this tension are relativism as embodied by Oliver Wendell Holmes, Jr. and traditionalism as embodied by Edmund Burke. For Berlin's Montesquieu the law cannot be modified but only overhauled. That is, when a law is found to be a violation of justice it must be thrown out. Following Hume on this point, Berlin's Montesquieu allows for no other conclusion but the, "chopping and changing of laws, and a new law specifically created by the legislative organ."[39] This method of legal change will lead to a continual weakening of the law by undermining its authority. Oddly enough, Berlin cites the common law tradition as seeming deeply abhorrent to Montesquieu. According to this section, and in fact this entire essay, it seems more reasonable to conclude that the judiciary allows for legal reform outside the direct view of the people. With reform via judiciary, as described by Montesquieu, history can be respected and laws can be changed without undermining the legitimacy of either. His silence is purposeful not because he is promoting anything inherently evil, but because his theory, if known by all, would lose its effectiveness. In crude terms, the judiciary helps to maintain the myth of the law. And what good is a myth if no one believes?[40]

Harvey Mansfield also explores the possibility of the hidden judge and why it is advantageous to keep the reform out of the sight of the people and to keep the power of judging hidden. "The detached judge who embodies the law and justice must be rendered as it were invisible and null, because the standard he enforces (ancient virtue) is too high or too low (modern fatality)...the opinion each has of his own security must be sheltered from the reason of judges who might demand too much from us, or who might remind us of our insignificance."[41] Mansfield concludes that the power of judging is given to the people in order to avoid these problems. I think Mansfield reads too literally Montesquieu's commitment to juries on this matter, and does not treat seriously enough Montesquieu's silence on the common law. Making assumptions about why an author does something can be risky, but I think it is safe to say that he treats the judiciary in *The Spirit of the Laws* in the same way he would like to see the judiciary operate. That is, he wants to show that the judiciary should operate out of the direct sight of the public, and to some degree the other branches.

Montesquieu remarks that "the masterwork of legislation is to know where to properly place the power of judging."[42] However, this statement about the judiciary is not the norm in Montesquieu's treatment of the judiciary; in fact, he makes his commitment to the judiciary less clear than some readers may like. He does not make his vision for the judiciary explicit. Book XI deals with the power of judging in England, but places the power of judging in various departments. The division of the judging power does not become clear to the reader who focuses exclusively on Book XI.6. While he says that the power of judging becomes "invisible and null" when in the hands of the jury, he says nothing of the judiciary being null, and he leaves the question open as to whether the judiciary should be invisible.[43]

Montesquieu gives a hint to the "visibility" of the judiciary in Book XIX.27 when he refers to the two visible powers. This reference is directed at the English constitution and the discussion in Book XI, "I have spoken in Book 11 of a free people, and I have given the principles of their constitution…in this state there would be two visible powers, the legislative power and the executive power…"[44] But when one goes back to Book XI to gain some insight into his vision of the judiciary, one notices that he does not mention "visible powers" per se, but he does make an effort to mask the judiciary. As Book XI progresses, the judiciary becomes conspicuously absent, as the three powers discussed in the opening chapters of Book XI, executive, legislative, and judiciary, become the executive and the two houses of the legislature. This point is not lost on Claus either. In fact Claus criticizes Montesquieu for not understanding the English model and the role the House of Lords served in the common law system.

"Apart from ignoring the Lords' jurisdiction to entertain appeals in civil disputes, Montesquieu failed to recognize that the Lords' decisions might change the common law."[45] Montesquieu did recognize this power, but did not comment on it directly. If Claus were not so concerned with correcting Montesquieu he would see that Montesquieu was referring to the House of Lords when he converts the three powers into two visible powers. By splitting the judiciary among traditional judges, juries, and members of parliament the power of judging is dispersed and hard to identify, if not invisible. That is, Montesquieu's method of separation of powers for the government in general is replicated in his discussion of judging. Moreover, by placing judicial power in the hands of the parliament, such as in the English model, reform through the judiciary is possible. But since the House of Lords only had appellate jurisdiction the reform could be moderated.[46] The English constitution is held to be the ideal by Montesquieu for a reason, and not because he misunderstood his subject.

Montesquieu makes other comments about the positive attributes of the judiciary. In his discussion of Saint Louis, there are a few passages in which Montesquieu openly addresses the role of the judiciary, he makes it clear that the judiciary is the proper institution to rely on as it is more in accord with the mores and traditions of a society, and it is typically less biased than any of the other branches.

> When one saw in his tribunals, and in those of the lords, a more natural, more reasonable way of proceeding, a way more in conformity with morality, religion, public tranquility, and the security of persons and goods, it was taken up and the other was abandoned.[47]

In Book II Montesquieu remarks that having an independent judiciary can prevent despotism. In fact, so long as the laws are protected and there is no infringement on the laws by the government, any form of government will do, but the judiciary is the only branch which can safely protect the rule of law.

> It is not enough to have intermediate ranks in a monarchy; there must also be a depository of laws. This depository can only be in the political bodies, which announce the laws when they are made and recall them when they are forgotten...In despotic states, where there are no fundamental laws, neither is there a depository of laws.[48]

The power of the judiciary is that it ensures the rule of law by providing a check on other government branches. The judiciary is naturally moderate, and its moderate tendency will permeate the rest of the government allowing for liberty to flourish.

> The bodies that are the depository of the laws never obey better than when they drag their feet and bring into the prince's business the reflection that

> one can hardly expect from the absence of enlightenment in the court concerning the laws of the state and the haste of the prince's councils.[49]

While none of the three powers is insignificant for Montesquieu's system of governance, it is the judiciary which has the most crucial role. It is the protector of the rule of law, and prevents a backslide into despotism.[50]

The judiciary works because it preserves the positive features of the nobility which existed in the English monarchy. The nobility tied the nation to its past and prevented radical change from the top or the bottom. It served as an anchor which resulted in moderate change.

> Intermediate, subordinate, and dependent powers constitute the nature of monarchical government, that is, of the government in which one alone governs by fundamental laws...The most natural intermediate, subordinate power is that of the nobility. In a way, the nobility is of the essence of monarchy, whose fundamental maxim is: no monarch, no nobility; no nobility no monarch; rather, one has a despot.[51]

This same role is served by the judiciary in Book XXVIII when Montesquieu traces the principle of *stare decisis* back to the Goths. While there was no guarantee that the nobility would serve as that anchor, a judiciary constructed in the manner which Montesquieu advises, would serve as the anchor, as it was through scientifically derived principles that he created the philosophical basis for its practical application. Furthermore, while the virtue of men cannot be relied upon to counteract and preserve liberty in a monarchy, republic, or democracy; a system that balances and divides the formal power of the government will combat the tendency of men and their agencies to expand their power and test the bounds of their authority. For Montesquieu there is much that can go wrong in a system that does not have an extensive set of regulations governing the actions of men, history, or nature; which leads him to devise a system which leaves little to chance and does not rely on virtue. It is not the institution or the system which is the novel innovation in Montesquieu's work; it is placing man above those effects of nature and history, putting man in a position to control his own fortune.

Section IIB: Common Law without the Common Law Name

Even if one rejects the claim that Montesquieu was not an advocate of a reform minded judiciary, one can still accept my second proposition that

Montesquieu did not want to mention the English common law given that it is not universally applicable. The common law in another country would be incomprehensible given its commitment to precedent. It would be impossible for one country to adopt the judicial precedents of another. The common law proper could not be instituted in any other country that was not colonized by England. One could imagine the resistance that his theory would have encountered in his native France—and elsewhere—if he had advocated for a dismissal of all French precedent in favor of English common law. Moreover, Montesquieu would not have condoned such a radical innovation. By treating the common law in the manner he did he was able to create a system that could be universally adopted.

Roman law tended towards centralization and Gothic law tended towards decentralization, and the competition between these two tendencies, present during the reign of Louis IX, led to a moderate regime. It appears that the centralizing tendency of Roman law is present in England, as it is the written component of Roman law that causes the centralization because written law must be universal and simple.[52] Montesquieu relies on England's Gothic heritage to counteract this tendency. And while France shares a similar Roman and Gothic heritage, no two histories are identical. Montesquieu hints that the common law proper would not work in France when he discusses the customs in France.[53] The path he traces of the civil laws among the French is quite similar to the path followed in England. Roman right and Germanic customs are as much a part of the French system as the English, but each country developed a different system of law despite having similar legal histories.

Montesquieu wants to develop a theory that is applicable to all nations.[54] For his plan to be successful he recognizes that different conditions demand different treatment.[55] While all may bow before his principles, Montesquieu is under no illusion that common law proper is applicable to all circumstances.[56] So while a common law system may be desirable, it may not always be practical. The common law is dependent upon, and developed through, England's history, traditions, and customs. It is a system of law nested within the cultural norms and formal institutions of England. Even though norms cannot be exported, institutions and principles can, and once adopted the new institutions can gradually institute reforms without being destructive.

The omission of the common law reinforces one of the most important teachings of the text: the development and adaptation of the law must be one which conforms to the society in such a way that it can give to a particular society what it needs to establish a moderate regime whose end is liberty. Thus, to assert that the English constitution including the common law is universal would be contrary to Montesquieu's thesis. The institutional structure of the English system could be implemented without upsetting the history and customs of a nation, particularly in new nations. And, countries that cannot replicate the institutions of the English model should, according to Montesquieu, adopt the principle of moderate reform that preserve both custom and the rule of law. This point is best illustrated through his discussion of Saint Louis.

Section III: A Role Model for Would-Be Reformers

Montesquieu's book is filled with examples of what to do and what not to do. The English model is the one most commentators take to be representative of his theory. Should the lesson be so easily taught then it would hardly seem necessary to write such a large text. I fully understand that there are space limitations that every study encounters. In this Section I try to convince the reader that there is another example equally deserving of study. Saint Louis does not provide a complete picture, but when it is studied in light of the comments made thus far about the English constitution it becomes clear that Saint Louis is a necessary component to uncovering the teaching of Book XI.6. Because the discussion of judging and reform are kept separate in the text, the design of the text reinforces in the reader's mind that the two should be kept separate in practice. But, as argued above, a fresh look at the two concepts shows they should be placed together conceptually and, according to Montesquieu, in practice. Saint Louis provides an example of how moderate reform can be achieved through legal institutions and that such reform preserves both the "mores and manners" and the legitimacy of the laws.

Montesquieu's positive view of the Germanic tradition is undeniable. The German tribes were dedicated to the principle of liberty. "The German nations who conquered the Roman Empire were very free, as is known."[57] Moreover, England, which was widely praised for its protection of liberty, had "taken their idea of political government from the Germans. This fine system was found in the forests."[58] This is indeed high praise for the Germanic tribes. The Roman law balanced Germanic law by bringing order and reason to it. Montesquieu shows how Germanic law and Roman law were combined under the rule of Saint Louis IX, who Montesquieu must have considered a good legislator since he was able to implement reform without disturbing the existing customs; and separated the power of judging from the other branches.[59]

Saint Louis took over a state in shambles; the rule of law was unclear; so too was the future of the state and the path it would take. The Germanic laws eventually became the basis for the French civil procedure. Prior to the rule of Saint Louis IX, the French courts adopted the practice of defending one's self by swearing an evangelical oath, against which there was no recourse in civil law, save for a test of endurance. The test of endurance rested on such things as combat or withstanding the burns from fire or boiling water. Such tests proved the authenticity of the defendant's claims as it would be only through God's power that they would be able to withstand the tests of endurance, and God would only support those whose oaths were truthful. This system is quite some distance from German procedure that had a trial by jury and an adversarial system. This again illustrates the point of what Montesquieu meant when he said "our fathers…constantly used proof that did not prove and that were linked neither to innocence nor the crime."[60]

When his reign began, Louis instituted reforms, reforms that would bring stability to the system through balance and moderation. The balance and moderation would be the result of a reformed justice system that would include Roman and Gothic law. The success of Louis's reforms was due to the gradual manner in which they were implemented. He did not eliminate the traditions and customs that already existed; instead he adapted new laws that would gently guide the traditions and customs. He integrated the new provisions with the old customs. Saint Louis took to making reforms through a trial and error approach. While he maintained a view of the big picture, he was not constrained by a single pedagogy. Montesquieu praises Saint Louis since this is the method of reform that Montesquieu endorses.[61] The method and target of Louis's reforms is the model for a prudent legislator who could implant reason and moderation in the laws. His method was subtle and gradual, "so that the change would be felt less," Saint Louis "removed the thing and let the terms continue to exist."[62] Louis was able to be successful, and held in such high regard by Montesquieu, for following the natural tendency of things, best exhibited in custom, and now in good rulers.

Saint Louis learned of the Roman law from the newly recovered Institutes of Justinian.[63] Saint Louis was able to accomplish something through moderate reform that the Romans were unable to do by force, which was, to institute Roman law in a land that was dominated by local custom and barbaric laws, while still preserving the spirit of the people.[64] One of his methods for injecting Roman law was so subtle that it could hardly be considered a reform. In order to persuade the men who practiced law he had the Roman laws translated so that they could be better understood by these men, it was through this process that there grew distaste for French law, and an affinity for Roman law.[65] The result was that the men who practiced and made the laws would perpetuate the reforms gradually as they unobtrusively influenced others. "There was an internal vice in this compilation: it formed an amphibious code, in which were mixed French jurisprudence and Roman law; things were brought together that had never been related and that were often contradictory."[66]

The aim of Book XXVIII is to draw the reader's attention to the balancing tendency of opposing forces when applied correctly, and the necessity of these opposing forces being present in order to achieve moderation. The success of Saint Louis ended when the adopted Roman law was allowed to proceed unconstrained. The aspects of Roman law that were subsequently adopted were from the Roman Empire, not the Roman Republic. This law limited the number of safeguards that were present in the French jurisprudence that had been adopted from the German tribes, whose goal was always to promote liberty. What made Saint Louis successful was his recognition of the need to balance liberty with stability, which he provided in the form of Roman law. But if stability is not balanced with liberty, then a system of restraint takes over at the cost of liberty.[67] French jurisprudence turned into a system, "which was employed everywhere…to regulate, limit, correct, and extend French jurisprudence."[68] The extension of Roman law led to a deterioration of both ancient Frankish law and Gothic customary procedures.[69]

Montesquieu makes the point clear that "the excess even of reason is not always desirable; and that men almost always accommodate themselves better in middles than extremes."[70] In Book XXII Montesquieu, through examples of Roman law, shows that "extreme laws for good produce extreme evil."[71] Reason and good must be moderated, and the pursuit of extreme reason and extreme good do not bring about positive ends. "I say it, and it seems to me that I have written this work only to prove it: the spirit of moderation should be that of the legislator; the political good, like the moral good, is always found between two limits."[72] Moderation cannot be found in Rome or the woods of the Germanic tribes. In Rome there were many extremes, including an unchecked pursuit of material interest that can hinder the protection of liberty. "This caused all honest means of borrowing and lending to be abolished in Rome, and a frightful usury, was repeatedly crushed only to rise again, became established."[73] Also, the Romans were too restrictive in their development and organization of the law. While they provided some checks to prevent the negative outcomes, the checks failed, especially when the Roman system was adopted by other countries. This is best exhibited by what

Montesquieu says happened in France after the reign of Louis IX when Roman law went unchecked.

Montesquieu clearly states that the Gothic system was, "the best kind of government men have been able to devise."[74] But, there are clearly problems with the Gothic system as it pursues liberty to the extreme which is why tempering the pursuit of liberty through procedural restraints leads to a moderate, and desired, system under Louis IX.[75]

Near the end of Book XXVIII Montesquieu asks

> What is this obscure, confused, and ambiguous code where one constantly mixes French jurisprudence with Roman law; in which one speaks as a legislator and reveals a jurist; where one finds a whole body of jurisprudence covering all situations, all the points of civil right?[76]

Montesquieu continues to explain, as he had done throughout Book XXVIII that the system was that instituted by Saint Louis. The system instituted by Saint Louis used the judiciary for reform, and the reform led to "a way more in conformity with morality, religion, public tranquility, and the security of persons and goods..."[77]

The lesson of Book XXVIII is that the judges were the ones to effectively bring about the reforms under Saint Louis. This point in Book XXVIII was previously made in Book XXVII when Montesquieu discusses the reform of inheritance laws. Book XXVIII teaches that it is only through the judiciary and the power of judging that reforms can be implemented without causing civil unrest. Furthermore, these changes that happen little by little are also quite reasonable, and it is only the changes brought about by the judiciary that receive the compliment from Montesquieu of being reasonable.[78]

Conclusion

This paper has found that Montesquieu's silence on the common law was not a mistake, and taking it seriously can be instructive. The lesson to be learned is that reform must be moderate and made out of sight of those who are ruled by the law, and some times out of the view of those who are to implement the reforms. In order to ensure security and liberty, the rule of law must be followed while still respecting the mores and manners of a people. This can be done via the power of judging.

By reading Montesquieu in this manner we are forced to reconsider formerly accepted truths about his teaching on representative government and separation of powers. We must also ask whether Montesquieu showed respect for local customs and mores because he saw intrinsic value in them, and recognized each society's right to govern itself as it saw fit, or whether he is simply advising the would-be reformer that one has to institute reforms in a manner that does not appear to disturb those customs already in place. That is, he has no objection to replacing certain customs with others, but simply advises the reader on how to do it successfully. In this regard, Montesquieu may be closer to Machiavelli that has previously been appreciated.

Continuing to examine Montesquieu's silence on the common law will allow scholars to untangle the tension between custom and reason in Montesquieu's writing as well as allow for a more thorough discussion of his constitutionalism and its link to moderation; not to mention the link between moderation and liberty. While these are topics I would like to have discussed more, one must draw the line somewhere. This treatment does not pretend to be exhaustive, nor does it even pretend to have raised all the relevant questions. The primary intention of this paper is to be an initial investigation into a previously uninvestigated topic in order to expand our understanding of Montesquieu and to suggest that there are still new avenues of investigation.

Notes

---

[1] Montesquieu. (1989) *The Spirit of the Laws*. Edited and Translated by Ann M Cohler, Basia C Miller, and Harold S Stone. Cambridge, UK: Cambridge University Press. I will refer to the *Spirit of the Laws* as *SL* in all citations below and I will give the book and chapter followed by the page number.

[2] Carrese, Paul O. (2003) *The Cloaking of Power*. Chicago, IL: The University of Chicago Press. p. 28.

[3] Shackleton, Robert (1961) *Montesquieu: A Critical Biography*. London: Oxford University Press.

[4] Carrithers, David W. (2001) "Introduction: An Appreciation of *The Spirit of the Laws*."

in David W. Carrithers, Michael A. Mosher, and Paul A. Rahe. *Montesquieu's Science of Politics: Essays on* The Spirit of the Laws. Lanham, MD: Rowman and Littlefield Publishers. Masterson, MP (1972) "Montesquieu's Grand Design: The Political Sociology of 'Espirit des Lois'" *British Journal of Political Science*. Vol 2:3. McMahon, Robert (2003) "The Numerological Structure of the *Spirit of the Laws*." *Interpretation*. Pangle, Thomas L. (1973) *Montesquieu's Philosophy of Liberalism: A Commentary on The Spirit of the Laws*. Chicago, IL: The University of Chicago Press.

[5] Carrese (2003).

[6] Berlin, Isaiah (1978) *Against the Current: Essays in the History of Ideas*. London: Hogarth Press. p. 154.

[7] Claus, Laurence (2005) "Montesquieu's Mistakes and the True Meaning of Separation." *Oxford Journal of Legal Studies*. Vo. 25:3.
[8] Claus (2005) p. 419.
[9] "I should like to seek out in all the moderate governments we know the distribution of the three powers and calculate thereupon the degrees of liberty each one of them can enjoy. But one must not always so exhaust a subject that one leaves nothing for the reader to do. It is not a question of making him read but of making him think" *SL* XI.20 p. 186.
[10] "Montesquieu's finished product was the result of continued and deliberate transference of sentences from one place to another, of intentional polishing, of conscious pursuit of the epigram and the paradox, of the constant suppression of the redundant and of the intermediate link between two ideas, of the rearranging of a sequence of ideas so that the consequence precedes the cause" Shackleton (1961), p. 238.
[11] Vile, M.J.C. (1998) *Constitutionalism and the Separation of Powers*. 2nd Edition. Indianapolis, IN: Liberty Fund, Inc. p. 87. Vile makes the point that Montesquieu was not writing about the reality of English government, but rather an idealized system.
[12] Krause, Sharon R. (2000) "The Spirit of Separate Powers in Montesquieu." *The Review of Politics*. Vol. 62:2.
[13] Ibid. p. 239
[14] Levy, Jacob T. (2006) "Beyond Publius: Montesquieu, Liberal Republicanism, and the Small-Republican Thesis." *History of Political Thought*. Vol. 27:1. p. 53.
[15] Carrithers, David W., Michael A. Mosher, and Paul A. Rahe. (2001) *Montesquieu's Science of Politics: Essays on* The Spirit of the Laws. Lanham, MD: Rowman and Littlefield Publishers.
[16] Carrithers, David W. (2001) "Democratic and Aristocratic Republics: Ancient and Modern." in David W. Carrithers, Michael A. Mosher, and Paul A. Rahe. *Montesquieu's Science of Politics: Essays on* The Spirit of the Laws. Lanham, MD: Rowman and Littlefield Publishers. Larrere, Catherine. (2001) "Montesquieu on Economics and Commerce." in David W. Carrithers, Michael A. Mosher, and Paul A. Rahe. *Montesquieu's Science of Politics: Essays on* The Spirit of the Laws. Lanham, MD: Rowman and Littlefield Publishers.
[17] Brockelbank, J.W. (1954) "The Role of Due Process in American Constitutional Law." *Cornell Law Quarterly*. Vol. 39:2. p. 562.
[18] Coke, Edward. (2004) *The Selected Writings of Sir Edward Coke*. 3 Volumes. Edited By Steve Sheppard. Indianapolis, IN: Liberty Fund, Inc. Vol. 1, p. 481.
[19] Hedley as quoted by Postema, Gerald. (2002) "Classical Common Law Jurisprudence: Part I." *Oxford University Commonwealth Law Journal*. Vol. 2:2. p. 166.
[20] Coke, Edward. (1979) *An Abridgement of the Lord Coke's Commentary on Littleton*. Edited by Sir Humphrey Davenport. New York, NY: Garland Publishing. p. 71.

[21] Stoner, James R. (1992) *Common Law and Liberal Theory: Coke, Hobbes, and the Origins of American Constitutionalism.* Lawrence, KS: The University Press of Kansas. p. 18.
[22] Stoner (1992), p. 22.
[23] Stoner (1992), p. 177.
[24] Coke, Edward. (1999) *The First Part of the Institutes of the Laws of England.* 18th Edition. Lawbook Exchange. p. 495.
[25] Stoner (1992), p. 23.
[26] Postema, Gerald. (2003) "Classical Common Law Jurisprudence: Part II." *Oxford University Commonwealth Law Journal.* Vol. 3:1. p. 6.
[27] Postema (2003), p. 9.
[28] Postema (2003), p. 10.
[29] When asked where common law originates, Coke writes, "that true it is that every precedent hath a commencement; but when authority and precedent is wanting, there is need of great consideration, before that any thing of novelty shall be established…" Coke, Edward (1727) *The Reports of Sir Edward Coke, etc.* Edited London: E. & R. Nutts and R. Gossling. XII, p. 24. "For reason is the life of the Law, nay the Common Law itself is nothing else but reason, which is to be understood of an artificial perfection of reason gotten by long study, observation, and experience and not every man's natural reason, for no one is born skillful. The legal reason is the highest reason." Coker, Edward (1628) *Institutes of the Laws of England.* Part I. London: Society of Stationers. p. 97.
[30] Stoner, James R. (2003) *Common-Law Liberty: Rethinking American Constitutionalism.* Lawrence, KS: University Press of Kansas. p. 8
[31] Hudson, John. (1996) *The Formation of the English Common Law: Law and Society in England from the Norman Conquest to Magna Carta.* Edinburgh Gate, UK: Addison-Wesley Longman Limited. p. 17
[32] Ibid. p. 23
[33] *SL* VI.1 p. 73
[34] *SL* XIX.4 p. 310
[35] *SL* XIX.5 p. 310
[36] *SL* XIX.14 p. 315. More on this point will be made in the section dedicated to Saint Louis.
[37] Montesquieu is a proponent of moderate reform, see comments in SL XXIX.1, XXII.21 (extreme laws for good produce extreme evil), and XI.6. In addition to Montesquieu's own comments on the matter, commentators from Hippolyte Taine, to Thomas Pangle, to Sharon Krause have recognized the importance of moderation in Montesquieu's thought
[38] Berlin (1978), p. 154.
[39] Berlin (1978), p. 154.
[40] The balance between law and history must be achieved through subtle reform without drawing too much attention to what is occurring, a practice that Montesquieu implements in his own writing. For those familiar with the work, my intellectual debt to Paul Carrese (2003) is undeniable.

[41] Mansfield, Harvey C. (1993) *Taming the Prince: The Ambivalence of Modern Executive Power.* Baltimore, MD: Johns Hopkins University Press. p. 235.
[42] *SL* XI.11 p. 169
[43] Carrese (2003) takes as its thesis that Montesquieu "hides" his treatment of the judiciary, and not only wishes to make the power of the judiciary invisible to the people who are governed by it, but Montesquieu also wishes to "hide" the role of the judiciary to the inattentive reader. Judith Shklar seems to agree, "The judicial power is so terrible to mankind that it must be made invisible in some way…" Shklar, Judith N. (1987) *Montesquieu.* Oxford, UK: Oxford University Press. p. 89. But Shklar does not say that Montesquieu hides this point from his readers.
[44] *SL* XIX.27 p. 325
[45] Claus (2005), p. 426
[46] I have not been the only one to recognize this distinction in Montesquieu's thought, as Thomas Pangle makes a similar point: "Although the juries will be supreme, the judges will uphold the law itself, and must therefore adhere strictly to the letter of the law. In order to provide for cases where the particular circumstances make this system too rigid or dangerous to an individual, it will be arranged so that the noble branch of the legislature can serve as a court of final appeal, bringing to bear its qualities of education and moderation" (Pangle 1973, p. 133).
[47] *SL* XXVIII.38 p. 591
[48] *SL* II.4 p. 19
[49] *SL* V.10 p. 56
[50] Montesquieu's heavy reliance on the judiciary to prevent despotism is further evidenced when he says, "In despotic states the prince himself can judge" (*SL* VI.5 p. 78).
[51] *SL* II.4 p. 17-8
[52] *SL* XXVIII and XXIX. More specifically Montesquieu states that "When many of these customs were rewritten, certain changes were made, either by removing all that was not compatible with current jurisprudence, or by adding certain things drawn from the jurisprudence" (*SL* XXVIII.45 p. 601).
[53] *SL* XXVIII.12 and 45
[54] Stoner (1992), p. 154
[55] *SL* I.3 p. 8
[56] *SL* XIV-XIX specifically *SL* XIX.5
[57] *SL* XI.8 p. 167
[58] Ibid. p. 166
[59] Ibid. p. 169
[60] *SL* XXVIII.17 p. 551
[61] *SL* XXVIII.37-38 especially p. 591
[62] *SL* XXVIII.29 p. 579
[63] *SL* XXVIII.42 p. 596
[64] The Romans used force, whereas Louis used moderate transitions. This is the important distinction; the method used determines what the result will be. This is the point that Montesquieu is making throughout Book XXVIII. "Thus the laws

made by Saint Louis had effects that could never have been expected of a masterpiece of legislation. Sometimes many centuries must pass to prepare for changes; events ripen, and then there are revolutions." (*SL* XXVIII.39 p. 593).
[65] *SL* XXVIII.38 p. 591
[66] Ibid. p. 592
[67] Pangle recognizes that, "The influential combination of canon and Roman law was generally more reasonable than either the canon law itself or the preexisting system of trial by combat" (Pangle 1973, 287).
[68] *SL* XXVIII.38 p. 592
[69] *SL* XXVIII.42
[70] *SL* XI.6
[71] *SL* XXII.21 p. 422
[72] *SL* XXIX.1 p. 602
[73] *SL* XXII.21 p. 421-2
[74] *SL* XI.8 p. 168
[75] Krause (2000) makes the point that unconstrained liberty is a bad thing for Montesquieu, with reference to the English Constitution.
[76] *SL* XXVIII.38 p. 590
[77] *SL* XXVIII.38 p. 590
[78] *SL* XXVIII.42-44 p. 596-599

HAYEK UNHEEDED: A CRITICAL APPROACH TO SOCIALISM AFTER HAYEK

GREGORY WOLCOTT

Abstract

Theodore Burczak's book, *Socialism after Hayek*, is one of the latest proposals for market socialism. Burczak takes F.A. Hayek's objections to central planning quite seriously, offering a "libertarian Marxist" critique of capitalism based upon Hayek's "postmodern" economics. However, Burczak's argument is wanting. First, his interpretation of Hayek's works is not uncontroversial, thus leading to questionable critiques of capitalism, liberalism, and Hayek. Second, his treatment of the major proposals—stakeholder grants and the abolition of wage labor—fails to take into account the full thrust of Hayekian objections. Last, Burczak's argument unravels on what appears to be a major contradictory note.

Introduction

This paper begins in reaction to recent laudatory remarks by various Austrian economists to Theodore Burczak's *Socialism after Hayek* (2006). Burczak promises to take Hayek seriously in his approach to socialism, and for that, various Hayekians are delighted that Hayek's devastating critiques of central planning are receiving their due. For example, Virgil Henry Storr says that the book is "well researched and thoughtfully argued….[It] seriously engages Hayek's work on the knowledge problem and offers provocative critiques of Hayek's conception of the rule of law and his critique of social justice….Burczak goes a long way toward *successfully* recasting socialism in the wake of Hayek's critiques" (Storr 2007, 316; my italics). Steven Horwitz argues that "Burczak…has produced a slim but very deep volume that contains the most fundamental challenge to Hayek's defenses of the market since the debates with the

Polish socialist Oscar Lange in the 1930s. The book should reopen some conversations that have been closed for too long" (Horwitz 2007, 65).

I agree with Horwitz that the book "reopens some conversations that have been closed for too long," but I disagree with his belief that Burczak offers a "fundamental challenge to Hayek's defenses of the market" and with Storr's contention that Burczak "goes a long way toward successfully recasting socialism in the wake of Hayek's critique." My reasons are actually quite simple: I do not think that Burczak, for all that he does understand within Hayek's canon, actually understands Hayek enough. In light of this, I will attempt to demonstrate why his argument fails. I will not attempt to reconstruct the ins-and-outs of Burczak's argument so much as underscore its most problematic aspects.

The Problem and Procedure

In his introductory chapter of *Socialism after Hayek*, Theodore Burczak asks three questions in the process of establishing what will ground his "'libertarian Marxist' conception of socialism, a socialism committed to forms of procedural and distributive justice that are central to the Marxian tradition and a socialism keenly aware of the factual and ethical knowledge problems emphasized by Hayek" (Burczak 2006, 3). Those three questions are:

> (1) Is there any meaningful notion of socialism that can answer Hayek's epistemological critique? (2) Can the goals of classical socialism be achieved without central planning and the abolition of private property? (3) Can there be socialism after Hayek? (Burczak 2006, 3; numbers inserted).

The goal of this paper is to argue that Burczak's failure to establish (3) leaves (1) and (2) unanswered. Actually, if Burczak fails to answer these questions, they could still be answered by someone, someday, and so (1) and (2) in particular are admittedly beyond my competence to address. Really, however, they are subsidiary to the central and practical question, which is (3). My belief is that Burczak actually does not comprehend the full thrust of Hayek's concerns regarding socialism. Burczak embraces the market (and the price system) for the reasons Hayek offers for its supremacy to planned systems in the coordination and distribution of dispersed and tacit knowledge, but he rejects the labor market in favor of Marx's hope for the "'abolition of the wages system'" (Marx, in Burczak, 2006, 3). This move by Burczak will prove fatal to his attempt to establish socialism after Hayek for reasons that Burczak cannot overcome, at least insofar as he presents the argument.

Interestingly enough, Burczak's failure to answer (3) is the result of a very peculiar problem: Hayek's ultimate concern with socialism was that, even if it could be made into a viable system for some level of economic activity, it could not produce or sustain anything like the level of civilization and progress that we now come to expect from our economic and social systems. So Burczak, by asking if there can be socialism *after* Hayek, sets for himself a very high bar: for his response to be adequate, his new system would have to result in, if not the same *type*, at least an equitable *level* of civilization and progress that generally liberal capitalist societies now produce. So, with this in mind, I will attempt to argue why Burczak's proposals would fail to meet Hayek's challenge to socialism with regard to the "factual and ethical knowledge problems emphasized by Hayek" (Burczak, 2006, 3) and with regard to the need *not* to regress in terms of the level of civilization and progress that we currently experience.[1]

My central argument in defense of my thesis is the following: I can see no way to abolish wage labor and respond effectively to the knowledge problem that Hayek poses for socialism. Burczak thinks that he can get around this through democratic leadership of firms. This is a mistake. We have no reason to suspect that the structure of the firm is a microcosm of the structure of society itself in the relevant way (which means, as I will show, with regard to its operation and use of knowledge). Furthermore, given the actual complex and seemingly chaotic structure of society—which reflects the actions of innumerable actors acting upon dispersed, tacit, and "man on the spot" knowledge (Hayek 1980, 77-80)—it is not clear why Burczak would think only democratically-run firms would maximize knowledge-use more than other institutions in a market society. (If anything, a firm organized along the lines of "market-based management" would be a better model for a firm [if the firm's correspondence to the Hayekian model of society—and the need to accommodate dispersed and tacit knowledge—should be the goal].[2]) Moreover, it is not clear that abolishing wages would abolish wage labor, for reasons I will offer and that depend, in part, upon Austrian insights regarding the "Regression Theorem."[3]

To begin, though, I will also note some of the major dialectical flaws of Burczak's book. I will then move to a more substantive critique of the central proposals in *Socialism after Hayek*. Despite the accomplishment it represents (indeed, there is much to be admired in this book—though, in the interest of space, I will attempt to avoid a comprehensive review of the book and focus instead upon its more problematic aspects with regard to (3) above), Burczak ends the book on a severely contradictory note—one which threatens the moral thrust of his major thesis. This problem just exacerbates another problem in the book, and that is Burczak's willingness to take certain unjustified liberties with regard to interpreting Hayek along the way—liberties which, while perhaps acceptable in other formats, distract from Burczak's promise that his approach does not "necessarily [fall] victim to Hayekian knowledge problems" (Burczak, 2006, 16). In other words, as Burczak argues that he will take Hayek seriously, then the minimal requirement would have been to represent Hayek accurately. This is not always the case, and thus we are reminded that Burczak's main question (3) truly is left unanswered.

Interpretative Disagreements and Dialectical Flaws

I should first begin by highlighting what I take to be major flaws in Burczak's reading of Hayek and in his argument structure. They involve the following three propositions that I take to be mistaken: (i) Hayek is a rule-utilitarian; (ii) Hayek cannot accommodate the capabilities approach to human flourishing in his account; and (iii) Hayek should value democracy more. I will treat each in turn, though I will note from the outset that all three are heavily interrelated in Burczak's account, and thus the reader should expect much overlap in my discussion of them.

(i) Is Hayek a rule-utilitarian?

The first flaw is actually quite subtle, but it affects Burczak's treatment of Hayek's philosophy, especially his legal philosophy, severely. Following Leland Yeager, Burczak argues that

> Hayek is best understood as a rule-utilitarian. A rule-utilitarian believes that laws consistent with the rule of law (i.e., well-announced, abstract, universally applicable rules) help to promote social cooperation and coordination....In addition, rule-utilitarians are reluctant to judge institutions and individuals' actions according to their ability to promote individual or aggregate well-being in particular cases. The pervasiveness of human ignorance renders impossible the full accounting of costs and benefits that would be necessary to decide whether (or how much) a particular activity contributes to happiness (Burczak 2006, 49).

This sounds more or less like Mill's arguments for reliance upon rules in *Utilitarianism*. There, Mill argues that we cannot know the effects of all our actions, so we rely upon rules developed over generations to serve as our *prima facie* guides for our activities (Mill 2001, 23-24). Let's suppose that Mill is a rule-utilitarian, though some may question it (and I am here not interested in endless rule- versus act-utilitarian debates). The important question is whether or not Hayek's argument for rules is a utilitarian argument.

The answer is no, Hayek's argument for rules is *not* a utilitarian argument for rules—and it especially is not Mill's argument. Though, like Hayek, Mill does say we rely upon rules because of our ignorance, his argument is that the rules we rely upon have been adapted because of their role in promoting our happiness: "Mankind must by this time have acquired positive beliefs as to the effects of some actions on their happiness; and the beliefs which have thus come down are the rules of morality for the multitude, and for the philosopher until he has succeeded in finding better" (Mill 2001, 24). In other words, *happiness* is the goal that Mill seeks, and the *happiness of specific and identifiable people* is the standard by which we accept and critique (and improve) our rules. For Hayek, this is lunacy: we have adopted rules because our ignorance of the ends (and happiness) of different people (identifiable or not) is *irremediable*; we never adopted them for happiness. Hayek states:

> The one 'utility' which can be said to have determined the rules of conduct is thus not a utility known to the acting persons, or to any one person, but only a hypostatized 'utility' to society as whole. The consistent utilitarian is therefore frequently driven to interpret the products of evolution anthropomorphically as the product of design and to postulate a personified society as the author of these rules....This basic error of utilitarianism has been most concisely expressed by Hastings Rashdall in the contention that "all moral judgments are ultimately judgments as to the value of ends." This is precisely what they are not; if agreement on particular ends were really the ground for moral judgments, moral rules as we know them would be unnecessary. The essence of all rules of conduct is that they label *kinds* of actions, not in terms of their largely unknown effects in particular instances, but in terms of their probable effect which need not be foreseeable by the individuals. It is not because of those effects of our actions which we knowingly bring about, but because of the effects of our actions have on the continuous maintenance of an order of actions, that particular rules have come to be regarded as important (Hayek 1978b, 22).

On Mill's view, rules can and should be changed according to a calculus in terms of their effects on the greatest number of people. In Hayek's view, rules can only be changed with respect to their promotion of the going order of society—which is to say their role within the social fabric that makes possible the coordinated activities of all within it, not the happiness of those people. (Thus he advocated "immanent criticism" of social structures and rules; see Hayek 1978b, 24.) Hayek's promotion of rules, then, is actually a teleological justification, as he explicitly rejects utilitarianism: rules should be evaluated insofar as they make possible the further order and free evolution of society.[4] Rule-utilitarians sacrifice this evolution by seeking policies that promote specific ends—even if the rules adopted occasionally fail to serve specific ends. (If anything, then, Hayek is broadly consequentialist, but who isn't on this definition?[5])

Why is this important for my discussion of Burczak? It is on this issue of labeling Hayek that Burczak's argument becomes muddled, for reasons I will explain. Generally speaking, Burczak employs an Aristotelian-Marxist approach to the promotion of human capabilities as Amartya Sen and Martha Nussbaum develop it (Burczak 2006, 85-100). Explicitly, such an approach stands in contradistinction to utilitarianism insofar as the classic formulation of utilitarianism is that one should promote "the greatest good for the greatest number." Because this formulation is open to the critique that the suffering of a few could be justified for the happiness of the majority—and thus our current systems of democracy, freedom, and opportunity may lack a robust normative basis that supports counterfactuals—Sen and Nussbaum offer an alternative to the utilitarian approach that will respect and promote individuals and their capacities for good lives substantially and non-contingently in a way that classic utilitarianism does not. Burczak, believing that the current capitalist order justifies the exploitation of some for the benefit of others, thus seeks a way to "search for an institutional structure—and the normative foundations to support that structure—that more fully promotes human well-being and the common good than does the market in a capitalist setting [and] a greater role for democratic processes than Hayek is willing to grant" (Burczak 2006, 78). And so he paints the alternative he will offer (abolition of wage-labor, end of exploitation, democratically-run firms; see Burczak 2006, chapter 6) as having the moral force that Hayek's supposed utilitarianism lacks, based upon that aforementioned capabilities approach.

In fact, these moral considerations drive Burczak's discussion, and rejection, of Hayek's legal philosophy. According to Burczak, Hayek argues, in his support of Anglo-American common law and the correlative market systems, that "the rule of law [is] an evolved principle that emerged spontaneously in the attempt of common law judges to frame their legal opinions to be consistent with existing rules. In order for their decisions to be accepted by the disputing parties, judges followed precedent and adhered to the inarticulate sense of justice prevailing in society" (Burczak 2006, 52). Furthermore, for Hayek, such an evolution went hand-in-hand with the development of the market, hence Burczak sees Hayek as arguing "that a market economy guided by the rule of law is an impartial, procedurally just system that improves the life chances of anyone chosen at random and thus that such an economy serves the common good more effectively than any other method of large-scale social cooperation" (Burczak 2006, 58). But Burczak, following American legal realism and the critical legal studies movement, argues that such impartiality and randomness are illusions:

> [T]he legal realist critique of legal neutrality shows that Hayek overstates the case for neutrality in a common law process. Hence the law may always be a servant of particular interests, or be biased against a particular group or certain types of people, thereby skewing the results of market processes. This possibility undermines Hayek's contention that a market process constrained by a common law system generally improves the life chances of any person chosen at random. Hayek's belief that the market serves the interests of the poor as well as the rich and the interests of people who perform wage labor as well as people who hire labor may not be correct if the law favors certain class interests (Burczak 2006, 66-67).

Here's where we have a muddle: Burczak argues that Hayek is a rule-utilitarian *and* he argues that Hayek supports the common law system and correlative market processes because they improve the chances of no particular person's enhanced life prospects. But these claims are actually inconsistent, at least for the reasons Burczak offers. If Hayek is rule-utilitarian and the legal realists are right that the law and the market have, at least up to now, only benefitted particular interests, then the critique that "Hayek overstates the case for neutrality" does not make any sense: given what I have argued about the utilitarian calculus, why would neutrality matter to Hayek? If he were a "good" utilitarian, he could settle for the law and the market serving the majority's (particular) interests over the common (general) good. (But he explicitly does *not* see that as the "goal"—metaphorically speaking—of the law and the market.[6]) However, if Hayek believes that the law and the market are neutral and impartial in the benefits they bestow, and they are not, then his mistake is simply empirical, and there is no actual argument against what Hayek believes that the law and the market *should* do—i.e., serve the common good neutrally and improve lives impartially.[7] The important point, moreover, is that if neutrality and impartiality are valuable regardless of any interests, then it does not follow that Hayek is a utilitarian and it does not follow that the law and the market should not be impartial.

Interestingly, the tables could be turned on Burczak. After he complains that the law and the market (especially the credit-rationing system) have mostly benefitted those who already have resources (on the law, see, for example, Burczak 2006, 78-79; on the market and credit-rationing, see, for example, 66-77), and that this oversight by Hayek is so egregious, he turns around and suggests that the state will have to benefit some people at the expense of others. À la Bruce Ackermann and Anne Alscott, Burczak states that when his new "socialistic" stakeholder plan is put into place (which will require generous state spending and monetary grants for citizens), something must be done "to prevent a massive influx of immigrants seeking a stake and to limit the stake of those citizens living inside the country" (Burczak 2006, 132). And so he embraces their idea that "the stake [a grant of at least $100,000 to be used for government-constrained purposes] should be given only to citizens who have lived for at least eleven years inside the country" (Burczak 2006, 132-133). I will return in the next section of the paper to why this is so problematic for another reason, but the obvious reason at this stage of my argument is that such a rule is patently utilitarian: it benefits the majority at the expense of others. By denying stakes to people who do not match the criterion, those who normally would immigrate to improve their lives would suffer enormously by being denied access to the services that natives receive and, should they still decide to attempt to enter, would find a grossly unequal, but engineered, economic playing field. Immigrants risk their lives to improve their situations by entering the United States now and they find economic opportunity in our relatively free labor market, but this is an opportunity that will evaporate in Burczak's model. And so, for the sake of the supposed natives of this country, Burczak's use of Ackermann and Alscott's proposal effectively closes the door to others (immigrants) seeking to improve their lives. This is a perfect example of a particularly selfish type of utilitarianism, and it is what Gordon Tullock labels "patriotic egalitarianism" (Cowen 2002, 51). Considering that the natives of the country have more resources than the immigrants seeking to enter, surely we should note that this form of protectionism benefits the wealthy at the expense of the worst off.

(ii) Can Hayek accommodate the capabilities approach in his philosophy?

This difficulty aside, a more sensible and interesting question is whether or not Hayek's approach is amenable to the capabilities approach Burczak adopts for his own theory. And we will see that this question also presents Burczak with some major problems. Now, it would take a book-length study to answer this fairly, and any affirmative answer to it would have to make a strong case for the role of communities and private institutions in supporting capabilities, as opposed to use of the state for such purposes (as it is embraced by Sen, Nussbaum, and Burczak). In fact, Burczak's assumption that the rejection of the state to support capabilities is *ipso facto* a rejection of the importance of supporting capabilities is an underlying but common interpretive error throughout his argument[8]--and I can see no *prima facie* reasons why Hayek's minimal governmental framework would prevent the promotion of capabilities between private individuals within communities. There are some more obvious errors, though, in Burczak's rejection of Hayek in favor of Sen and Nussbaum. Though Burczak is right to argue that "[a]mong the attributes of Hayek's thought, the first and in many ways most significant that is common to most varieties of liberalism is his skepticism regarding the possibility that individuals in a modern society can reach any principled agreement about the substantive characteristics of a good life" (Burczak 2006, 85), his subsequent line of criticism falls apart at the seams; one must wonder *whom* Burczak really critiques on this front: Hayek, or any other liberal and/or libertarian thinkers he can name? What should be a critique of Hayek in favor of Sen and Nussbaum (on the reasonable assumption that Burczak is mounting a critique against Hayek) actually turns out to be a critique *not only* of Hayek (as the supposed rule-utilitarian), but principally of John Rawls, Deirdre McCloskey, Robert Nozick, amorphous "liberals," "cultural relativists," and Israel Kirzner (Burczak 2006, 85-94). At this point then, the critique against Hayek loses force, for Hayek is, in many ways, *sui generis*. (Put differently, a critique of Rawls or of Nozick will not always apply to Hayek.) Still, at times, Burczak actually notes agreement between Hayek and Sen and Nussbaum (on provisions against starvation, for example), but he thinks Hayek's views are "unprincipled and groundless in a framework that elevates equality under the law as the guiding normative principle for modern society" (Burczak 2006, 91-92). Burczak's conclusion is unwarranted and is based upon the mistake I highlighted above: to believe that the state should be limited in its substantive support of human capabilities is not to render support of human capabilities "groundless." (If Hayek were a utilitarian, perhaps Burczak's argument would have a little more strength, but as I have shown, this is not the case.)

(iii) Should Hayek value democracy more?

Earlier I mentioned that Burczak seeks to make a stronger case for the role of democratic decision making than Hayek will allow. This is part of Burczak's general argument for the use of human capabilities to gauge and construct social and economic institutions. It is true that Hayek believed that democracy was valuable primarily for its role in peaceful transitions of power and as a vehicle of change, and not as an expression of human capabilities (Hayek 1978a, 104-109). Hayek fully rejected the growing tendency to view democracy as "an end in itself" and felt instead that it must be "limited," lest it degenerate into "demagoguery" (Hayek 1978a, 106, 107). Burczak is far more sanguine, however, in his approach to democracy—particularly in the workplace—and sees it as a means for the extension of human capabilities, especially when one contrasts it with the exploitation of wage labor in the traditional capitalist labor market. In fact, it is here that Burczak turns into a consequentialist and judges labor arrangements by whether or not they generate good consequences; with the appropriate caveats regarding human nature, Burczak adopts Nussbaum's belief that "a policy, a right, or any other institution generates good consequences if it promotes the capability for people to function in a mode that is consistent with a fully realized human nature that is defined in a conjective, intersubjective, or internalist essentialist manner. A fully realized human nature includes more than happiness…the exercise of practical reason is essential" (Burczak 2006, 116). Incorporating David Ellerman's and Karl Marx's arguments, Burczak states:

> …certain essential human characteristics—in particular, responsibility and decision making—are factually inalienable….Yet in the capitalist firm, workers do not have legal responsibility for their actions, insofar as they do not appropriate the entire product for which their labor is factually responsible. Thus workers in a capitalist enterprise assume the legal status of things and are often treated similarly. Marx characterizes an employee of a capitalist this way: "in his human functions he no longer feels himself to be anything but an animal"….While participating in a capitalist work process, the worker loses his or her dignity (Burczak 2006, 117).

So Burczak sees a human capability, use of mental powers—such as decision making abilities and responsibility—as made possible for actualization within democratically-run, worker managed firms. Wage labor, on his account, exploits the worker and hinders his or her capacities to be fully human. By definition, one who is exploited is used in an unfair way—by being forced to do something without his or her consent, for example. The questions we should ask are whether or not Hayek is amenable to the human capability of use of mental powers and whether or not Hayek should have embraced some form of worker democracy in the actualization of such a capacity.

Hayek would not deny that being treated as a mere means does degrade a human being; in fact, he would *agree* that use of one's capabilities is important in what it means to be a human being. For example, he states: "Coercion thus is bad because it prevents a person from using his mental powers to the full and consequently from making the greatest contribution that he is capable of to the community" (Hayek 1978a, 134). Or, elsewhere, "Coercion is evil precisely because it thus eliminates an individual as a thinking and valuing person and makes him a bare tool in the achievements of the ends of another" (Hayek 1978a, 21). Notice, however, that Hayek thinks that *coercion* is the method by which one is prevented from actualizing one's possibilities (though he will admit of inescapable soft coercion via irreducible social forces). Is wage labor coercive? As unfortunate as some persons' circumstances may be, the voluntary contract between two individuals (the wage laborer and the firm) is not coercive, and to insist otherwise—by arguing that wage labor is exploitation when there is no coercion—is to engage in gross moral equivocation.[9] But even if wage labor were exploitative, would it follow that democratically-run firms actually (or necessarily) promote the use of one's mental powers more fully?

The answer to this, from Hayek, is no: there is no reason to suspect that democratic firms make possible capabilities actualization in the relevant sense. (I will presume that for democracy to promote human capabilities, it must produce results that correspond to measured desires for cooperation, active achieving of goals, and arriving at consensus deliberately.) As hinted above, Hayek argues at length about the limits of democracy, but, as his thesis is partially empirical, we can test it by asking if democracy delivers on more than its promise to make change peaceful by the hope that it will promote human capabilities (especially use of one's reason and mental powers). The evidence thus far does not favor Burczak. It is surprising to me that Burczak would ignore, for example, Kenneth Arrow's Impossibility Theorem (Arrow 1951) or the vast amounts of literature flowing from public choice economists, especially one of the main founding documents, James Buchanan and Gordon Tullock's 1962 *The Calculus of Consent*. Social and public choice economists have demonstrated time and time again that it is incredibly difficult to order preferences rationally and consistently[10] and that different types of voting procedures will produce contradictory results.[11] Furthermore, these theorists have demonstrated how the democratic political process is quite irrational insofar as it promotes voter ignorance and cunning and manipulation by factions and special interest groups. Moreover, game theorists and cognitive scientists have shown that there is thus far little empirical basis for the belief that "deliberation" improves decision making processes; in fact, the strength of the hope of relying upon deliberation for ideal democratic procedures rests on dubious assumptions that "participants will speak to each other, listen to each other, respect each other, and then learn from each other's statements" (McCubbins and Rodriguez 2006, 11). So what, we should ask, does democracy offer in terms of substantially promoting human capabilities, especially the capacity to use one's mental powers, other than what Hayek suspected it could offer (i.e., a reliable framework of reasonable expectations of peaceful change)?[12] How would a democratic firm serve as an improvement upon the putatively degrading irrationality of exploitative wage labor? I do not wish to suggest that there is no other case to be made for democracy, or that current theorems and statistics are the last words on its value. There may be other benefits to democracy in the workplace (though, I suspect, the benefits are short-term and will cause more harm than good in the future). However, on this issue, Burczak's account could benefit from some acknowledgement of the possible limits of democracy and deliberation—limits that Hayek understood all too well.

The Central Problems: Stakeholder Grants and Wage Labor

I have thus far danced around the issue of Burczak's proposal to seek a "constitutional amendment to prohibit the capitalist employment relation" (Burczak 2006, 122)—i.e., to prohibit wage labor—in my discussion of interpretive disagreements with Burczak and his dialectical flaws. This is the central proposal in Burczak's argument, though it is very much connected to his proposal to offer stakeholder grants to all citizens. It is now time to see whether or not Burczak's proposal fully takes into account Hayek's understanding of dispersed and tacit knowledge. My belief, as stated earlier, is that it does not.

Burczak's proposal to amend the constitution to ban wage labor (based upon Jaroslav Vanek's ideas) would effect the following plan:

> [The] amendment requires that workers in a common enterprise democratically appropriate the results of their labor and democratically manage their collective efforts. Private ownership of capital is not prohibited, but capital ownership conveys no possibility—through right or contract—of control rights over workers. [The] amendment would thus

> result in the elimination of two markets: the market in which people rent control over their labor time, in exchange for wage or salary, and the market for common stock, in which claims to the firms capital stock entail control rights over workers (Burczak 2006, 122).

It is important to note that Burczak sees this approach as desirable for its role in promoting human capabilities and *not,* necessarily, to eliminate inequalities (in other words, he seems aware of the Nozickian insight that patterns need not produce desired outcomes). However, he does propose, through the aforementioned stakeholder grants and government programs, to make possible the robust economic participation by all citizens in a way that current credit-rationing models do not:

> A socialist, stakeholder society should therefore promote nonexploitative forms of good living. It would do so by providing a social inheritance to finance investments in human and physical capital: postsecondary education, vocational training, equipment to become an independent contractor, and potential membership fees to join a labor-managed firm. Perhaps the stake could be used to purchase real estate, since it could readily be used as collateral to finance self-managed work opportunities. But using the stake to buy a car or to travel around the world...would be prohibited by a socialist stakeholder society (Burczak 2006, 133).

Let's start with the restrictions on use of the stakeholder grants that Burczak favors, and then we'll work back to the prohibition of wages. We'll see that Hayek's concerns have gone unheeded by Burczak. (It does not matter that Burczak acknowledges departure from Hayek; what matters is his claim to have taken Hayek seriously and to have answered Hayek.)

(i) Stakeholder grants and free societies

In what is now common knowledge, Hayek's argument in the *Road to Serfdom* was that central government planning could lead to central direction over people's personal lives, as evidenced by the forced labor, for example, in the history of totalitarian regimes. Burczak, however, is so well-intentioned that he ignores the force of the skepticism inherent in Hayekian thought about the good life. So he neglects this sort of passage from Hayek:

> The choice open to us is not between a system in which everybody will get what he deserves according to some absolute and universal standard of right, and one where the individual shares are determined partly by accident or good or ill chance, but between a system where it is the will of

> a few person that decides who is to get what, and one where it depends at least partly on the ability and enterprise of the people concerned and partly on unforeseeable circumstances (Hayek 1994, 112-113).

Why do unforeseeable circumstances matter so much? They do not just skew the results of patterns. They also create situations where restrictions on private activity create undue burdens on individuals and where those restrictions prohibit creative solutions to problems. Let us offer the example of a person, let's name her Jane, who would like to use her government stake to purchase an automobile, something that is prohibited by Burczak's proposal. Ostensibly this prohibition is the result of the desire to prevent people from wasting the resources that could better their lives. But what if Jane has a job as a traveling salesperson? A car would be quite useful to her. Burczak's prohibition, at this point, presents burdens to Jane and *manipulates* her into utilizing her capabilities in a governmentally favored way.

But I am being too harsh on Burczak. He did say that "equipment" for one's job could be part of government provisions, and a car—in this case—appears to fit this definition of "equipment." (Though, let us acknowledge, this set-up forces Jane to make a case for her decisions before some sort of lending or grant institution, and so how it is an improvement over the current credit-rationing system—which supposedly only favors some—is not entirely clear.) So let's take the harder case: the person, let's call him John, who seeks to use his grant or his loans to travel the world but is prohibited from doing so. Is this prohibition also ill-advised on Hayekian grounds?

Absolutely. It is the very essence of Hayek's Adam Smith-inspired philosophy that the unintended consequences of self-interested (not to be confused with selfish) activity (such as travel) have the greatest impact on those whom we are incapable of helping directly. One example of a positive externality associated with a self-interested activity (such as travel) is the benefit travel brings to those places that are visited: "travel, tourism, and hospitality" is a major industry and all the travelers of the world—by patronizing businesses surrounding this industry—support the innumerable people, local economies, and nations that depend upon the revenue generated by those travelers. For example, consider these recent statistics from the Embassy of France's website regarding the number of accommodations available to visitors of France (and note this does not include all the bars, restaurants, museums, souvenir shops, airlines and transportation businesses, and tourist sites that benefit from travelers):

- 18,884 hotels,
- 8,138 camping sites,

- 914 holiday villages,
- 177 youth hostels,
- 1,389 Tourist residences,
- 34,848 chambres d'hôtes (bed and breakfast).

France's tourism sales in 2004 totaled €66 million. France's income from tourism (€66 billion) is the third largest in the world, after the United States and Spain. The trade surplus in this sector is over €8.9 billion (http://www.info-france-usa.org/atoz/economy.asp).

Now, we, following Hayek, can pose the following question to Burczak: why doesn't support for France's (or any other nation's) travel, tourism, and hospitality industry (which, we see, is a huge sector in France's economy) promote the capabilities of innumerable French people involved with this industry? (We can also offer the automobile industry, too, on this line of reasoning. Don't automobile manufacturers need customers as well?) Why is it that only overtly traceable and identifiable activities that promote capabilities matter to Burczak, when it is so obvious that human capabilities can also be promoted by unintended consequences of self-interested behavior *and* that the attempt to thwart such self-interested behavior could wreak absolute havoc on the capabilities of others? (This latter clause is the ultimately damning question.)

Burczak could respond that people could use their own income from their employment at a democratic firm for self-interested activity, but that they could not use that aforementioned stakeholder grants for it—and so the travel industry (as an example) need not be destroyed. But this response is too *ad hoc* and entirely unprincipled. Why should the government draw a line between the acceptable and unacceptable use of stake funds based upon the origin of those funds? Once the state is granted the power to direct the use of money, anything that could be deemed as interfering with human capabilities could be prohibited. In fact, a plausible and frightening scenario, based upon Tullock's patriotic egalitarianism (as described above), would be a situation where a government would allow travel within one's own country (for the promotion of national interests) and would prohibit foreign travel (lest too much money flow outside one's own country). We are now traveling (!) on the "road to serfdom" and have returned full-circle to Hayek's critique of utilitarianism: for utilitarianism to work, we must overcome epistemic limitations and be capable of identifying the particularly relevant consequences sufficiently in a way that would override unforeseen consequences. As it were, we are not capable of this on such a large scale as a complex world, though Burczak seems to think that we are. (Or, at least he leaves his position open to this critique.) And so Burczak ends up sounding more utilitarian than Hayek.

(ii) Prohibitions of wage labor and adaptations

Still, let's suppose that the stakeholder grants will not ruin economies or destroy industries. Burczak is rather convinced that his proposal to ban wage labor will not do significant damage to national economies (how else could he propose it?) and that no harmful or uncomfortable changes would be required in the way business as usual proceeds. Is there a Hayekian answer to this? Or, put differently, does Burczak respect Hayek's knowledge problem sufficiently? There are two ways of answering this, and neither will affirm that Burczak treats Hayek's objections seriously enough. The first way is to question whether democratically-run firms are the appropriate analogues of complex economies. The second way is to conjecture that the wage labor framework is sufficiently "sticky" enough in a complex, dynamic economy that attempts to eradicate it would not be successful. I'll begin with the first way.

A common error in interpreting Hayek is to suppose that all organizations should be as structured as loosely as possible in order to facilitate the best transmission of knowledge possible: if every member of a firm, for example, could utilize his or her local knowledge in a way that he or she sees fit, then the firm would benefit from the use of that knowledge in a way greater than it would should the firm be organized along stricter operational lines. For Hayek, this is a mistake. Firms, families, sports teams, businesses, churches, etc., are all purpose-driven organizations that may or may not benefit from decentralized structuring. Societies, we have learned, benefit from decentralization, but it does not follow that all organizations *within* such societies need to be structured so loosely. And it makes sense: small organizations have far greater identifiable purposes and attainable plans than do amorphous and complex societies, and the structure of such organizations can reflect that. Burczak, however, in his support for the abolition of wage labor, believes that the democratically-run firm can take advantage of localized, dispersed knowledge in a way that capitalist firms cannot. He states:

> Hayek's idea of the importance of tacit, local knowledge in the production process suggests there might be other efficiency-promoting benefits of a system of labor-appropriating firms. There is reason to think that the labor-appropriating firm will give more workers incentive to report their subjective perceptions of economic opportunity—such as more efficient technologies, since they share in the profits these technologies might

> allow. Insofar as capitalist firms often do not provide incentives to all employees to notice and report improvements in a firm's technology, the labor-appropriating firm may be more innovative than the capitalist firm. In addition, if workers participate in appropriation and act as the residual claimant, they might be more willing to invest in firm-specific forms of human capital (Burczak 2006, 119).

What Burczak describes is the sort of entrepreneurial activity within the microcosm of the firm: the use of one's special epistemic perspective for the benefit of oneself and for one's firm. The problem, however, is that the workers are only one portion of the entrepreneurial process. Burczak does not take into account that owners of firms or entrepreneurs with good ideas about new businesses may see that certain types of organizational structures are more advantageous than others in the pursuit of their business goals. In other words, though it may be true that *a* democratically-run firm can "capitalize" on its workers' local knowledge in a beneficial way, it does not follow from this that *every* firm can capitalize on dispersed decision making. Furthermore, it is quite possible that some firms would need a wage-labor framework in order to be competitive and to offer services efficiently. For example, a person running an ice cream shop during a few hot summer months a year probably would benefit most from hiring high school kids on summer vacation seeking to earn a few extra dollars—this is hardly the type of business that one would expect could be democratically-run and efficient. But this can also apply to larger businesses, and the reason—to speak in terms of the worker's capabilities—is that the worker is also, in his or her own way, an entrepreneur. Seen in this light, it is plausible that some workers will find it advantageous to change jobs or careers every so often (for whatever reason)—and the prohibitive costs of exit and entry into democratically-run firms could thwart such job and career change opportunities. In other words, when Hayek spoke of the knowledge problem—and the nature of dispersed and tacit knowledge—his solution to the issues it created was to seek as much flexibility as possible in the ability to respond to it. This flexibility, however, cannot be applied only within the firm. It also has to applied to the economy and business environment as a whole. Abolishing wage labor destroys this flexibility.

I will now move to the second way of asking if Burczak responds to Hayek's knowledge problem, and that way is my conjecture that the market—as a locus for exchange—is a "sticky" institution in a modern society and attempts to eradicate it would not work. Now, Burczak embraces the market for goods and services—we must be clear about that—but he does hope to abolish both the common stock market and the labor market. I will only address the latter. Before doing so, however, I must flesh out this concept of "institutional stickiness."

"Institutional stickiness"—"the ability or inability of new institutional arrangements to take-hold where they are transplanted"—is a concept employed by Austrian economists to evaluate whether exogenously and endogenously imposed institutional arrangements (whether "indigenously" or "foreign-introduced") actually reflect the practices, mores, and customs of people upon whom, or from whom, such institutions develop (Boettke, Coyne and Leeson 2008, 332). It was developed further by Ludwig von Mises with his "Regression Theorem." According to Boettke, Coyne, and Leeson,

> The Regression Theorem maintains that the stickiness, and therefore the likely success, of any proposed institutional change is a function of that institution's status in relationship to indigenous agents in the previous time period (2008, 331).

Furthermore, when changes are sought for the promotion of certain goals, and there is accordance of emergent and imposed institutions with extant practices, efficient results are more likely to follow than in the case of imposed institutions that agree less with practices:

> The idea that [spontaneously-ordered] institutions tend to be tend to be efficient and most effective in promoting the ends of indigenous agents is not original to us. On the contrary, Hayek…was among the first to emphasize these aspects of spontaneously-emergent institutions, and in particular, law (Boettke, Coyne, and Leeson 2008, 333).

The mention of Hayek here is quite important. In Hayek's discussion of spontaneous order, any activities by intentional agents produce institutional effects. Money, law, language, and morality—when understood generally—are all examples of the institutions that have emerged spontaneously from the actions of states, private individuals, communities, businesses, and so on.[13] And, some specific institutional arrangements can and have been imposed. From Hayek's perspective, the institutions that "stick," as it were, are the ones that reflect and accord with, in some robust sense, the practices of actual individuals. An imposed piece of legislation, for example, that does not reflect the values of citizens, probably won't stick—one can imagine laws that people ignore (such as drug laws). However, laws that encourage the monogamous, two-person relationships of marriage, for example, "stick" because such laws reflect the desires and willingness of individuals to commit to one another exclusively.[14]

Now, as Boettke, Coyne, and Leeson are quick to point out, "institutional stickiness is *not* equivalent to institutional 'goodness'....[i]t is not the case that every endogenously-created institution in all circumstances is efficient or conducive to economic development" (Boettke, Coyne, and Leeson 2008, 345). We can take this one step further: according to Hayek, the fact that an institution or practice survives is no indication of its *moral* goodness (Hayek 1991, 27). But the point is that stickiness must be accounted for when one attempts to impose or change institutional arrangements; it's a constraint—for better or for worse—on the aspirations for social change: "Stickiness is therefore a necessary though not sufficient institutional attribute for creating economic growth" (Boettke, Coyne, and Leeson 2008, 345). My suspicion is that wage labor is too sticky simply to be eradicated—not because people demand to receive wages *per se*—but because it is a central feature of the very entrenched market activity of exchange we find in modern societies—as Hayek describes it—and that even Burczak recognizes.

Why should the stickiness of wage labor matter, though? Couldn't we still abolish it? Economists know that attempts to eradicate certain behaviors through the law are never quite as successful as lawmakers would hope: the attempt to abolish legitimatized markets only paves the way for black markets. Thus markets for drugs and prostitution, for example, though (mostly) outlawed, still thrive in black markets despite the enormous costs involved with being caught for engaging in drug use or prostitution. There just is no easy way to parse activities of mutually beneficial exchange in complex markets to eradicate the undesirable from the desirable activities. Given that most people probably have no serious moral qualms with selling their labor in exchange for payment, especially those who do so successfully (and by this I mean simply those for whom wage labor does *not* make them feel exploited—which is probably the vast majority of well-paid wage earners), it would be absurd to suggest to those people that some form of "false consciousness" prevents them from seeing their true interests.

I could be wrong about this, of course, but my intuition is that even if wage labor were abolished officially, there would be, especially in the case of low-value jobs, a massive market for illegal services. As in the case of illegal prostitutes who are in danger of abuse and real exploitation while "working" because they have no recourse to the law, lest they admit engagement in prohibited activities and face legal penalties, Burczak's proposal would foster a *de facto* nation of prostitutes in constant peril. We also already see this in the case of the illegal immigrants who work for "under the table" pay–and who are willing to do this because, comparatively, their options in their native countries are worse. Given this, the reasonable and, dare I say, truly moral thing to do would be to accept the inescapable situation as it is and seek ways to improve the lives of those within the systems already in place. So instead of abolishing wage labor, perhaps, to borrow a Popperian idea, "piecemeal" improvements within current institutions and attempts to provide greater flexibility for wage earners to improve their lives are in order instead. Hayek understood this and thus emphasized the limits of rationalistic social construction attempts—attempts that could stifle the level of progress and civilization that we now come to expect in our modern world. One must wonder if Burczak absorbed this lesson in his reading of Hayek, or if he is truly capable of meeting the challenge posed by Hayek.

Conclusion: An Inherent Contradiction?

For all its flaws, Burczak's proposal does at least recognize many of Hayek's objections to socialism and his plan incorporates many of the *sine quibus non* of modern society, civilization, and progress, though in modified forms: markets (in certain sectors, at least), private property (despite restrictions on the use of it), and the rule of law (however artificial and imposed the laws are). In this way, Burczak's proposal is an advance toward a rapprochement between Hayekians and socialists. This may be a problem for socialists; at the end of *Socialism after Hayek*, Burczak recognizes that "[m]ost socialists will probably find this Hayekian socialism thin soup. They will insist, correctly, that while worker cooperatives may enhance the capability of laborers to work with dignity and responsibility, they larger system of competitive markets is unlikely to yield a distribution of resources that effectively satisfies human needs" (Burczak 2006, 139). And so Burczak, realizing that this objection is a formidable one, skims a few other alternatives to liberal capitalism offered by various socialists. But, because he respects Hayek's arguments in favor of markets too much, he rejects any of the more anti-market approaches, and he lands upon an alternative offered by Samuel Bowles and Herbert Gintis. According to Burczak, they

> propose a vision of market socialism similar to the one advocated in this book: they advocate workplace democracy and asset redistribution. They do not, however, support a rule banning the capitalist firm....They seek to encourage worker self-management through government provision of credit to self-managed enterprises at competitive interest rates, government provision of insurance to labor-managed firms that face bankruptcy due to

> a hostile economic environment…, and a high level of unemployment insurance… (Burczak 2006, 144).

Despite what I see as obvious problems with their approach—which, we should add, is not very much different than what current laws support and what government-backed institutions already look like—the salient aspect of their proposal is that "worker self-management would evolve naturally in cases where it was more efficient than capitalist enterprises" (Burczak 2006, 144). In other words, Bowles and Gintis will work toward achieving small goals and toward molding the legal and business climate in favor of socialistic enterprises. (It should be noted that Hayek offers no argument why a natural evolution toward worker self-management should be halted so long as capitalist firms are also allowed to coexist. And there is no legitimate reason why he would; but he would object to the government having such an active role in that evolution, for reasons that should be clear.)

Burczak reviews Bowles and Gintis's proposal favorably, and he concludes his account rather pragmatically and, I will add, problematically:

> The question we need to ask is which vision offers more hope for a post-capitalist society: the asset redistribution advocated by Bowles and Gintis or a post-Hayekian socialism comprised of Ackermann and Alscott's stakeholder grant and Vanek's amendment? ….Most people in [wealthy] countries are not ready to vote to abolish wage labor or to establish sizable, universal wealth grants. It thus seems prudent for practical socialists to be open to market-friendly, evolutionary proposals—such as those advanced by Bowles and Gintis—that promise to move us toward more extensive worker appropriation and the expansion of capabilities equality (Burczak 2006, 145, 146).

Though we can appreciate Burczak's prudence on this matter and his eagerness to experiment, his willingness to concede that a slow, trial and error approach to socialism—given that we are now supposedly sufficiently industrialized to move to socialism—creates a contradiction within his account. The reason is as follows: up until these concluding remarks, we have been told that capitalism is now known to be morally unacceptable, now that we know that workers are denied their dignity through wage labor exploitation. If this is true, how can anything other than a complete eradication of "exploitation" be justified? In other words, if it is so wrong to permit wage labor, how is it that an evolutionary approach to abolishing wage labor is acceptable? If wage labor is wrong, it is wrong regardless of whether or not a solution that abolishes it will be feasible. Maybe for a utilitarian such a compromise between alternatives is permissible, but we already know that Burczak considers his account of human dignity to be far superior to anything utilitarians could offer. So what grounds his concession to practicality? There is nothing.

And so, for this reason and many others, we must conclude that Burczak's model, though laudable for its attempt to take Hayek seriously, does not comprehend fully the Hayekian challenge to socialism. Can there be socialism after Hayek? The question, we must conclude, has been left unanswered.[15]

Works Cited

Arrow, Kenneth. 1951. *Social Choice and Individual Values*. New York: Wiley.

Baldas, Tresa. 2005. "States Ride Post-'Kelo' Wave of Legislation," *The National Law Journal*, reprinted on "Law.com": www.law.com.

Boettke, Peter J., Christopher J. Coyne, and Peter T. Leeson. 2008. "Institutional Stickiness and the New Development Economics," *American Journal of Economics and Sociology* 67 (2): 331-358.

Buchanan, James and Gordon Tullock. 1962. *The Calculus of Consent*, Ann Arbor, MI: The University of Michigan Press.

Burczak, Theodore A. 2006. *Socialism after Hayek*, Ann Arbor, MI: The University of Michigan Press.

Coleman, John, Tadd Wilson, and Tony Woodlief. Unpublished, "The Knowledge Problem and the Firm: New and Existing Critiques of Graduate Management Education."

Cowen, Tyler. 2002. "Does the Welfare State Help the Poor?" *Social Philosophy and Policy* Vol. 19, No. 1: pp. 36-54.

Hayek, F.A. 1978a. *The Constitution of Liberty*, Chicago: University of Chicago Press.

—. 1978b. *Law, Legislation, and Liberty, Vol. 2: The Mirage of Social Justice*, Chicago: University of Chicago Press.

—. 1980. "The Use of Knowledge in Society," reprinted in *Individualism and Economic Order*, Chicago: University of Chicago Press.

—. 1991. *The Fatal Conceit: The Errors of Socialism*, Chicago: University of Chicago Press.

—. 1994. *The Road to Serfdom*, Fiftieth Anniversary Edition, Chicago: University of Chicago Press.

Horwitz, Steven. 2007. "Leftists for Hayek," *Reason* 39 (3): 65-69.

de Jouvenel, Bertrand. 1989. *The Ethics of Redistribution*, Indianapolis, IN: Liberty Fund.

Koch, Charles. 2007. *The Science of Success: How Market Based Management Built the World's Largest Private Company*, San Francisco, CA: Berrett-Koehler.

Mack, Eric. 2006. "Hayek on Justice and the order of actions," in Edward Feser, ed., *The Cambridge Companion to Hayek*, Cambridge/New York: Cambridge University Press.

McCubbins, Matthew and Daniel Rodriguez. 2006. "When Does Deliberating Improve Decisionmaking?" *Journal of Contemporary Legal Issues* 15 (9): 9-50.

Mill, John Stuart. 2001. *Utilitarianism*, Second Edition, George Sher, ed., Indianapolis, IN: Hackett Publishing Company.

Mises, Ludwig von. 1980. *The Theory of Money and Credit*, Indianapolis, IN: Liberty Fund.

Murray, Charles. 1988. *In Pursuit: Of Happiness and Good Government*, New York: Simon & Schuster.

Nozick, Robert. 1974. *Anarchy, State, and Utopia*, New York: Basic Books.

Searle, John R. 1995. *The Construction of Social Reality*, New York: Free Press.

Shepsle, Kenneth and Mark Bonchek. 1997. *Analyzing Politics: Rationality, Behavior, and Institutions*, New York/London: W.W. Norton & Company.

Storr, Virgil Henry. 2007. Review of Theodore A. Burczak's *Socialism after Hayek*, *Review of Austrian Economics* 20 (4): 313-316.

Taylor, Charles, 1982. "The diversity of goods," in Amartya Sen and Bernard Williams, eds., *Utilitarianism and Beyond*, Cambridge/New York: Cambridge University Press.

Notes

---

[1] "Need" as I employ it here is a relative term. One might argue that we do not "need" to progress at the rate at which we currently progress. That's debatable, but it's not unreasonable. Much harder, though, would be to establish that we could do without the benefits of civilization and progress that we currently enjoy: increased life expectancies and standards of living, developments that enable us to provide better and more efficient goods and services (like life-saving medical technologies), and the unexpected discoveries that can be utilized for improving the environment and for increasing the possibility of, or opening more paths for, new discoveries. (This latter point is especially important: for this reason, Hayek argued that "progress is movement for movement's sake, for it is in the process of learning, and in the effects of having learned something new, that man enjoys the

gift of his intelligence" [Hayek 1978a, 41].) So, such benefits are part of the tradition of modern order of discovery. Thus Hayek's concerns with socialism were not only that it might slow down progress, but also that we might, in our attempts to "save" the world by directing progress, destroy a large part of it: "I do claim that, whether we like it or not, without particular traditions, the extended order of civilization could not continue to exist; and that if we discard these traditions, out of ill-considered notions of what it is to be reasonable, we shall doom a large part of mankind to poverty and death. Only when these facts are fully faced do we have any business—or are we likely to have any competence—to consider what the right and good thing to do may be" (Hayek 1991, 27).

[2] "Market-based management" is developed in Koch (2007) and in an unpublished paper by Coleman, Wilson, and Woodlief, offered to me in correspondence with Woodlief. I am not espousing market-based management so much as offering it as an alternative response to the knowledge problem in the firm (versus Burczak's proposal).

[3] The Regression Theorem is found in Mises (1980); my use of it depends upon its application to development economics as it is formulated by Boettke, Coyne, and Leeson (2008).

[4] Eric Mack (2006) has developed this argument thoroughly in his contribution to the *Cambridge Companion to Hayek.*

[5] Hayek believed that a concern for consequences did not make one a utilitarian necessarily, otherwise nearly every moral philosopher could be labeled a utilitarian. Charles Taylor offers a similar critique of a too-broad understanding of consequentialism (bracketing technical differences between utilitarianism and consequentialism): if consequentialism is "taken so widely as to lose all its meaning," we may end up with a non-theory (Taylor 1982, p. 144).

[6] The entire first chapter of Hayek's second volume of *Law, Legislation, and Liberty* (1978b, 1-30) is an extended discussion of the difference between what it means to serve the common good, or the "general welfare," versus particular purposes; in other words, it's a critique of the utilitarian methodology. Why Burczak neglects this is a mystery to me.

[7] Hayek did not think that judges always acted impartially and consistently with the prevailing sense of justice, and Burczak recognizes this. Hayek thought the corrective to errors in this realm was legislation. I think a great example of this is the reaction to the U.S. Supreme Court's recent decision in *Kelo v. City of New London*, in which the Supreme Court, against the prevailing sense of justice, decided to expand the government's ability to use eminent domain to promote economic development. Immediately after that decision, states governments on both sides of the political spectrum drew up legislation limiting the use of eminent domain, as public sentiment prevailed against the decision. According to an article in *The National Law Journal* : "Just five weeks after the U.S. Supreme Court upheld the use of eminent domain to seize private property for economic development, more than half of the states have introduced legislation to thwart potential abuses" (Baldes 2005).

[8] Whether or not one agrees with it, one must respond to the common argument from classic liberals, libertarians, and conservatives that the use of the state to promote human capabilities in a substantive way has destroyed sentiments of personal responsibility and community. Hayek states: "The present tendency of governments to bring all common interests of large groups under their control tends to destroy real public spirit; and as a result an increasing number of men and women are turning away from public life who in the past would have devoted much effort to public purposes. On the European continent the over-solicitude of governments has in the past largely prevented the development of voluntary organizations for public purposes and produced a tradition in which private efforts were often regarded as the gratuitous meddling of busybodies, and modern developments seem progressively to have produced a similar situation even in the Anglo-Saxon countries where at one time private efforts for public purposes were so characteristic a feature of social life" (Hayek 1978c, 152). Charles Murray (1988) supports this thesis empirically with regard to how the state is destroying the "tendrils of community." Bertrand de Jouvenel, along these lines, goes further; he argues that the socialist project is inherently contradictory: by turning to the state to foster interdependence and responsibility, socialists attempts to capitalize upon "brotherly love" for materialistic purposes without the voluntaristic "faith" that originally sustained that love but that was oriented to non-materialistic *other-worldliness* (de Jouvenel 1989, 14-15).

[9] In Storr's critique of Burczak's book, he says, "Burczak's condemnation of wage-labor is clearly too sweeping. Are all wage laborers exploited? Is Roger Clemens exploited? Is Kobe Bryant? Is the computer programmer earning six figures a year who works remotely from home? On the flip side, would we say that the textile worker in Bangladesh who works by the piece is not exploited? By the definition of exploitation that Burczak embraces, the computer programmer is the exploited one because he was not the first owner of his labor product or the last owner of his labor time. The textile piece worker is both the first owner of her labor product and the last owner of her labor time. For exploitation to be a meaningful category, however, it cannot call the programmer exploited and the piece worker not exploited" (Storr 2007, 315.)

[10] I would suggest that there is an ordinary difference between preferences and values that is useful for this discussion (bracketing the technical philosophical distinctions between the two). Hayek did not doubt that we could agree upon our values in a formal, general sense—though not, necessarily, in our ranking scale (see, for example, Hayek 1944, 66). And it would be odd to think most people do not value education, health care, employment opportunities, and so on. But there is a big difference between that proposition and the idea that we could rationally order such things when considered on a more substantive level—when such values turn into preferences (for example, in valuing education, young person A may prefer a liberal arts college education, while young person B may prefer vocational training, and young person C may consider job experience more important than attending either college or vocational schools; and all these preferences might be irrelevant to an elderly person who values retirement and health care). My example

is very simple, but in a complex economy and society, it will become even more complicated.

[11] A recent statement of this and some empirical work can be found in Kenneth A. Shepsle and Mark S. Bonchek's 1997 *Analyzing Politics*, especially chapter 7.

[12] One could argue that what matters is that the workers *feel* as if they are actually using their mental powers and effecting positive change, and in fact I suspect that they do feel this way (and not entirely unjustifiably, either). But this would be a dangerous argument indeed if it is taken too far: by supporting the illusion of robust level of rationality, the argument falls prey to Nozick's critique of the mental desire account of utilitarianism as he describes it through his famous "experience machine" (Nozick 1974, 42-45).

[13] In my estimation (and I am not the first to have noted this), Hayek's views on this matter resonate quite well with John Searle's positions in *The Construction of Social Reality* (1995).

[14] This example may seem questionable due to high rates of divorce, but I think it works. The very fact that people continue to get married, even if marriage was primarily an economic arrangement in past societies, should adduce my claim that monogamous marriages reflect the beliefs, desires, intentions, and activities of individuals.

[15] I would like to acknowledge the assistance and comments of David Schweickart. Though we found ourselves disagreeing over the relative merits and demerits of socialism and capitalism, his enthusiasm and assistance for my project are testaments to his integrity as a scholar.